Theory of International Politics

KENNETH N. WALTZ
University of California, Berkeley

Boston, Massachusetts   Burr Ridge, Illinois
Dubuque, Iowa   Madison, Wisconsin   New York, New York
San Francisco, California   St. Louis, Missouri

McGraw-Hill

A Division of The McGraw·Hill Companies

THEORY OF INTERNATIONAL POLITICS
First Edition

24 25 26 27 28 29   BKM BKM   0 9 8 7 6

ISBN-13: 978-0-07-554852-2

ISBN-10: 0-07-554852-6

Preface

Theory is fundamental to science, and theories are rooted in ideas. The National Science Foundation was willing to bet on an idea before it could be well explained. The following pages, I hope, justify the Foundation's judgment. Other institutions helped me along the endless road to theory. In recent years the Institute of International Studies and the Committee on Research at the University of California, Berkeley, helped finance my work, as the Center for International Affairs at Harvard did earlier. Fellowships from the Guggenheim Foundation and from the Institute for the Study of World Politics enabled me to complete a draft of the manuscript and also to relate problems of international-political theory to wider issues in the philosophy of science. For the latter purpose, the philosophy department of the London School of Economics provided an exciting and friendly environment.

Robert Jervis and John Ruggie read my next-to-last draft with care and insight that would amaze anyone unacquainted with their critical talents. Robert Art and Glenn Snyder also made telling comments. John Cavanagh collected quantities of preliminary data; Stephen Peterson constructed the Tables found in the Appendix; Harry Hanson compiled the bibliography, and Nadine Zelinski expertly coped with an unrelenting flow of tapes. Through many discussions, mainly with my wife and with graduate students at Brandeis and Berkeley, a number of the points I make were developed.

Most of Chapters 2 and 3, and some of Chapters 1 and 6, appear in my 1975 essay; they were parts of the original plan for this book. Here and there I have drawn passages from other essays and from an earlier book. These and other sources appear in the bibliography near the end of the book.

Because a theory is never completed, I have been reluctant to declare the manuscript done. I do so now—without a sense of completion, but with a deep sigh of relief and a deep sense of gratitude to the many organizations and individuals who helped me.

Harborside, Maine   K. N. W.
July 1978

Contents

1

Laws and Theories

I write this book with three aims in mind: first, to examine theories of international politics and approaches to the subject matter that make some claim to being theoretically important; second, to construct a theory of international politics that remedies the defects of present theories; and third, to examine some applications of the theory constructed. The required preliminary to the accomplishment of these tasks is to say what theories are and to state the requirements for testing them.

I

Students of international politics use the term "theory" freely, often to cover any work that departs from mere description and seldom to refer only to work that meets philosophy-of-science standards. The aims I intend to pursue require that definitions of the key terms *theory* and *law* be carefully chosen. Whereas two definitions of theory vie for acceptance, a simple definition of law is widely accepted. Laws establish relations between variables, variables being concepts that can take different values. If *a*, then *b*, where *a* stands for one or more independent variables and *b* stands for the dependent variable: In form, this is the statement of a law. If the relation between *a* and *b* is invariant, the law is absolute. If the relation is highly constant, though not invariant, the law would read like this: If *a*, then *b* with probability *x*. A law is based not simply on a relation that has been found, but on one that has been found repeatedly. Repetition gives rise to the expectation that if I find *a* in the future, then with specified probability I will also find *b*. In the natural sciences even probabilistic laws contain a strong imputation of necessity. In the social sciences to say that persons of specified income vote Democratic with a certain probability is to make a law-like statement. The word *like* implies a lesser sense of necessity. Still, the statement would not be at all like a law unless the relation had so often and so reliably been found in the past that the expectation of its holding in the future with comparable probability is high.*

By one definition, theories are collections or sets of laws pertaining to a particular behavior or phenomenon. In addition to income, for example, associations may be established between voters' education, their religion, and their parents' political commitment, on the one hand, and the way they vote, on the other hand. If the probabilistic laws thus established are taken together, higher correlations are achieved between voters' characteristics (the independent variables) and choice of party (the dependent variable). Theories are, then, more complex than laws, but only quantitatively so. Between laws and theories no difference of kind appears.

This first definition of theory supports the aspiration of those many social scientists who would "build" theory by collecting carefully verified, interconnected hypotheses. The following story suggests how most political scientists think of theory:

Homer describes the walls of Troy as being eight feet thick. If his account is true, then millenia later one should be able to find those walls by careful digging. This thought occurred to Heinrich Schliemann as a boy, and as a man he put the theory to empirical test. Karl Deutsch uses the story as an example of how new-style theories are tested (1966, pp. 168–69). A theory is born in conjecture and is viable if the conjecture is confirmed. Deutsch regards theories of the simple if-then sort as "special theories," which may "later on become embedded in a grand theory." He then gives other examples and in doing so shifts "from a yes-or-no question to a how-much question." We should try to find out how much of a contribution "different variables" make to a given result (1966, pp. 219–21).

What is possibly useful in such a pattern of thinking, and what is not? Everyone knows that a coefficient of correlation, even a high one, does not warrant saying that a causal relation exists. Squaring the coefficient, however, technically permits us to say that we have accounted for a certain percentage of the variance. It is then easy to believe that a real causal connection has been identified and measured, to think that the relation between an independent and a dependent variable has been established, and to forget that something has been said only about dots on a piece of paper and the regression line drawn through them. Is the correlation spurious? That suggests the right question without quite asking it. Cor-

---

*One must be careful. The above statement is law-like only if it can be verified in various ways. Counterfactual conditions, for example, would have to be met in this way: Person b is in the income category of likely Republicans; if b's income were reduced to a certain level, he would probably become a Democrat. More precisely, the law-like statement establishes these expectations: If b is an R with probability x, and if a is a D with probability y, then if b becomes a, he thereby becomes a D with probability y.

relations are neither spurious nor genuine; they are merely numbers that one gets by performing simple mathematical operations. A correlation is neither spurious nor genuine, but the relation that we infer from it may be either. Suppose someone propounds a law, for example, by carefully establishing the relation between the amount of push imparted to a cart and the amount of its movement. The relation established, if conditions are kept constant and measurement is careful, is simply a fact of observation, a law that remains constantly valid. The *explanation* offered for that relation of push and movement, however, is radically different depending on whether we consult Aristotle or Galileo or Newton. The uncritical acceptance of a number as indicating that a connection obtains is the first danger to guard against. To do so is fairly easy. The next problem is more important and harder to solve.

Even if we have satisfied ourselves in various ways that a correlation points to a connection that reliably holds, we still have not accounted for that connection in the sense of having explained it. We have accounted for it in the way—and only in the way—that Aristotelian physics accounted for the relation between push and movement. From a practical standpoint, knowledge of the high correlation between push and movement is very useful. That descriptive knowledge may suggest clues about the principles of motion. It may as easily be grossly misleading, as indeed it turned out to be. Numbers may describe what goes on in the world. But no matter how securely we nail a description down with numbers, we still have not explained what we have described. Statistics do not show how anything works or fits together. Statistics are simply descriptions in numerical form. The form is economical because statistics describe a universe through manipulation of samples drawn from it. Statistics are useful because of the variety of ingenious operations that can be performed, some of which can be used to check on the significance of others. The result, however, remains a description of some part of the world and not an explanation of it. Statistical operations cannot bridge the gap that lies between description and explanation. Karl Deutsch advises us "to formulate, or reformulate, a proposition in terms of probability and to say *how much* of the outcome could be accounted for by one element and how much of the outcome could be accounted for from other elements or is autonomous and free" (1966, p. 220). If we follow that advice, we will behave like Aristotelian physicists. We will treat a problem as though it were like the one of trying to say to what extent a cart's movement results from push and slope and to what extent its movement is impeded by frictions. We will continue to think in sequential and correlational terms. By doing so, results that are practically useful may be achieved, although students of international politics have disappointingly little to show for such efforts, even in practical terms. And if useful information were uncovered, the more difficult task of figuring out its theoretical meaning would remain.

The "inductivist illusion," as structural anthropologist Lévi-Strauss terms it, is the belief that truth is won and explanation achieved through the accumulation of more and more data and the examination of more and more cases. If we gather more and more data and establish more and more associations, however, we will not finally find that we know something. We will simply end up having more and more data and larger sets of correlations. Data never speak for themselves. Observation and experience never lead directly to knowledge of causes. As the American pragmatist, C. S. Peirce, once said, "direct experience is neither certain nor uncertain, because it affirms nothing—it just *is*. It involves no error, because it testifies to nothing but its own appearance. For the same reason, it affords no certainty" (quoted in Nagel 1956, p. 150). Data, seeming facts, apparent associations—these are not certain knowledge of something. They may be puzzles that can one day be explained; they may be trivia that need not be explained at all.

If we follow the inductivist route, we can deal only with pieces of problems. The belief that the pieces can be added up, that they can be treated as independent variables whose summed effects will account for a certain portion of a dependent variable's movement, rests on nothing more than faith. We do not know what to add up, and we do not know whether addition is the appropriate operation. The number of pieces that might be taken as parts of a problem is infinite, and so is the number of ways in which the pieces may be combined. Neither observationally nor experimentally can one work with an infinity of objects and combinations. In the following example, Ross Ashby offers an apt caution. Astrophysicists seek to explain the behavior of star clusters with 20,000 members. The beginner, Ashby observes, "will say simply that he wants to know what the cluster will do, i.e., he wants the trajectories of the components. If this knowledge, however, could be given to him, it would take the form of many volumes filled with numerical tables, and he would then realise that he did not really want all that." The problem, Ashby concludes, is how to find out what we really want to know without "being overwhelmed with useless detail" (1956, p. 113). The old motto, "knowledge for the sake of knowledge" is an appealing one, perhaps because one can keep busy and at the same time avoid the difficult question of knowledge for what. Because facts do not speak for themselves, because associations never contain or conclusively suggest their own explanation, the question must be faced. The idea of "knowledge for the sake of knowledge" loses its charm, and indeed its meaning, once one realizes that the possible objects of knowledge are infinite.

Today's students of politics nevertheless display a strong commitment to induction. They examine numerous cases with the hope that connections and patterns will emerge and that those connections and patterns will represent the frequently mentioned "reality that is out there." The hope apparently rests on the conviction that knowledge begins with certainties and that induction can uncover them. But we can never say with assurance that a state of affairs inductively arrived at corresponds to something objectively real. What we think of as reality is itself an elaborate conception constructed and reconstructed through the ages. Reality emerges from our selection and organization of materials that are available in infinite quantity. How can we decide which materials to select and how to arrange them? No inductive procedure can answer the question, for the very problem is to figure out the criteria by which induction can usefully proceed.

Those who believe, oddly, that knowledge begins with certainties think of theories as edifices of truth, which they would build inductively. They define theories as hypotheses that are confirmed and connected. But empirical knowledge is always problematic. Experience often misleads us. As Heinrich Hertz put it, "that which is derived from experience can again be annulled by experience" (1894, p. 357). Nothing is ever both empirical and absolutely true, a proposition established by Immanuel Kant and now widely accepted at least by natural scientists. And since empirical knowledge is potentially infinite in extent, without some guidance we can know neither what information to gather nor how to put it together so that it becomes comprehensible. If we could directly apprehend the world that interests us, we would have no need for theory. We cannot. One can reliably find his way among infinite materials only with the guidance of theory defined in the second sense.

Rather than being mere collections of laws, theories are statements that explain them (cf. Nagel 1961, pp. 80–81; Isaak 1969, pp. 138–39). Theories are qualitatively different from laws. Laws identify invariant or probable associations. Theories show why those associations obtain. Each descriptive term in a law is directly tied to observational or laboratory procedures, and laws are established only if they pass observational or experimental tests. In addition to descriptive terms, theories contain theoretical notions. Theories cannot be constructed through induction alone, for theoretical notions can only be invented, not discovered. Aristotle dealt with real motion, that is with the ratios of effort to movement that are matters of common experience. Galileo took bold steps away from the real world in order to explain it. Aristotle believed that objects are naturally at rest and that effort is required to move them; Galileo assumed that both rest and uniform circular motion are natural and that an object remains in either of these conditions in the absence of outside forces. Newton conceived of a uniform rectilinear motion. The theory he devised to explain it introduced such theoretical notions as point-mass, instantaneous acceleration, force, and absolute space and time, none of which can be observed or experimentally determined. At each step, from Aristotle through Galileo to Newton, the theoretical concepts became bolder—that is, further removed from our sense experience.

A theoretical notion may be a concept, such as force, or an assumption, such as the assumption that mass concentrates at a point. A theoretical notion does not explain or predict anything. We know, and so did Newton, that mass does not concentrate at a point. But it was not odd of Newton to assume that it did, for assumptions are not assertions of fact. They are neither true nor false. Theoretical notions find their justification in the success of the theories that employ them. Of purported laws, we ask: "Are they true?" Of theories, we ask: "How great is their explanatory power?" Newton's theory of universal gravitation provided a unified explanation of celestial and terrestrial phenomena. Its power lay in the number of previously disparate empirical generalizations and laws that could be subsumed in one explanatory system, and in the number and range of new hypotheses generated or suggested by the theory, hypotheses that in turn led to new experimental laws.

Aristotle concluded that, within limits, "a given body can be displaced in a set time through a distance proportional to the effort available" (Toulmin 1961, p. 49). Whether by ancient or modern mechanics, the high correlation of push and movement holds true. But how is it to be explained? Such facts have remained constant; the theories accepted as adequate for their explanation have changed radically. Laws are "facts of observation"; theories are "speculative processes introduced to explain them." Experimental results are permanent; theories, however well supported, may not last (Andrade 1957, pp. 29, 242). Laws remain, theories come and go.

Since I see no reason for wasting the word "theory" by defining it as a set of two or more laws, I adopt the second meaning of the term: Theories explain laws. This meaning does not accord with usage in much of traditional political theory, which is concerned more with philosophic interpretation than with theoretical explanation. It does correspond to the definition of the term in the natural sciences and in some of the social sciences, especially economics. The definition also satisfies the need for a term to cover the explanatory activity we persistently engage in. In order to get beyond "the facts of observation," as we wish irresistibly to do, we must grapple with the problem of explanation. The urge to explain is not born of idle curiosity alone. It is produced also by the desire to control, or at least to know if control is possible, rather than merely to predict. Prediction follows from knowledge of the regularity of associations embodied in laws. Sunrises and sunsets can be reliably predicted on the basis of empirical findings alone, without benefit of theories explaining why the phenomena occur. Prediction may certainly be useful: The forces that propel two bodies headed for a collision may be inaccessible, but if we can predict the collision, we can at least get out of the way. Still, we would often like to be able to exert some control. Because a law does not say why a particular association holds, it cannot tell us whether we can exercise control and how we might go about doing so. For the latter purposes we need a theory.

A theory, though related to the world about which explanations are wanted, always remains distinct from that world. "Reality" will be congruent neither with a theory nor with a model that may represent it. Because political scientists often think that the best model is the one that reflects reality most accurately, further discussion is needed.

Model is used in two principal ways. In one sense a model represents a theory. In another sense a model pictures reality while simplifying it, say, through omission or through reduction of scale. If such a model departs too far from reality, it becomes useless. A model airplane should look like a real airplane. Explanatory power, however, is gained by moving away from "reality," not by staying close to it. A full description would be of least explanatory power; an elegant theory, of most. The latter would be at an extreme remove from reality; think of physics. Departing from reality is not necessarily good, but unless one can do so in some clever way, one can only describe and not explain. Thus James Conant once defined science as "a dynamic undertaking directed to lowering the degree of the empiricism involved in solving problems" (1952, p. 62). A model of a theory will be about as far removed from reality as the theory it represents. In modeling a theory, one looks for suggestive ways of depicting the theory, and not the reality it deals with. The model then presents the theory, with its theoretical notions necessarily omitted, whether through organismic, mechanical, mathematical, or other expressions.

Some political scientists write of theoretical models as though they were of the model airplane sort. For example, they first criticize the state-centric model of international politics because it has supposedly become further and further removed from reality. Then they try earnestly to make models that mirror reality ever more fully. If their efforts were to succeed, the model and the real world would become one and the same. The error made is the opposite of the one Immanuel Kant so cogently warned against, that is, of thinking that what is true in theory may not be so in practice. As Kant well understood, his warning did not imply that theory and practice are identical. Theory explains some part of reality and is therefore distinct from the reality it explains. If the distinction is preserved, it becomes obvious that induction from observables cannot in itself yield a theory that explains the observed. "A theory can be tested by experience," as Albert Einstein once said, "but there is no way from experience to the setting up of a theory" (quoted in Harris 1970, p. 121). To claim that it is possible to arrive at a theory inductively is to claim that we can understand phenomena before the means for their explanation are contrived.

The point is not to reject induction, but to ask what induction can and cannot accomplish. Induction is used at the level of hypotheses and laws rather than at the level of theories. Laws are different from theories, and the difference is reflected in the distinction between the way in which laws may be discovered and the way in which theories have to be constructed. Hypotheses may be inferred from theories. If they are confirmed quite conclusively, they are called laws.

Hypotheses may also be arrived at inductively. Again, if they are confirmed quite conclusively, they are called laws. Ebb and flood tides were predicted by ancient Babylonians with an accuracy unsurpassed until the end of the nineteenth century. Highly reliable knowledge of the law-like movement of tides did not enable one to explain them. Hypotheses about the association of this with that, no matter how well confirmed, do not give birth to theories. Associations never contain or conclusively suggest their own explanation.

Though in itself induction leads to a theoretical dead end, we nevertheless need some sense of the puzzling connections of things and events before we can worry about constructing theories. At the same time we need a theory, or some theories, in order to know what kind of data and connections to look for. Knowledge, it seems, must precede theory, and yet knowledge can proceed only from theory. This looks much like the dilemma suggested by the Platonic proposition that we cannot know anything until we know everything. Take this thought literally, and one is driven to despair. Take it instead as a statement of the strategic problem of gaining knowledge, and no more is suggested than the difficulties in any field of getting onto an intellectual track that promises to lead to some progress.

If induction is not the way to get onto a useful track, what is? The leap from law to theory, from the fashioning of hypotheses to the development of explanations of them, cannot be made by taking information as evidence and seeking more of it. The leap cannot be made by continuing to ask what is associated with what, but rather by trying to answer such questions as these: Why does this occur? How does that thing work? What causes what? How does it all hang together?

If a theory is not an edifice of truth and not a reproduction of reality, then what is it? A theory is a picture, mentally formed, of a bounded realm or domain of activity. A theory is a depiction of the organization of a domain and of the connections among its parts (cf. Boltzman 1905). The infinite materials of any realm can be organized in endlessly different ways. A theory indicates that some factors are more important than others and specifies relations among them. In reality, everything is related to everything else, and one domain cannot be separated from others. Theory isolates one realm from all others in order to deal with it intellectually. To isolate a realm is a precondition to developing a theory that will explain what goes on within it. If the precondition cannot be met, and that of course is a possibility, then the construction of theory for the matters at hand is impossible. The question, as ever with theories, is not whether the isolation of a realm is realistic, but whether it is useful. And usefulness is judged by the explanatory and predictive powers of the theory that may be fashioned.

Theories, though not divorced from the world of experiment and observation, are only indirectly connected with it. Thus the statement made by many that theories can never be proved true. If "truth" is the question, then we are in the realm of law, not of theory. Thus the statement made by James B. Conant, a chemist, that "a theory is only overthrown by a better theory" (1947, p. 48). Thus the statement made by John Rader Platt, a physicist, that "the pressure of scientific determinism becomes weak and random as we approach the great unitary syntheses. For they are not only discoveries. They are also artistic creations, shaped by the taste and style of a single hand" (1956, p. 75). And these statements can all be read as glosses on the famous proof of the mathematician Henri Poincaré that if one mechanical explanation for a phenomenon can be given, then so can an infinity of others.* Theories do construct *a* reality, but no one can ever say that it is *the* reality. We are therefore faced with both an infinity of data and an infinity of possible explanations of the data. The problem is a double one. Facts do not determine theories; more than one theory may fit any set of facts. Theories do not explain facts conclusively; we can never be sure that a good theory will not be replaced by a better one.

I have said what theories are and what they are not, but I have not said how theories are made. How are they made? The best, but unhelpful, short answer is this: "creatively." The word sets the problem without saying how to solve it. How does one move between observations and experiments and theories that explain them? The longest process of painful trial and error will not lead to the construction of a theory unless at some point a brilliant intuition flashes, a creative idea emerges. One cannot say how the intuition comes and how the idea is born. One can say what they will be about. They will be about the organization of the subject matter. They will convey a sense of the unobservable relations of things. They will be about connections and causes by which sense is made of things observed. A theory is not the occurrences seen and the associations recorded, but is instead the explanation of them. The formula for the acceleration of a freely falling body does not explain how the body falls. For the explanation one looks in classical physics to the whole Newtonian system—a package of interconnected concepts, an organization of the physical world in which the pertinent happenings become natural or necessary. Once the system is understood, once its principle of organization is grasped, the phenomena are explained. All of this is well summed up in words that Werner Heisenberg attributes to Wolfgang Pauli: " 'Understanding' probably means nothing more than having whatever ideas and concepts are needed to recognize that a great many different phenomena are part of a coherent whole" (1971, p. 33).

By a theory the significance of the observed is made manifest. A theory arranges phenomena so that they are seen as mutually dependent; it connects

---

*The proof is simply presented by Nagel (1961, p. 116n). One should add that the explanations will not be equally simple and useful.

otherwise disparate facts; it shows how changes in some of the phenomena necessarily entail changes in others. To form a theory requires envisioning a pattern
where none is visible to the naked eye. The pattern is not the sum of the substance
of our daily world. Scientific facts are highly special and relatively few as compared to all of the things that could conceivably be brought within explanatory
systems. A theory must then be constructed through simplifying. That is made
obvious by thinking of any theory, whether Isaac Newton's or Adam Smith's, or
by thinking of the alternative—to seek not explanation through simplification but
accurate reproduction through exhaustive description. Simplifications lay bare
the essential elements in play and indicate the necessary relations of cause and
interdependency—or suggest where to look for them.

Even by those who have authored them, the emergence of theories cannot be
described in other than uncertain and impressionistic ways. Elements of theories
can, however, be identified. The difficulty of moving from causal speculations
based on factual studies to theoretical formulations that lead one to view facts in
particular ways is experienced in any field. To cope with the difficulty, simplification is required. This is achieved mainly in the following four ways: (1) by isolation, which requires viewing the actions and interactions of a small number of
factors and forces as though in the meantime other things remain equal; (2) by
abstraction, which requires leaving some things aside in order to concentrate on
others; (3) by aggregation, which requires lumping disparate elements together
according to criteria derived from a theoretical purpose; (4) by idealization,
which requires proceeding as though perfection were attained or a limit reached
even though neither can be. Whatever the means of simplifying may be, the aim
is to try to find the central tendency among a confusion of tendencies, to single
out the propelling principle even though other principles operate, to seek the
essential factors where innumerable factors are present.

In addition to simplifications, or as forms of them, theories embody theoretical assumptions. Imagining that mass concentrates at a point, inventing genes,
mesons, and neutrinos, positing a national interest, and defining nations as unitary and purposive actors: These are examples of common assumptions. Theories
are combinations of descriptive and theoretical statements. The theoretical statements are nonfactual elements of a theory. They are not introduced freely or
whimsically. They are not introduced in the ancient and medieval manner as fic-
tions invented to save a theory. They are introduced only when they make explanation possible. The worth of a theoretical notion is judged by the usefulness of
the theory of which it is a part. Theoretical notions enable us to make sense of the
data; the data limit the freedom with which theoretical notions are invented. Theorists create their assumptions. Whether or not they are acceptable depends on
the merit of the scientific structure of which they are a part.

Constructing theories involves more than the performance of logically permissible operations on observed data. By deduction nothing can be explained, for the results of deduction follow logically from initial premises. Deduction may give certain answers, but nothing new; what is deduced is already present either in theoretical major premises or in empirical minor premises dealing with matters previously observed. Induction may give new answers, but nothing certain; the multiplication of particular observations can never support a universal statement. Theory is fruitful because it goes beyond the necessarily barren hypothetico-deductive approach. Both induction and deduction are indispensable in the construction of theory, but using them in combination gives rise to a theory only if a creative idea emerges. The task of constructing theories becomes both more consequential and more complicated, and so does the task of verifying them. The relation between theory and observation, or between theory and fact, becomes puzzling.

As an example of this puzzling relation, consider the problem of defining the terms used in a theory. Think of the distinct meanings in different physical theories of space, energy, momentum, and time. Obviously such notions have no meaning outside of the theory in which they appear (Nagel 1961, pp. 17, 127f.). That theoretical notions are defined by the theory in which they appear is easily understood. In the field of international politics, think of the different meanings commonly attached to the words in the following list: power, force, pole, relation, actor, stability, structure, and system. The meanings of such terms vary depending on their user's approach to the subject. This is necessarily so in any field where theories are contradictory. The contradiction of theories creates differences in the meanings of terms across theories. In international politics, as in the social sciences generally, theories turn out to be weak ones. The weakness of theories creates uncertainty of meanings even within a single theory. In international politics, whether because theories are contradictory or weak, discussion and argument about many important matters—the closeness of national interdependence, the stability of particular configurations of power, the usefulness of force—are made difficult or useless because the participants are talking about different things while using the same terms for them. Movement toward a remedy is impeded by disinclination to treat the question of meaning as a problem that can be solved only through the articulation and refinement of theories. The tendency instead is to turn the problem of meaning into the technical one of making terms operational. That won't help. Any of the above terms can be made operational in most of the meanings our discourse assigns to them. "Poles" have clear empirical referents, for example, whether defined as blocs or as great powers. By either definition, "poles" can become descriptive terms in the statement of laws. The technical usability of terms is unfortunately a weak criterion.

Though it is easy to see that theoretical notions are defined by the theory in which they appear, it is easy to overlook that even descriptive terms acquire different meanings as theories change. Stephen C. Pepper refers to the "close interdependence of fact and theory" (1942, p. 324). Thomas S. Kuhn specifies what happens precisely in terms of the change of "similarity relations" in the transition from one theory to the next. Objects of the same or of different sets in one theory may be grouped in different or in the same sets by another theory, as with the sun, the moon, Mars, and the earth before and after Copernicus. As Kuhn remarks, if two men are committed to different theories, "we cannot say with any assurance that the two men even see the same thing, [that they] possess the same data, but identify or interpret it differently" (1970, pp. 266–76). Do we only know what we see, one may wonder, or do we only see what we know? Our minds cannot record and make something of all of the many things that in some sense we see. We are therefore inclined to see what we are looking for, to find what our sense of the causes of things leads us to believe significant.

Changes of theory produce changes in the meaning of terms, both theoretical and factual ones. Theories not only define terms; they also specify the operations that can rightly be performed. In the sense used a moment ago, the operational question is a minor or merely a practical one. In another sense, the operational question is fundamentally important. Theories indicate what is connected with what and how the connection is made. They convey a sense of how things work, of how they hang together, of what the structure of a realm of inquiry may be. If the organization of a realm affects the interactions of variables within it, it makes no sense to manipulate data until the question of how variables may be connected is answered. Nevertheless, correlational labors proceed as though in the international realm variables are directly connected without structural constraints operating on them—as though the phenomena we deal with are all at one level. Coefficients of correlation are amassed without asking which theories lead one to expect *what kind* of a connection among *which* variables.

Much pointless work is done because the three questions that should be asked at the outset of an inquiry are so often ignored. They are:

- Does the object of investigation permit use of the analytic method of classical physics—examining the attributes and interactions of two variables while others are kept constant?

- Does it permit the application of statistics in ways commonly used when the number of variables becomes very large?

- Does the object of study permit neither approach, but instead require a systemic one?

The answer to the last question will be "yes" if the object of study is both complex and organized. Organized complexity, to use Warren Weaver's term, precludes the use of traditional modes of investigation (1947, pp. 6–7). One must choose an approach that is appropriate to the subject matter. The rules by which one's inquiry proceeds vary from one approach to another. "Due process of inquiry," as Martin Landau has said, requires one to follow the logic and procedures that one's methodology prescribes (1972, pp. 219–21). Most students of international politics have not observed "due process of inquiry." Worse still, they have not been able to figure out what the due process of their inquiries might be. They have been much concerned with methods and little concerned with the logic of their use. This reverses the proper priority of concern, for once a methodology is adopted, the choice of methods becomes merely a tactical matter. It makes no sense to start the journey that is to bring us to an understanding of phenomena without asking which methodological routes might possibly lead there. Before setting out we need to ask what different theoretical maps of the subject matter might show. If we are not to waste time laboring without any idea of whether the labor is mere muscular exercise, theoretical questions must be raised at the outset of inquiry.

II

In examining international-political theories in the next two chapters, we shall rely on the above discussion of the meaning of theory. If we should find some constructions that look like theories, we will of course want to know how good the explanations they offer may be. I conclude this chapter, therefore, by examining the problem of testing theories.

In order to test a theory, one must do the following:

1 State the theory being tested.
2 Infer hypotheses from it.
3 Subject the hypotheses to experimental or observational tests.
4 In taking steps two and three, use the definitions of terms found in the theory being tested.
5 Eliminate or control perturbing variables not included in the theory under test.
6 Devise a number of distinct and demanding tests.
7 If a test is not passed, ask whether the theory flunks completely, needs repair and restatement, or requires a narrowing of the scope of its explanatory claims.

The apparent failure of a theory may result from the improper accomplishment of one of these steps. Several of them require special emphasis. Since a hypothesis derived from a theory is being tested (there being no way to test a theory directly), a hypothesis proved wrong should lead one to reexamine the second and seventh operations. Was the hypothesis rightly inferred from the theory? How, and to what extent, does the invalidation of a properly drawn hypothesis bring the theory into question? The unfavorable results of tests should not lead to the hasty rejection of theories. Nor should favorable results lead to their easy acceptance. Even if all tests are passed, one must remember that a theory is made credible only in proportion to the variety and difficulty of the tests, and that no theory can ever be proved true.*

Efforts by political scientists to infer hypotheses from theories and test them have become commonplace. Much of the testing is done in basically the same way. One effort to test propositions, an effort more careful than most, can therefore serve as an illustration of how the above requirements go unobserved. Singer, Bremer, and Stuckey (1972) set out to evaluate "a number of equally plausible, but logically incompatible, theoretical formulations" about certain conditions that are said to be associated with peace and stability, or, alternatively, with war and instability. Having consolidated the "viewpoints" of the opposing "schools," they offer "predictive models" in which concentration of capability within the set of major powers, changes of that concentration, and changes of capability among the powers are the three independent variables. They then reach conclusions about whether and when the "parity-fluidity" model or the "preponderance-stability" model makes the better predictions. The questions asked are these: Will international politics be more or less peaceful and stable if power is more or less closely concentrated and if the ranking of great powers changes more or less rapidly? What can one make of the answers given? Very little. The deficiencies that account for this disappointing answer are revealed by running down our list of rules for the testing of theories.

Many testers of theories seem to believe that the major difficulties lie in the devising of tests. Instead, one must insist that the first big difficulty lies in finding or stating theories with enough precision and plausibility to make testing worthwhile. Few theories of international politics define terms and specify the connection of variables with the clarity and logic that would make testing the theories worthwhile. Before a claim can be made to have tested something, one must have something to test. In testing their models, Singer, Bremer, and Stuckey fail to examine the theories they have attempted to model. The theories the authors apparently have in mind are contradictory and confused about whether it is war and peace, or conflict and harmony, or instability and stability that are the expected alternative outcomes. One may, for example, think of a stable system as one that survives the waging of wars. Singer and his associates nevertheless finesse the question of what outcome should be expected by identifying war with

---

*For consideration of testing procedures and explanation of their importance, see Stinchcombe (1968, Chapter 2).

instability and letting it go at that. They fail to explain how their expectations accord with expectations derived from any particular theory.

The authors claim to be systematically and quantitatively evaluating contradictory "theoretical formulations." In gathering their data they necessarily fix upon certain definitions of the variables involved. As their key independent variable they choose concentration of power or of capabilities. They mention no theory that in fact employs such a variable, and I know of none that does. The well-known theories dealing with these matters refer to numbers of great powers or to polarities. "Polarity," moreover, is variously defined in terms of countries or of blocs. "Poles" are counted sometimes according to the physical capabilities of nations or of alliances, sometimes by looking at the pattern of national interrelations, and sometimes by awarding or denying top status to those who get or fail to get their ways. Unless the confused, vague, and fluctuating definitions of variables are remedied, no tests of anything can properly be conducted. The authors have nevertheless arbitrarily introduced their new variables without even considering how they may alter one's expectation of outcomes. Though this crucial problem is not even discussed, Singer and his associates announce that correlations between power-concentration variables, on the one hand, and war, on the other hand, confirm or disconfirm the expectations of the two schools they so vaguely refer to.

Rules one, two, and four are thus blithely ignored. The theories being tested are not stated. How hypotheses may have been inferred from them is not explained. Observations are made and data are generated without any effort to define variables as they were defined in the theories presumably being dealt with. The authors may be accomplishing something, but that something cannot be the confirming or disconfirming of any school's expectations.

In the face of such failures, one finds it hard to believe that here, as so often in the correlational labors undertaken by students of international politics, no thought is given to the possible presence of perturbing variables. An exception does not prove a rule or a theory, but if something can be shown to be exceptional, it does not provide any disproof either. One would expect variation in results achieved to prompt a search for possible sources of perturbation omitted from the models. In the instance before us, the "findings" for the nineteenth century differ from those for the twentieth. The discrepancy leads the authors only to the barest speculation about what may have been omitted and to no speculation at all about what may have gone wrong in the way variables were originally defined and interconnected. Rule five is no more heeded than the preceding ones.

Rule six calls for a number of different tests and for demanding ones. One might think this instruction more than usually important since the model consists merely of three highly similar and arbitrarily chosen variables and since the results of the tests are inconclusive. The dubious quality of the results, however, does not lead the authors to devise or to suggest further tests that might challenge their models with some force.

The seventh rule calls for care in the drawing of conclusions from the negative results of tests. Do they defeat the theory, require its amendment, or call for a narrowing of explanatory claims? Singer and his associates fail to consider such questions. Instead they simply report the different correlations between power-concentration and war in the nineteenth and twentieth centuries. Their conclusions are modest enough, but then what more could they say?

A general word of caution should be added to the many words of caution just uttered. One would be scientifically most satisfied if rigorous, experimental tests could be made. If a theory is stated in general terms, however, and if it gives rise to expectations that fall within a range that is identifiable but unfortunately wide, then to draw precise inferences and to try to check them experimentally is to place more weight on the theory than it can bear. Rigorous testing of vague theory is an exercise in the use of methods rather than a useful effort to test theory. The early application of demanding tests may, moreover, cause poorly developed theories to be discarded before their potential has unfolded (cf. Rapoport, 1968).

What then can one do? Simply negotiate the seven steps set forth above in ways appropriate to the theory at hand. Ask what the theory leads one to expect rather than fixing arbitrarily on expectations that one's data and methods can cope with. Check expectations against one's (often historical) observations before trying for precise refinements and using elaborate methods. Unless a theory is shown to be logical, coherent, and plausible, it is silly to subject it to elaborate tests. If a theory is seen to be logical, coherent, and plausible, the rigor and complication of tests must be geared to the precision or to the generality of the expectations inferred from the theory.*

III

I have dealt so far with the meaning of theory and with theory construction and testing. Theories do not emerge from efforts to establish laws, even when those efforts succeed. The construction of theory is a primary task. One must decide which things to concentrate on in order to have a good chance of devising some explanations of the international patterns and events that interest us. To believe that we can proceed otherwise is to take the profoundly unscientific view that everything that varies is a variable. Without at least a sketchy theory, we cannot

---

*See Chapter 6, part III, for further thoughts about testing.

say what it is that needs to be explained, how it might be explained, and which data, how formulated, are to be accepted as evidence for or against hypotheses (cf. Scheffler 1967, pp. 64–66; Lakatos 1970, pp. 154–77). To proceed by looking for associations without at least some glimmering of a theory is like shooting a gun in the general direction of an invisible target. Not only would much ammunition be used up before hitting it, but also, if the bull's-eye were hit, no one would know it!

The trick, obviously, is to link theoretical concepts with a few variables in order to contrive explanations from which hypotheses can then be inferred and tested. Our problem in the next two chapters is to see to what extent, and how well, this has been done by students of international politics.

2

Reductionist Theories

Among the depressing features of international-political studies is the small gain in explanatory power that has come from the large amount of work done in recent decades. Nothing seems to accumulate, not even criticism. Instead, the same sorts of summary and superficial criticisms are made over and over again, and the same sorts of errors are repeated. Rather than add to the number of surveys available, I shall concentrate attention in the critical portion of this work on a few theories illustrating different approaches. Doing so will incline our thoughts more toward the possibilities and limitations of different types of theory and less toward the strengths and weaknesses of particular theorists.

I

Theories of international politics can be sorted out in a number of ways. Elsewhere I have distinguished explanations of international politics, and especially efforts to locate the causes of war and to define the conditions of peace, according to the level at which causes are located—whether in man, the state, or the state system (1954, 1959). A still simpler division may be made, one that separates theories according to whether they are reductionist or systemic. Theories of international politics that concentrate causes at the individual or national level are reductionist; theories that conceive of causes operating at the international level as well are systemic. In Chapter 2, I shall focus on reductionist theories.

With a reductionist approach, the whole is understood by knowing the attributes and the interactions of its parts. The effort to explain the behavior of a group through psychological study of its members is a reductionist approach, as is the effort to understand international politics by studying national bureaucrats and bureaucracies. Perhaps the classic reductionist case was the once widespread effort to understand organisms by disassembling them and applying physical and chemical knowledge and methods in the examination of their parts. Essential to the reductionist approach, then, is that the whole shall be known through the study of its parts. It also often happens that the reductionist finds himself using the methods of other disciplines in order to apprehend his own subject matter. A priori, one cannot say whether reduction will suffice. The question of adequacy has to be answered through examining the matter to be explained and by observing the results achieved.

The onetime rage for reduction among biologists may have been unfortunate.* One can nevertheless understand how the success and attendant prestige of physics and chemistry made the reductionist path enticing. In our field, the reductionist urge must derive more from failures of work done at the international-political level than from the successes of other possibly pertinent disciplines. Many have tried to explain international-political events in terms of psychological factors or social-psychological phenomena or national political and economic characteristics. In at least some of these cases, the possibly germane factors are explained by theories of somewhat more power than theories of international politics have been able to generate. In no case, however, are those nonpolitical theories strong enough to provide reliable explanations or predictions.

The positive temptation to reduce is weak, yet in international politics the urge to reduce has been prominent. This urge can be further explained by adding a practical reason to the theoretical reason just given. It must often seem that national decisions and actions account for most of what happens in the world. How can explanations at the international-political level rival in importance a major power's answers to such questions as these: Should it spend more or less on defense? Should it make nuclear weapons or not? Should it stand fast and fight or retreat and seek peace? National decisions and activities seem to be of overwhelming importance. This practical condition, together with the failure of international-political theories to provide either convincing explanations or serviceable guidance for research, has provided adequate temptation to pursue reductionist approaches.

The economic theory of imperialism developed by Hobson and Lenin is the best of such approaches.† By "best" I mean not necessarily correct but rather most impressive as theory. The theory is elegant and powerful. Simply stated and incorporating only a few elements, it claims to explain the most important of international-political events—not merely imperialism but also most, if not all, modern wars—and even to indicate the conditions that would permit peace to prevail. The theory offers explanations and, unlike most theories in the social

---

*Alfred North Whitehead at least thought so (1925, p. 60).

†Hobson's and Lenin's theories are not identical, but they are highly similar and largely compatible.

sciences, predictions as well. Moreover, it has successfully performed the other tasks that a good theory should accomplish: namely, stimulating and guiding research and provoking counter-theories that claim to account for the same phenomena. All in all, the literature that can be attributed to the Hobson-Lenin theory of imperialism, both in support of the theory and against it, is as extensive and as sophisticated as the literature associated with any other school in the field of international politics. For these reasons, the theory can well be used to illustrate reductionist approaches.

II

From Chapter 1, we know that theories contain theoretical (nonfactual) assumptions and that theories must be judged in terms of what they pretend to explain or predict. From what I have said about reductionist approaches, it follows that the assumptions of the Hobson-Lenin theory will be economic, not political. Its standing as an explanation of imperialism and of war hinges on (1) whether the economic theory is valid, (2) whether the conditions envisioned by the theory held in most of the imperialist countries, and (3) whether most of the countries in which the conditions held were in fact imperialist. I have specified most, rather than all, countries not in order to weaken the tests that economic theories of imperialism must pass but because exceptions fail to invalidate a theory if their occurrence can be satisfactorily explained. A wind that wafts a falling leaf does not call Newton's theory of universal gravitation into question. So also with Hobson's and Lenin's theories; the assigned causes may operate, yet other causes may deflect or overwhelm them. Hobson's and Lenin's theories may explain imperialism when it occurs, yet not be refuted even if all advanced capitalist countries do not at all times practice imperialism.

Hobson's *Imperialism*, first published in 1902, still merits close study. Indeed, students will save much time and trouble by mastering the sixth chapter of Part I, where they will find all of the elements of later economic explanations of imperialism from Lenin to Baran and Sweezy. "Overproduction," "surplus capital," "maldistribution of consuming power," "recurrent gluts," "consequent depressions": Hobson thickly populates his pages with such concepts, which he develops and combines systematically. In doing so, moreover, he hits upon notions that later authors have taken up—the role of advertising and the importance of trusts, for example, and even the possibility of what is now known as the imperialism of free trade.

Hobson's economic reasoning is impressive. Like Malthus, he anticipates Keynes by questioning the classical economists' belief that if only government would leave the economy alone, effective demand would strongly tend toward sufficiency, that the money demand for goods would clear the market of all that is produced and thus provide suppliers with the incentive to employ the factors of production fully through continued investment. Surpassing Malthus, Hobson was able to explain why effective demand might be deficient and thus to provide reasons for the proposition later established by Keynes: namely, that a free-enterprise economy may come to rest at a point representing less than full employment of the factors of production.

Because of the concentration of wealth in the hands of the few, Hobson argues, consumption cannot keep pace with increases of productive power; for "the rich will never be so ingenious as to spend enough to prevent overproduction." At a price level that returns a profit, demand will be insufficient to clear the market. There are then, in Hobson's words, "goods which cannot get consumed, or which cannot even get produced because it is evident they cannot get consumed." As for Keynes, the malfunctioning of the economy is caused by a maldistribution of wealth. As for Keynes, the sensible solution is for the government, through its taxing and spending powers, to contrive a more equitable distribution of income in order to bring about an aggregate demand that will sustain the economy in a condition of full employment. As for Keynes, the approach is macroeconomic, examining relations among system-wide aggregates in order to explain the condition of the economy as a whole.*

We now have the economic elements of Hobson's theory of imperialism in hand. Faced with a falling rate of profit at home and with underused resources, would-be investors look abroad for better opportunities. Those opportunities are found where they have been least fully exploited—that is, in economically backward countries. Put differently, to say that a country is economically underdeveloped means that it is short of capital. Where capital is scarce, it commands the highest premium. With similar impulses to invest abroad felt by nationals of different capitalist countries, their governments are easily drawn into backing the claims of their citizens for fair treatment by, or for special privileges from, the native rulers in whose countries they are operating. If one government supports its businessmen abroad, can other governments do less? If one government places tariff walls around its colonies, can other governments stand idly by and watch their citizens being discriminated against in more and more of the world's markets? The governments of capitalist states felt the force of the reasoning implied in

---

*The above three paragraphs are a summary of part I, Chapter 6, of Hobson (1902). Keynes gives Hobson full credit for anticipating the major elements of his general theory, though with strictures upon Hobson's lack of a theory of the rate of interest and his consequent excessive emphasis on the oversupply of capital rather than the lack of demand for it. See Keynes (n.d., pp. 364–70) and the references there given. In an otherwise excellent article, Boulding and Mukerjee (1971) remark that it is possible to make some sense of Hobson's theory of surplus capital by interpreting it in a Keynesian light. They can believe that a special interpretation is required only because they have missed the close similarity of Hobson to Keynes.

such rhetorical questions. And so the urge to invest abroad, and the competition among the nationals of different countries responding to that urge, led naturally, it was thought, to waves of imperialist activity. Thus Hobson reached his conclusion: Imperialism "implies the use of the machinery of government by private interests, mainly capitalists, to secure for them economic gains outside their country." Other forces do operate—patriotism, missionary zeal, the spirit of adventure, for example. But the economic factor is the "taproot," the one cause without which the imperialist enterprise withers. Economic forces are the "true determinant in the interpretation of actual policy." Directly or indirectly, moreover, imperialism was thought to account for most, if not all, modern wars (1902, pp. 94, 96, 126; cf. pp. 106, 356ff.). As Harold J. Laski later put it: War's "main causes lie in the economic field. Its chief object is a search for a wealth obtainable by its means that is deemed greater by those who push the state to its making than will be obtained if peace is preserved" (1933, p. 501).

Though imperialism promotes employment through the export of surplus capital and labor, losses suffered by an imperialist nation far exceed gains. Gains are insignificant partly because most of them go to businessmen and investors, a tiny minority of the nation. They reap the profits of imperialism; the nation as a whole bears its considerable expense. In the words Hobson borrowed from James Mill, imperialism is "a vast system of outdoor relief for the upper classes." Redistribution of income would put factors of production to more profitable use. If imperialist activity, moreover, causes all wars and not just the directly imperialist ones, then the costs of the entire "war system," the costs of preparing for wars as well as of fighting them, must be charged to the imperialist enterprise. By such reasoning, costs must vastly exceed gains.* In addition to costs counted in pounds, the pursuit of imperialist policies produces unfortunate social and political effects at home. It leads either to the development of militarism in England or to her dependence on native troops; it sets forces in motion that are antagonistic to social and economic reform and that undermine representative government; it sustains and enlarges an effete aristocracy dependent on tribute from Asia and Africa and may ultimately turn most West Europeans into a parasitic people (1902, pp. 51, 130–52, 314–15).

That, in Hobson's view, defines one major part of the loss to the imperialist nation. The other major part of the loss comes through the effects of imperialism abroad. The imperialist nation, in exporting its capital goods and its know-how, enables backward countries to develop their resources. Once that is done, there is

---

*By a more restrictive accounting, relative gains and losses are still problematic even for Britain in its modern imperialist heyday. See the judicious calculations of Strachey (1960, pp. 146–94), and cf. Brown (1970, p. x). Brown especially writes of imperialism from a Marxist standpoint. See also Boulding and Mukerjee (1971).

nothing to prevent, say, China from using foreign capital, and increasingly her own capital, combined with her labor, to produce goods that may supplant "British produce in neutral markets of the world." She may finally "flood" even Western markets with cheap "China goods," reverse the flow of investment, and gain "financial control over her quandom patrons and civilizers" (1902, pp. 308f., 313). The imperialist country's own actions undermine its position of superiority.

Lenin drew heavily on Hobson and differed from him on only two important points. Hobson believed that the impetus to imperialism could be eliminated by governmental policies designed to redistribute wealth (1902, pp. 88–90). Lenin believed that the capitalists who control governments would never permit such policies. Imperialism was then inevitably a policy of capitalist states in their monopoly stage (1916, pp. 88–89). Hobson believed that imperialist contention was the cause of most conflicts among the imperialist countries themselves and the principal reason for their vast expenditures on armaments. Hobson did, however, see the horrible possibility of capitalist states cooperating in the exploitation of backward peoples (1902, pp. 311f., 364f.). Lenin believed that cooperative arrangements would never endure, given the shifting fortunes of capitalist states and the changing pattern of opportunities for external investment. Capitalism inevitably produces imperialism. That in turn inevitably leads to war among capitalist states, a thought that later supported the belief that socialism could survive in one country (1916, pp. 91–96, 117–20).

Using Hobson's analysis, Lenin tried to prove that the effects Hobson thought probable were necessary products of capitalism. Lenin, moreover, liked what Hobson foresaw and deplored: Imperialism is part of the dialectic that brings the demise of the capitalist world by sapping the energies of the advanced states and sharpening the antagonisms within them, on the one hand, and by promoting the economic development of backward areas, on the other.* Lenin here fit comfortably into the Marxist mold. In the *Communist Manifesto*, Marx and Engels had sounded a paean to capitalism that would have seemed embarrassingly pretentious had it come from a bourgeois apologist.

> National differences, and antagonisms between peoples [they wrote] are daily more and more vanishing, owing to the development of the bourgeoisie, to freedom of commerce, to the world-market, to uniformity in the mode of production and in the conditions of life corresponding thereto (1848, p. 39).

Adapting Hobson's explanation of imperialism, Lenin was able to retain both Marx's vision of a benign future and his conviction that capitalist societies contained its seed.

---

*Lenin makes the first point by quoting Hobson, among others, and the second point largely by quoting Rudolf Hilferding (Lenin, 1916, pp. 102–104, 121).

We can now check the economic theory of imperialism against the three questions raised at the beginning of part II. First, how good is the economic theory itself? Here we must distinguish between the general merits of Hobson's Keynesian-style theory and its ability to explain the push to export capital that supposedly produces imperialism. Both Hobson and Lenin attribute imperialism to the push that originates in underconsumption at home combined with the pull provided by the lure of higher profits through investment abroad. It is the higher profits that are wanted, however they may be gained, as both Hobson and Lenin would readily say. Hobson's economic theory cannot in itself lead to the conclusion that the building of empires is needed. Capital may flow out of a country in search of higher profits, but whether imperial conquest is required, or is thought to be required, in order to secure them depends on political as well as on economic conditions at home and abroad. Showing how capitalist states may generate surpluses does not determine how those surpluses will be used. Economic reasoning can do no more than explain the appearance of specified surpluses under designated conditions. The question shifts, then, from whether the economic theory explains capital surpluses to whether internal economic condition determines external political behavior. That question cannot be answered by a theory about the working of national economies. Despite this fatal difficulty, one may believe, as I do, that the persuasiveness of the economic reasoning has helped to carry the theory as a whole, despite its failure to pass the second test and its difficulty with the third one.

The second and third tests can be considered together. Recall that for the economic theory of imperialism to be valid, most of the imperialist countries must be both capitalist and surplus-producing and that most of the countries so described must be imperialist. From about 1870 onward, which is the period when the theory is said to apply, all or practically all of the states that could reasonably be called "capitalist" did engage in at least a bit of imperialist activity. Some of the imperialist states, however, exported little capital to their own colonies; and some of them did not produce surpluses of capital at all. A number of imperialist states, moreover, were not capitalist states. The diversity of the internal conditions of states and of their foreign policies was impressive. Their conformity to the stipulations of the theory was not. England, the premier imperialist state, had about half of its capital invested outside of its colonies at the end of the nineteenth century. That the largest single amount was invested in the United States is at least mildly disconcerting for scrupulous adherents of the theory. France consistently ranked second or third in investments in, and trade with, the territories she owned (Feis 1930, p. 23). Japan in Asia, and Russia in Asia and Eastern Europe, were certainly imperialist, but they were neither capitalist nor surplus-producing. Those few cases illustrate the variety of conditions associated with imperialism, a variety fully sufficient to refute the theory.

These anomalies, from the theory's point of view, awaken further doubts. Imperialism is at least as old as recorded history. Surely it is odd to learn that the cause (capitalism) is much younger than the effect it produces (imperialism). Admittedly, Hobson and Lenin pretend to explain imperialism only in the era of advanced capitalism. But one must then wonder what caused imperialism in bygone periods and why those old causes of imperialism no longer operate, why they have been replaced as causes by capitalism. If there were new things in the world in the late nineteenth century, imperialism was not one of them. Not the phenomenon, but only its cause, was said to be new. It is as though Newton claimed to have discovered the explanation for the free fall of bodies only from 1666 onward, as though he left it to someone else to explain how such objects fell before that date, and as though his newly discovered gravitational effect were something that did not exist or did not operate earlier.

The theory of Hobson and Lenin cannot deal with these problems and did not try very seriously to do so.* The acceptance of the theory, which spread and endured marvelously, rested instead on the attractiveness of its economic reasoning and on the blatant truth that the advanced capitalist states of the day were, indeed, among history's most impressive builders of empire. The advanced capitalist states were fiercely imperialist. Then why not identify capitalism and imperialism? The identification was obviously easy to make, for so often one reads of capitalist states forcing their surplus goods and capital on unsuspecting natives, and of the mad scramble of capitalist states for colonies.

If the implied assertions of cause are convincing at all, they are so only until one realizes that in Hobson's day, as in ours, most of the leading states were capitalist. This question is then raised: Are the advanced countries "imperialist" because they are *capitalist* or because they are *advanced*? The growth of industrial economies in the nineteenth century spawned a world-girdling imperialism. Was the hegemony of the few over the many produced by the contradictions of capitalism or by the unlocking of nature's secrets, the transmuting of science into technology, and the organization of the powers of technology on a national scale? Is imperialism the highest stage of capitalism or are capitalism *and* imperialism the highest stage of industrialism? For any theory that attempts to account for imperialism, the answers to these questions are critical.†

Some will respond by saying that the burst of imperialist activity in the late nineteenth century can be explained only by economic changes within imperialist

---

*One way out is to argue that the "new imperialism" was different from the old because of capitalism. That there were some differences is of course true, but theoretically trivial. For an example of the argument, see O'Connor (1970).

†Wehler (1970) provides a striking example of how the analysis of causes becomes muddled when industrialization is equated with capitalism.

countries and that this provides evidence in support of Hobson's and Lenin's theory. The argument misses the point. In rejecting the theory, I am not arguing that capitalism had nothing to do with British and French imperialism. Doing so would be as silly as saying that authoritarian rule had nothing to do with Russian and Japanese imperialism. Particular acts have particular causes, which account for some part of the outcomes that interest us. In dealing with particular causes, however, we are dealing with matters that are more interesting historically than theoretically. To claim that a theory contemplating only the internal condition of states does not sufficiently explain their external behavior is not to claim that external behavior can be explained without reference to internal condition. Capitalist economies were efficient generators of surpluses. Governments of capitalist states therefore had wide ranges of choice and effective means of acting internationally. How they would choose to act, however, cannot be explained by internal conditions alone. External conditions must be part of the explanation since the variety of conditions internal to states is not matched by the variety of their external behaviors.

Through history, the famous three "surpluses"—of people, of goods, and of capital—are associated with imperialist movements. In various versions, they are identified, respectively, as the imperialism of swarming, the imperialism of free trade, and the imperialism of monopoly capitalism. Two points need to be made. First, a country that sustains an imperialist movement must produce one or a combination of such "surpluses" in the specific sense that the imperial country requires a margin of superiority over the people it controls. How else can control be exercised? Second, how the "surplus" is produced, and the nature of the state producing it, appear to be quite unimportant. Republics (Athens and Rome), divine-right monarchies (Bourbon France and Meijian Japan), modern democracies (Britain and America) have all at times been imperialist. Similarly, economies of great variety—pastoral, feudal, mercantilist, capitalist, socialist—have sustained imperialist enterprises. To explain imperialism by capitalism is parochial at best. Rather than refer to capitalist imperialism one might more aptly write of *the imperialism of great power.* Where gross imbalances of power exist, and where the means of transportation permit the export of goods and of the instruments of rule, the more capable people ordinarily exert a considerable influence over those less able to produce surpluses. In a shot that is supposed to tell heavily against Joseph Schumpeter, Murray Greene accuses him of tacking this thought onto his sociological theory of imperialism: What may "look like capitalist imperialism just happens to occur in the era of capitalism" (1952, p. 64). Greene hit precisely upon an important point, although he wholly misunderstood it. Historically, imperialism is a common phenomenon. Where one finds empires, one notices that they are built by those who have organized themselves and exploited their resources most effectively. Thus in its heyday mercantilism was the cause of imperialism in just the same spurious sense that capitalism was later.

If capitalist states, the most advanced states of their day, did not affect others more than others affected them, and at least occasionally engage in outwardly imperialist activity, that would be odd. In this sense, the absence of imperialism in the face of unbalanced power would sorely require explanation. Weakness invites control; strength tempts one to exercise it, even if only for the "good" of other people.* The phenomenon is more general as well as older than the theory offered to explain it. The phrase that expresses the root cause that operates across differently organized economies is "the imperialism of great power." The economic organization that will "cause" imperialism (in the sense of enabling a country to pursue imperialist policies) is whatever economic form proves most effective at the given time and within the pertinent area. To complete the comparison suggested above: Newton's gravitational force did work earlier, though it had not been fully identified; the causes of imperialism, present in advanced capitalism, were present earlier, though identification of capitalism with imperialism has obscured this.

III

After World War 1, Lenin and his followers could try out their thesis in its strongest form. Capitalism produces imperialism, and the leading capitalist state will be the fiercest imperialist country. Thus Trotsky foresaw America becoming the world's most imperialist nation and this development as touching off "military collisions" of "unprecedented scale" (1924, p. 29). Not only must the leading capitalist state be the most imperialistic, but also its imperialist policies must be the major cause of war in the world.

In the same period, Joseph Schumpeter wrote his well-known essay, giving an explanation of imperialism contrary to the economic one. "Precapitalist elements, survivals, reminiscences, and power factors" propel states into imperialist ventures. Military classes, once needed for the consolidation and extension of their states, do not disappear upon the completion of their tasks. They live on. They seek continued employment and prestige. They are supported by others who become imbued with their spirit. Such atavistic forces give rise to imperialist tendencies, which are not lacking even in the United States. But, Schumpeter asserts, "we can conjecture that among all countries the United States is likely to

---

*Cf. Nkrumah's warning to Africans that the weakness of disunity invites imperialist control (Grundy, 1963, p. 450).

exhibit the weakest imperial trend" (1919, p. 72). Like Veblen, and by similar reasoning, Schumpeter assigns the causes of war to the continued vogue of an out-
moded militarism and believes that Germany and Japan—countries in which
capitalist forces have not fully supplanted feudal elements—will constitute the
greatest danger of war.*

Does imperialism wither away as capitalism, inherently pacifistic, fully
assimilates anachronistic social elements, or is imperialism the last malignant
expression of capitalism prior to the advent of socialism? Judged by the accuracy
of predictions, Veblen and Schumpeter carry the day. But prediction is an insufficient criterion for accepting a theory's validity, for predictions may be right or
wrong for many different and accidental reasons. Veblen and Schumpeter nevertheless posed the problem that latter-day Marxists had to cope with: how to salvage Lenin's theory of imperialism when capitalist states fail to pursue colonial
policies—indeed, when none of them any longer clings to its colonies.

The solution is found in the concept of neocolonialism as it developed from
the early 1950s onward. Neocolonialism separates the notion of imperialism from
the existence of empires. Lenin offers some basis for this separation. He had
defined imperialism as an internal condition of certain states rather than as a
policy, or a set of actions, or a result produced. Imperialism is simply "the
monopoly stage of capitalism." But for Lenin that condition necessarily found
political expression. Imperialism originated privately but expressed itself pub-
licly. A policy of imperialism could be pursued only if soldiers and sailors were
available to implement it. Empires without colonies, and imperialist policies that
require little if any force to back them up, were unimaginable to Lenin.

The first big difference between the old and the new Marxist theses on
imperialism is found in the divorce of imperialism from governmental policies
and actions. One sees this difference clearly in the quick change of conclusions by
Harry Magdoff, one of the leading neocolonial writers. In his 1969 book he
emphasizes America's dependence on foreign resources and on profits earned
abroad. The nation's economic dependence then requires governmental action to
establish a position of dominance that will make the world secure for the operations of American capital. In a 1970 article he joins what is now the neocolonial
mainstream. References to America's dependence fade away, and private business supplants government as the engine that drives the imperial machine. The
neocolonial thesis contains the ultimate economic explanation of international
politics, asserting, as it does, that in capitalist states private economic instruments have become so fully developed that their informal use is sufficient for the
effective control and exploitation of other countries' resources (1969, Chapters 1,

---

*Schumpeter fails to mention Germany apparently because of the constraints of wartime
censorship. Veblen's essay was first published in 1915.

5; 1970, p. 27).* Multinational corporations now operate on such large scales and over such wide areas that they can both develop their own leverage against economically less powerful countries and pursue their own bet-hedging strategies by distributing their operations across countries, some with more and some with less predictably safe and stable governments. The outward thrust of business is so strong, and its ability to take care of itself is so great, that businesses develop their "invisible empires" ordinarily without the support of governmental policies or of national force.

The second big difference between the old and the new Marxist theses on imperialism is found in the estimates of the effects of imperialism on less-developed countries. Older Marxists believed that capitalists dug their own graves in various ways, one of which was by contributing to the economic development of their empires through capitalist investment abroad. An un-Marxist despair has replaced Marx's and Lenin's optimism. Capitalists operating in foreign parts are now said to have the effect either of freezing economic development at relatively low levels or of distorting that development disadvantageously. Backward countries remain the suppliers of raw materials for the more developed countries or are kept at the level of comparatively crude manufacture.† In the latter sense, even the relation between the most advanced capitalist country, the United States, and the comparatively less-developed economies of Western Europe are included.

Neocolonial theorists claim to identify and explain yet another "new" imperialism. An examination of neocolonial thought will lead to several important points about international-political theory. They are suggested by the following headings: (1) self-verifying theories, (2) structure without behavior or the disappearance of function, (3) over-explanation and the problem of change.

1. SELF-VERIFYING THEORIES

Imre Lakatos uses the phrase "auxiliary theories" to describe theories that are devised "in the wake of facts" and that lack the power to anticipate other facts (1970, pp. 175–76). Suppose, for example, that I begin with the conviction that

---

*With more similarities than differences, the points just made and those to follow are common to the neocolonial school. I use "school" broadly to suggest a similarity of conclusions among authors who arrive at their conclusions in different ways, whether through historical, political, or economic approaches, and whose commitment to Marxism varies. Some of the more interesting sources, in addition to Magdoff, are Baran and Sweezy (1966), Brown (1970), Galtung (1971), Hymer (1970), Williams (1962), and Wolff (1970).

†These points are made in an influential early article, whose author is not of the school we are examining. See H. Singer (1950).

certain types of states are imperialist. Suppose I believe that my theory explains why this is so. Suppose further that I want to maintain my theory substantially intact, even though the activity explained, and those who engage in it, change a good deal over time. To reach that end, I need to do two things: first, redefine the old word to cover the new activity, and second, revise the old theory in order to cover new elements. The evolution of theories about imperialism nicely illustrates both procedures.

According to Hobson and Lenin, if a country builds an empire in order to control the external arena of its economic operations, that is imperialism. According to a later notion, if a country is able to operate abroad economically *without* building an empire, that is also imperialism. The latter definition is embodied in the idea of "the imperialism of free trade," associated most often with the nonMarxist, historically impressive work of Gallagher and Robinson. They emphasize the use of free trade as a technique of British expansion, especially in the middle of the nineteenth century, and they argue that whatever the method used, British interests throughout the century continued to be safeguarded and extended (1953, pp. 11, 13). Now it may well be that Britain's interest in formal empire dwindled in the middle years of the nineteenth century precisely because her dominance of world markets guaranteed that sufficient quantities of her goods would be bought by foreigners whether or not she ruled them. Similarly, one can say that America's foreign economic operations have not required the traditional apparatus of empire and certainly do not now.*

The neocolonial school's acknowledgment that American economic operations abroad require little if any backing by military force closely corresponds to reality. Imperialist policies, old style, have languished; empires have nearly disappeared. Now as ever, the superior economic capability of wealthy peoples nevertheless has its impact on those who are poor. Calling the influence of the rich over the poor "imperialism" is the first step toward saving Lenin's theory. Asserting that what capitalists do abroad *is* imperialism—whether or not they do it through empires and by force—helps to turn the theory into a self-verifying one. The theory did not anticipate the facts. It did not lead anyone to expect the decline of visible empires. Instead the definition of what the theory supposedly explained was changed to accommodate what had actually happened. Neocolonialists, in redefining the behavior that capitalist states are expected to display, strikingly show the validity of the point made earlier: namely, how national economies produce surpluses and how surpluses are used are different questions, and the second cannot be answered by a theory about national economies.

---

*Cf. William's notion of what one might call "open-door imperialism" (1962). Cf. also Michael Barratt Brown's attempt to complete the neocolonialist logic by arguing that in the later nineteenth century as well as today imperial control depended more on economic domination than on political rule (1970, pp. xxxiv–xxxv).

2. STRUCTURE WITHOUT BEHAVIOR,
OR THE DISAPPEARANCE OF FUNCTION

The new definition of imperialism strongly affects the way in which the traditional economic theory of imperialism has been amended in order to cover recent practices, as can easily be seen by looking at Johan Galtung's "structural" theory of imperialism. By pushing neocolonial theory to its logical end, Galtung unwittingly exposes its absurdity. Imperialism, in Galtung's view, is a relation between more harmonious and richer states, on the one hand, and less harmonious and poorer states, on the other. He makes imperialism into a structural affair, but his structural theory is arrived at partly through reduction. In his definition of international structure he combines a national attribute, degree of harmony, with an international structural characteristic, distribution of capability. The former is an element of national structure, if it is a structural element at all. Because Galtung includes a national attribute in his international structure, his approach becomes reductionist. Structure is a useful concept if it is seen as conditioning behavior and as affecting the way in which functions are performed.* Defining international structure partly in terms of national attributes identifies those attributes with the outcomes one is trying to explain. Because Galtung defines structure in that way, behavior and function disappear; a country is called imperialist by virtue of its attributes and aside from the acts it commits. The observation of behavior, its connection with events, and the problem of alternative outcomes—all such complex and difficult matters can be left aside. Thus Galtung can say about Japan in southeast Asia that "there is no doubt as to the economic imperialism, but there is neither political, nor military, nor communication, nor cultural ascendancy." Imperialism, perfected, employs no military force whatsoever, neither direct force nor threat of violence (1971, pp. 82–84, 101). Rather than being a hard-to-unravel set of activities, imperialism becomes an easily seen condition: the increase of the gap in living conditions between harmonious rich countries and disharmonious poor ones.

Galtung's construction, offered as a theory, merely asserts that the cause of the widening gap in living conditions is the exploitation of the poor by the rich. "Vertical interaction," he claims, is "the major source of the inequality of this world" (1971, p. 89). Why that should be so is not explained but instead is reasserted in various ways. The asymmetry of international trade, the difference of situation between those who make goods and those who merely purvey the products of nature, the different degrees of processing that various nations' exports receive: In unspecified ways such factors supposedly cause the interactions of nations to enrich advanced states while impoverishing backward ones.

---

*For a discussion of these matters, see Chapter 4, part III.

To show how, under what circumstances, and to what extent the rich have enriched themselves by impoverishing the poor would require careful analysis, including examination of changes in the terms of trade and of the composition of exports and imports across countries and over time.* Such examinations reveal that at times some primary producers do very well. Are they then imperialistically exploiting others? In 1974, exporters of oil and of foodstuffs prospered. Underdeveloped Arab nations and highly developed North American ones fared well in contrast to most other countries. The former are pre-eminently examples of Galtung's exploited countries. They fall into his category of "being" rather than "becoming," of countries selling nature's goods rather than fashioning their own. At the same time, the United States is the world's major exporter of foodstuffs *and* Galtung's very model of an imperialist country. Not only does Galtung's theory offer descriptions rather than explanations, but also his descriptive categories fail to correspond to realities.

Galtung has apparently drawn unwarranted conclusions from a tendency of the terms of trade to move from the early 1950s to the early 1970s against primary products and in favor of manufactured goods. But such trends are not the same for all products nor do they last indefinitely. As variations in the terms of trade occur, some countries gain more from international trade; others gain less. The terms of trade move against countries offering products that are already plentifully supplied by others. Internationally as domestically, the poor are alienated and frustrated because they are so little needed. How can the unemployed be said to be exploited? How can countries offering materials that are in plentiful supply be said to be subsidizing rich nations through low commodity prices? If rich nations stopped buying their products, poor countries would surely be poorer.

Galtung nevertheless believes the rich exploit and impoverish the poor, impede their economic development, and keep them internally and externally disunited as well (1971, pp. 89–90). His conclusion, first put into his theory and later drawn from it, is that the imperialist relation between the rich and the poor is the major explanation for the well-being of the few and the suffering of the many. One must then ask whether the northern and western parts of the world have indeed impoverished the southern and eastern ones, and whether exploitation of the latter in turn enriched the former. Did imperialism bring economic exploitation, poverty, and strife to people who had not previously suffered those afflictions? Does imperialism now serve to perpetuate those ills? Exploitation and strife

---

*Rather than do this, Galtung offers examples that often turn out to be odd ones. "When a nation exchanges tractors for oil," he says, "it develops a tractor-producing capacity," with a tank-producing capacity as a possible spin-off (1971, p. 98). He leaves aside the fact that a country exports tractors for oil only if it already has developed an automotive industry. He apparently wants to make it seem that the poor enable the rich to develop their industries.

are not recent misfortunes, nor is poverty. Those who attribute disunity to imperialism might well recall the earlier condition of most colonial people. Until the middle of the nineteenth century, moreover, nearly everyone everywhere lived at a subsistence level or very close to it.* Marx and the earlier Marxists seem to be nearer the truth in believing that without the intervention of dynamic capitalist countries the nonwestern would might have remained in its backward condition forever.†

The causes of poverty are many and age-old, and so are the causes of wealth. Those who believe that imperialism is so highly profitable that it accounts for much of the wealth of the wealthy confuse private with national gain, fail to consider the costs of the imperial country including the cost of exporting capital, and forget that for most imperial countries any imperial gain is at best small when measured against its own economy. As markets for goods and as places for investment, moreover, other wealthy nations have been more important to advanced countries, whether or not they were imperialist, than backward countries have been. To say that imperialism has not returned some profits would be wrong. The main point, however, so compelling that it can be said in one sentence, is this: Surely the major reasons for the material well-being of rich states are found within their own borders—in their use of technology and in their ability to organize their economies on a national scale.

Nevertheless, for many of those who explain imperialism economically, the notion that the poor make the rich rich has become a cherished belief. That the rich make the poor poor, and inflict numerous other ills on them, is a belief perhaps as deeply revered. These despairing thoughts, momentary for old-fashioned Marxists because causes embedded in the system were to bring about its destruction, become permanent for today's neocolonialists for reasons that I shall set forth in the next section.

3. OVER-EXPLANATION AND THE PROBLEM OF CHANGE

The effort to save Lenin's thesis has led to such a broadening of the definition of imperialism that almost any relation among unequals can be termed "imperialism." The broadening was required to cover the successive refutation by events of

---

*Cf. Emmanuel (1972, pp. 48–52). The book advances the odd thesis that the increase of wages is the cause of national economic development.

†Mao Tse-tung's ambivalence on these points is interesting. China was not a colony but a semi-colony shared by several imperial masters. No one imperial country therefore had the incentive to promote China's development, and that, Mao remarks, helps to explain her uneven "economic, political and cultural development" (1939, p. 81). The conflict among imperial masters, however, promoted China's national and revolutionary struggles (1936, pp. 193–98).

key points in Lenin's theory. Marxists used to view foreign investment as a means of breaking through the inevitable stagnation of a laissez-faire economy. But once foreign investment brings capitalist countries a return greater than the amount of their new investment abroad, the "push" principle can no longer be said to operate. Some neocolonialists now point out that the net flow of funds is *to* the United States, and they add that much of the new investment of corporations operating abroad comes from capital borrowed locally.*

How then do capitalist states avoid economic stagnation? A simple answer is often given: by spending a lot on defense. Defense budgets are ideal absorbers of surplus capital because defense expenditures are sterile. This explanation, however, ill applies to Japan or to West Germany, the world's second and third ranking capitalist states. Even applied to the United States, the explanation itself admits that any additional objects of large-scale private or public expenditure would do as well, as Baran and Sweezy themselves point out (1966, pp. 146–53, 223). For our purposes, all that need be noticed is that the foreign investment of states is effectively separated from the Marxist analysis of capitalist economies once foreign investment is no longer seen as a way of compensating for underconsumption internally.

Thus one of the two principal elements of dialectic development is eliminated. The second element has also ceased to operate, for, as explained above, the underdeveloped countries are no longer thought to be uplifted economically through the flow of foreign capital to them. They therefore do not acquire the ability to resist the encroachments of capitalist states in the future. Capitalism does not reproduce itself abroad through its imperialist policies and therefore does not create the conditions from which socialism classically is supposed to emerge.

As the ultimate economic explanation, neocolonialism divorces imperialism from governmental policy. Imperialism now, resting on an economic imbalance in favor of capitalist states, is a condition that endures so long as that imbalance lasts. Putting it that way reveals the important common quality between Britain's "imperialism of free trade" in the middle of the nineteenth century and America's recent "imperialism of business expansion abroad." Each case is an instance of "the imperialism of great power." When a country produces a third or a quarter of the world's goods, it is bound to affect others more than others affect it. The vehicles of influence—whether they be commodity trade, financial instruments, or multinational corporations—produce their far-reaching effects because of the vast national capabilities that lie behind them.

---

*See, e.g., Baran and Sweezy (1966, pp. 105–109); Magdoff (1969, p. 198). Marxists have it both ways: earlier, the dependence of richer on poorer countries to absorb surplus capital; later, the exploitation of poorer by richer countries through the repatriation of profits on investment.

The only prescription for ending this so-called imperialism is one that tells the poor to become richer and/or the rich to become poorer.* And yet the present system is seen as producing, perpetuating, and enlarging the gap between rich nations and poor ones. Those who accept the neocolonial analysis must either end in despair or indulge in fantasy. The fantasy of their prescriptions for undoing imperialism is easily seen. Having defined imperialism as the exploitation of the weak by the strong or of the poor by the rich, Galtung, for example, can see an end to imperialism only through the weak and the poor cooperating and uniting in order to become strong and rich, though the complication of his statements somewhat obscures this prescription (1971, pp. 107ff.). Be strong! Become rich! Advice of that sort is difficult to follow. On occasion, the weak and poor may gain something by combining; but the occasions are few, and the gains are difficult to achieve. The dramatic increase of oil prices promoted by the cartel of oil exporting countries in the middle 1970s suggests that highly special conditions are prerequisites of success. The example mainly shows that those who are well-endowed with a resource in heavy demand prosper at the expense of many others, the more so if some regulation of supply is possible. The example confirms the colloquial saying that "them that's got, git" rather than supporting the hope that poor countries can improve their lots by concerting their efforts. Misery may like company, but when the poor and the weak join hands they gain little if anything in prosperity and strength.

IV

We can now reflect on the theories of imperialism examined above. Hobson, Lenin, and the neocolonialists offer economic explanations of the external behavior of states, with greater differences between the neocolonial school and Lenin than between Lenin and Hobson. Hobson and Lenin saw the expansion and consolidation of empires proceeding along with the development of capitalism. They argued that capitalism caused imperialism, and they concluded that the regulation or elimination of capitalism would abolish imperialism. They made the understandable error of thinking that the solution, even if it were such, of the specific problem of imperialism in the late nineteenth and early twentieth centuries would be a solution to the general and age-old problem of imperialism and also to the problem of war. Latter-day Marxists and other neocolonialists make different and less easily excused errors. They reinterpret the world to make it fit their misinterpretations of an old theory. "Theories" of the neocolonial sort can be

---

*As Robert Jervis pointed out in commenting on this chapter, a depression in rich countries that narrowed the gap would end imperialism as Galtung defines it so long as the depression lasted!

rejected as offering not explanations but redefinitions designed less to account for the phenomena than to salvage a theory.

The examination of neocolonial writers alerts us to the common practice of claiming to construct or to reconstruct theories while instead engaging in definitional exercises designed to make descriptive categories correspond to changes in observed events. The examination of Hobson and Lenin leads to thoughts about why reductionist approaches may be inadequate for the construction of international-political theory.

Hobson and Lenin concentrated attention on important attributes of some of the major imperialist states of their day. Examining those attributes in the light of Hobson's economic theory does tell us something about changes in national policies and in international politics from the late nineteenth century onward. But what claimed to be a general theory turned out to be only a partial one. As Eugene Staley commandingly demonstrated, although the theory does help to explain some imperialist policies, it is woefully misleading for others (1935). Economic considerations enter into most, if not into all, imperialist ventures, but economic causes are not the only causes operating nor are they always the most important one. All kinds of states have pursued imperialist policies. One who claims that particular types of states cause imperialism would, to be cogent, have to add that at other times and places quite different types of states were also imperialistic. Yet the theories we have examined claim that an imperial relation exists precisely because the imperial state has certain economic attributes. Such theories require one to believe that a condition of international imbalance accords an amount of influence and a degree of control that is usefully described as imperialism only if the more powerful parties possess the prescribed attributes. Thus, according to most of the economic theories, the baleful influence of the strong over the weak is to be found only if the strong states are capitalist. But that is hard to believe. One wonders, for example, if Mao Tse-tung thought of capitalist states as the unique cause of imperialism, and we know that Chou En-lai did not.* Conversely, the necessary implication of economic theories is that the strong and the weak can coexist without an imperial connection developing if the strong are properly constituted. If they are, then the autonomy of the weak will be secured by the self-interested wisdom of the strong.

Theories that make such assertions also contain, at least implicitly, the wider assertion that there are no good international-political reasons for the conflict and the warring of states. The reasons for war, as for imperialism, are located within some, or within all, of the states. But if the causes were cured, would the

---

*In his report to the Tenth Congress of the Chinese Communist Party, Chou identified the US and the USSR as the two imperialist countries "contending for hegemony" and referred to the latter as a "social-imperialist country" (Chou, September 1, 1973, p. 6).

symptoms disappear? One can hardly believe that they would. Though economic theories assign specific causes of war, we know that all sorts of states with every imaginable variation of economic and social institution and of political ideology have fought wars. Internationally, different states have produced similar as well as different outcomes, and similar states have produced different as well as similar outcomes. The same causes sometimes lead to different effects, and the same effects sometimes follow from different causes. We are led to suspect that reductionist explanations of international politics are insufficient and that analytic approaches must give way to systemic ones.

The failure of some reductionist approaches does not, however, prove that other reductionist approaches would not succeed. The defects of economic theories of imperialism and war, though they may suggest general problems met in concentrating explanations of international politics at national or lower levels, cannot be taken to indicate that all reductionist theories of international politics will be defective. Doubts about the adequacy of reductionist approaches would deepen if, one after another, such approaches were tried and found wanting. Even so, we would have no compelling reason to stop hoping that the next try would lead to a viable reductionist theory. We would be more nearly persuaded of reduction's inadequacy by either or both of the following: the construction of a useful nonreductionist, or system's level, theory, a task which is begun in Chapter 5; an explanation of why reductionist theories fail, a task better postponed until after some avowedly systemic theories have been examined in the next chapter.

3
Systemic Approaches and Theories

Skepticism about the adequacy of reductionist theories does not tell us what sort of systems theory might serve better. Explaining international politics in nonpolitical terms does not require reducing international to national politics. One must carefully distinguish between reduction from system to unit level and explanation of political outcomes, whether national or international, by reference to some other system. Karl Marx tried to explain the politics of nations by their economics. Immanuel Wallerstein tries to explain national and international politics by the effects "the capitalist world-economy" has on them (September 1974). One useful point is thereby suggested, although it is a point that Wallerstein strongly rejects: namely, that different national and international systems coexist and interact. The interstate system is not the only international system that one may conceive of. Wallerstein shows in many interesting ways how the world economic system affects national and international politics. But claiming that economics affects politics is no denial of the claim that politics affects economics and that some political outcomes have political causes. Wallerstein argues that "in the nineteenth and twentieth centuries there has been only one world-system in existence, the capitalist world-economy" (p. 390). The argument confuses theory with reality and identifies a model of a theory with the real world, errors identified in Chapter 1. An international-political theory serves primarily to explain international-political outcomes. It also tells us something about the foreign policies of states and about their economic and other interactions. But saying that a theory about international economics tells us something about politics, and that a theory about international politics tells us something about economics, does not mean that one such theory can substitute for the other. In telling us something about living beings, chemistry does not displace biology.

A systems theory of international politics is needed, but can one be constructed? Alan C. Isaak argues that political science has no theories and no theoretical concepts (1969, p. 68). The preceding discussion may have strengthened that argument by considering only economic and social theories, theories that claim to explain political outcomes without the use of political concepts or variables. "If capitalism, then imperialism" is a purported *economic* law of politics, a law that various economic theories of imperialism seek to explain. Can we find *political* laws of politics and political theories to explain them? Those who have essayed systems theories of international politics implicitly claim that we can, for a theory of international politics is systemic only if it finds part of the explanation of outcomes at the international-political level.

This chapter examines approaches to international politics that are both political and systemic. What is a systems approach? One way to answer the question is to compare analytic with systemic approaches. The analytic method, preeminently the method of classical physics and because of its immense success often thought of as *the* method of science, requires reducing the entity to its discrete parts and examining their properties and connections. The whole is understood by studying its elements in their relative simplicity and by observing the relations between them. By controlled experiments, the relation between each pair of variables is separately examined. After similarly examining other pairs, the factors are combined in an equation in which they appear as variables in the statement of a causal law. The elements, disjoined and understood in their simplicity, are combined or aggregated to remake the whole, with times and masses added as scalars and the relations among their distances and forces added according to the vector laws of addition (see, e.g., Rapoport 1968, and Rapoport and Horvath 1959).

This is the analytic method. It works, and works wonderfully, where relations among several factors can be resolved into relations between pairs of variables while "other things are held equal" and where the assumption can be made that perturbing influences not included in the variables are small. Because analytic procedure is simpler, it is preferred to a systems approach. But analysis is not always sufficient. It will be sufficient only where systems-level effects are absent or are weak enough to be ignored. It will be insufficient, and a systems approach will be needed, if outcomes are affected not only by the properties and interconnections of variables but also by the way in which they are organized.

If the organization of units affects their behavior and their interactions, then one cannot predict outcomes or understand them merely by knowing the characteristics, purposes, and interactions of the system's units. The failure of the reductionist theories considered in Chapter 2 gives us some reason to believe that a systems approach is needed. Where similarity of outcomes prevails despite changes in the agents that seem to produce them, one is led to suspect that analytic approaches will fail. Something works as a constraint on the agents or is interposed between them and the outcomes their actions contribute to. In international politics, systems-level forces seem to be at work. We might therefore try conceiving of political systems in ways compatible with usage in systems theory and in cybernetics.* A system is then defined as a set of interacting units. At one level, a system consists of a structure, and the structure is the systems-level component that makes it possible to think of the units as forming a set as distinct from a mere collection. At another level, the system consists of interacting units.

The aim of systems theory is to show how the two levels operate and interact, and that requires marking them off from each other. One can ask how A and B affect each other, and proceed to seek an answer, only if A and B can be kept distinct. Any approach or theory, if it is rightly termed "systemic," must show how the systems level, or structure, is distinct from the level of interacting units. If that is not shown, then one does not have a systems approach or a systems theory at all. Definitions of structure must omit the attributes and the relations of units. Only by doing so can one distinguish changes of structure from changes that take place within it.

What systems theories seek to reveal is often misunderstood by their critics. Some claim that systems theory seeks only to define equilibrium conditions and show how they can be maintained, that systems theory deals only with systems as wholes. Others claim that systems theory seeks to show how systems determine the behavior and interaction of their units, as though causes worked only downward. Because some theorists have limited themselves to the first purpose or adopted the second one is no reason for limiting or condemning systems theory as such. In international politics the appropriate concerns, and the possible accomplishments, of systems theory are twofold: first, to trace the expected careers of different international systems, for example, by indicating their likely durability and peacefulness; second, to show how the structure of the system affects the interacting units and how they in turn affect the structure.

A systems approach conceives of the international-political system as shown in Fig. 3.1. In order to turn a systems approach into a theory, one has to move from the usual vague identification of systemic forces and effects to their more precise specification, to say what units the system comprises, to indicate the com-

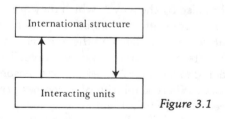

Figure 3.1

---

*I have found the following works bearing on systems theory and cybernetics especially useful: Angyal (1939), Ashby (1956), Bertalanffy (1968), Buckley (1968), Nadel (1957), Smith (1956 and 1966), Watzlawick *et al.* (1967), Wiener (1961).

parative weights of systemic and subsystemic causes, and to show how forces and effects change from one system to another. I shall examine the works of three prominent systems theorists to see whether, or how well, these tasks are accomplished.

I

To Richard Rosecrance, the international-political system looks like Fig. 3.2 (1963, p. 229). His framework is made up of four elements: (1) a disruptive source or input, (2) a regulator, and (3) a table of environmental constraints that translates numbers one and two into (4) outcomes (1963, pp. 220–21). States are the disrupters—more so, for example, if their elites are revolutionary and are insecurely in control of a good quantity of disposable resources; less so if their elites are conservative and are securely in control of a restricted supply of resources. The regulator appears in different historical periods as an institution, such as the Concert of Europe and the League of Nations, or as an informal process by which some states oppose the disturbing actions of others, perhaps through alliances and balance-of-power politics. The environment is the set of physical constraints that influences policy—the supply of colonizable land, for example, in an era of imperialist action (1963, pp. 224–30). Where in this formulation is there a notion of something at the systems level that conditions the behavior of states and affects the outcomes of their interactions? The answer is "nowhere." Rosecrance has not developed a theory; he has outlined a framework. Whatever seem to be the most important factors in a particular period of history are fitted into this framework. Systems language is then used to describe interactions and outcomes.

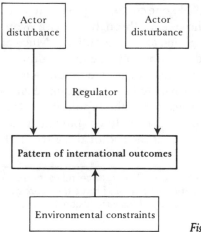

Figure 3.2

He has, moreover, constructed his framework in a way that determines the kind of conclusion he reaches. He announces a "finding" that he believes to be contrary to venerable and current views alike: namely, that the domestic insecurity of elites tends to correlate with international instability (1963, pp. 304–305). The correlation is apparently not a very high one. According to Rosecrance, neither Napoleon nor Hitler feared a "reversal of domestic constitutions," yet they were the biggest disturbers during the 220 years that Rosecrance covers. In the period of 1945–1960 the neutralist bloc, with insecure elites, appears alongside of the United Nations as the system's regulator (1963, pp. 210–11, 266). Nevertheless, however high or low the presumed correlation, Rosecrance can come to no conclusion other than that actors' behavior determines international outcomes. For states, his framework prescribes the role of "disturber"; states are also prominently included among the systems' regulators. Since the environment is purely physical and since no other element operating at the systems level is identified or postulated, international systems can be determined only by their units viewed as actors.*

For the most part, the above remarks are not criticisms of Rosecrance; they are instead descriptions of what he has done. He presents the components of his systems and then, in his words, seeks to show "how changes in these components make for changes in the international system." He terms his enterprise "systematic empirical analysis." It is empirical and analytic, but not systematic unless that word is used merely to suggest that an orderly method is followed. It is not systematic in any other sense, for the components produce all of the changes, and none of the components is at the systems level. "System-change, stability, and instability," as he puts it, "are not interdependent" (1963, pp. 220, 232). Systems as he describes them have no affect on the actions and the interactions of states. This is made obvious by his description of the international-political system in various eras. International politics from 1789 to 1814 and from 1918 to 1945, for example, is called "bipolar." No one could, or at least no one should, believe that bipolarity characterized those eras throughout, else why was Napoleon so pleased by the prospect of fighting against coalitions? Much of the politics of both periods centered on one side's trying to make and maintain coalitions while the other side tried to prevent or break them. Coalitions were finally forged in the crucible of war and even so proved to be of uncertain reliability, especially in the earlier period. What Rosecrance terms the bipolarity of these quarter centuries cannot possibly help to explain their politics. Bipolarity is used as a term that describes the alignment of states at the end of these eras rather than a term that

---

*In a later book (1973), a college text, Rosecrance relies more on common sense and strives less for theoretical innovation and rigor. I have therefore not commented on it, but I should mention that he modifies many of his earlier conclusions.

describes a political structure that conditions the acts of states and influences outcomes. At the systems level, we find results; at the subsystems level, causes.

Rosecrance's approach is reductionist, not systemic. His work does, however, represent one of the principal uses of a systems approach in international politics: namely, as a source of vocabulary and as a set of categories for the organization of a complex subject matter. How useful is the taxonomy? How good is the historical writing? His work should be judged in those terms rather than as a systems theory.

II

Especially in his earlier work, Stanley Hoffmann seems to differ decisively from Rosecrance, his former student. Hoffmann defines "an international system" as "a pattern of relations among the basic units of world politics." The "pattern is largely determined by the structure of the world," among other things (1961, p. 90). This seems to point toward a systems theory containing a structure conceived of as a truly systems-level element. That structure, unfortunately, comes to be so inclusively and vaguely defined that all distinct meaning is lost. This is not an accidental misfortune but a necessary consequence of Hoffmann's objectives and methods. Let me explain.

First, in Hoffmann's view, "the international system is both an analytic scheme and a postulate." As an "analytic scheme," or an "intellectual construct," system is a way of organizing plentiful and complex data. Systems are abstractions. As a postulate, system is an assertion "that there are distinguishable patterns of relations and key variables that can be discerned without artificiality or arbitrariness." Systems are then also realities, and that notion dominates Hoffmann's work. The following passage is a key expression of his method and aspiration:

> A historical sociology of international politics must try to study the international systems that have emerged in history just as political scientists study real (by contrast with imagined) domestic political systems.

The existence of domestic systems he believes to be certain; the existence of international systems is "more hypothetical." The student of international politics must all the more earnestly search for reality. He must look for relations among units that are "regular" and that "reach a certain amount of intensity," for units that have "a modicum of awareness of their interdependence," and for a specific international component that is distinct and separable from the internal affairs of the units (1961, pp. 91–92; cf. 1968, pp. 11–12).

These points reveal the fundamentals of Hoffmann's method. When he writes that the "existence" of the domestic political system is "certain," he is both assuming that a systems approach to politics requires the student to define and describe the political system as "real" and adopting a particular definition of system. What he takes as obvious is instead problematic. It is by no means apparent that one should take the existence of the domestic political system as being certain. Governments exist, but one may well think of political systems as being merely intellectual constructs (cf. Manning 1962, Chapter 3). Indeed, unless one does that, there is no reason for, or meaning to, system as a concept, as an approach, or as a possible theory.

Hoffmann nevertheless moves quickly from writing of political systems as intellectual constructs to hot pursuit of those systems as realities. Indeed he dwells so little on the scheme that the meaning and the very notion of system as construct remains elusive. If one is to pursue real international systems, what route must one follow? From a knowledge of the parts, one must draw inferences about the whole. Only the parts can be observed, the course of their actions traced, their purposes discerned. Thus Hoffmann praises Raymond Aron for his "rejection of any science that gives to the forms of behavior it studies explanations *contrary* to or *divorced* from the meaning understood by the participants." And, Hoffmann adds, "one must begin with the characteristic agents and forms of behavior" (1963a, p. 25). Hoffmann describes himself as a disciple of Montesquieu, de Tocqueville, and Aron (1964, p. 1269). The method of the masters is historical sociology, and that is an inductive approach.

The preceding comments enable one to understand both how Hoffmann thinks of systems and why he conceives of them as he does. These comments also explain why Hoffmann's approach breaks down. To sustain a systems approach, one must be able to say which changes represent the normal working of the system's parts and which changes mark a shift from one system to another. Hoffmann can only arbitrarily distinguish between those different kinds of changes because he has mingled elements at the unit level with elements at the systems level in his definition of structure. The mingling of elements necessarily takes place because one cannot inductively develop both a description of a system and criteria by which changes within a system are distinguished from changes between systems. Since the entities one looks at and the interactions among them *are* the system, it becomes impossible by any theory or logic to separate changes within systems from changes between them.

How then can Hoffmann distinguish one system from another? He believes that through historical comparisons important changes stand out, and that one can say that every important change is a change of system. Big changes *within* systems he takes to be changes *of* system. Economic examples easily show why this won't do. If economists confused unit-level with system-level changes, they would declare that a competitive economy, or an oligopolistic sector, changes its character as major technological breakthroughs occur or as managerial revolutions within firms take place. Theories of a competitive economy or of an oligopolistic sector may be improved or may be replaced by better ones, but the applicability of such theories is not called into question by technological change or by changes within firms. To call changes within systems changes *of* systems makes developing the notion of system into a theory of some explanatory power wholly impossible. And yet Hoffmann follows just that practice in writing about international politics. He sees a new system emerging every time the "units in potential conflict" change in form, every time "a fundamental innovation in the technology of conflict" occurs, and every time "the scope of the units' purposes" shrinks or expands (1961, pp. 92–93). Systems will proliferate wildly if these criteria are applied. Their energetic application is in fact discouraged by the complexity that would result. The generality of Hoffmann's criteria does, however, permit the student to announce the birth of a new system at any moment that suits him. "System" with an adjective prefixed—revolutionary, moderate, stable, bipolar, multipolar, or whatever—becomes a tag or title given to an era after it has been imaginatively drawn and finely described. "System" then does not explain anything; rather the exhaustive description of everything defines the system, and a new system is said to emerge every time there is reason to change the description in any important respect. Systems multiply to the point where different political systems are said to exist at one time and within a single arena (Hoffmann 1968, pp. 356–57; cf. Rosecrance 1966, pp. 320–25). Where the phenomena requiring explanation seem to be distinct, different systems are summoned into existence supposedly in order to explain them. Actually the systems merely reflect the variations that have been observed and described.

Progressively Hoffmann manages to get everything into the structure. In "International Systems and International Law," what states are like internally and the weapons technology at their disposal do not seem to be structural elements (1961). In *Gulliver's Troubles*, they have become so (e.g., pp. 17, 33). A structural cause is invented for every effect, and this is done in a way that makes the approach largely reductionist. Because the attributes and the behavior of units are said to be structural elements, systems-level causes become entangled with unit-level causes and the latter tend to become dominant. Although Hoffmann does not reach the Rosecrance extreme, he does come close to it. Hoffmann defines structure partly according to the arrangement of parts (the pattern of power) and partly according to the characteristics of those parts (the homogeneity or heterogeneity of states). The concrete characteristics of states— the ambitions of rulers, the means they employ, the extent of national integration, the properties of political institutions—all of these are part of his definition of structure (1961, pp. 94–95; 1968, pp. 17–18). In practice, his explanation of national policies and of international events rests almost entirely on what states and statesmen are like.

In effect, Hoffmann defines "structure" as a collection of items presumed somehow to have an important bearing on the conduct of foreign policy and on the outcomes of national interactions. In doing so he produces a confusion of causes and a mingling of causes and effects. To place the configuration of power and the homogeneity or heterogeneity of states in a single definition of structure is to combine elements at different levels of abstraction. "Configuration of power" abstracts from all of the characteristics of states except their capabilities. Including the homogeneity and heterogeneity of states as structural elements brings more content into the definition and thus lowers the level of abstraction. It requires us to ask not only what states are physically capable of doing but also how they are organized politically and what their ideologies and aspirations may be. The structure then contains elements at the unit level that may themselves be affected by the characteristics of the structure at the systems level.

The practical effect of combining different levels in one definition of structure is to make it impossible to answer, and even to impede asking, such important questions as these: How does the structure defined as configuration of power affect the characteristics of states—their aspirations, their choice of means, and possibly even their internal organization? And, conversely, how sensitive are different international structures to variations in the internal organization and behavior of the separate states? Hoffmann's method permits him only to describe international systems, or rather to convey his impression of them. It does not enable him to explain what happens to systems or within them. And yet he claims to do that. He draws a distinction, for example, between "moderate" systems and "revolutionary" ones. The former are multipolar in the distribution of power and homogeneous in terms of the aims of states and the methods they employ. The latter are bipolar in the distribution of power and heterogeneous in terms of the qualities of states (1968, pp. 12–14; cf. 1965, pp. 89–100). If the causal factors have been identified with care, then the categories should be useful. The categories are useful if they give rise to a range of expectations that correspond to the historical fate that different international systems have experienced. It is then somewhat unnerving to read that "the present system is also one of relative moderation," and to learn further that this "stability is achieved *despite* revolutionary aims and *despite* apparent bipolarity" (1968, pp. 20, 33, his emphasis).*

---

*The obvious but unhelpful response would be to say that nuclear weaponry makes a bipolar world moderate, and Hoffmann has sometimes said that. But the answer only begs the question or shows that a systems approach has been abandoned, for one immediately wants to know what differences in the effects of nuclear weaponry are to be expected as systems vary (see below, Chapter 8).

This conclusion makes it clear that for Hoffmann structure as a systems-level concept is neither going to explain much nor tell us that international outcomes are likely to fall within particular, definable ranges. Hoffmann has trouble thinking of bipolar and multipolar structures as themselves affecting the aspirations and behavior of states. He cannot very long or very consistently pursue such a line of thinking for reasons revealed in a comment he makes about earlier international systems: A "system's moderation or immoderation could," he writes, "be measured by examining the goals of the major units" (1968, p. 33). Admittedly, he does sometimes allow for systemic influences, but they always seem to be easily overcome—by the effects of weapons technology if not by the ambitions of rulers. His system is so rigged that he is free to select any of many elements of structure—most of which are at the subsystems level—and to say that in *this* case *that* element accounts for the outcome. What is important then are Hoffmann's evocations of systems, for their effects are subjectively and quite arbitrarily assigned.

Hoffmann consistently displays himself as Aron's disciple. Their theoretical commitments are identical; both pull persistently toward explanations of the inside-out variety. As Aron puts it, "the principal actors have determined the system more than they have been determined by it" (1966, p. 95). For Hoffmann as for Aron, outcomes are much more nearly unit determined than they are system influenced. Perhaps they are right. One would, however, think that a basic question to be explored is precisely whether system and unit effects vary in strength from one type of system to another. Aron and Hoffmann have arbitrarily given a particular answer to this question. Only by giving that arbitrary answer are they able to insist that the theorist preserve an assumed correspondence between the meaning of participants and the forms of their behavior.

So profound is Hoffmann's commitment to inside-out explanations that he recasts even Rousseau in his own image. Preeminently among political theorists, Rousseau emphasized the impossibility of inferring outcomes from observation merely of participants' attributes and behavior. The context of action must always be considered, whether dealing with men or with states, for the context will itself affect attributes and purposes and behavior as well as alter outcomes. Hoffmann, however, believes that Rousseau's "solution to the problem of war and peace" is this: Establish "ideal states all over the world, and peace will follow—without the need for a world league *a la* Kant" (1963b, p. 25). Interestingly enough, Rousseau rejects that belief and comes close to ridiculing it.*

---

*"Thus it is not impossible," so reads a representative statement from Rousseau's works, "that a Republic, though in itself well governed, should enter upon an unjust war" (1762, pp. 290–91; cf. Waltz 1959, pp. 145–86).

One can, however, find evidence to support almost any interpretation in an author who writes profoundly and at length about complicated matters. When Rousseau indicates a hope for peace among highly self-sufficient states having little contact with each other, Hoffmann attributes to Rousseau the notion that the internal qualities of such states—their goodness—would be the cause of peace among them. Rousseau is instead giving an environmental explanation: States can experience little conflict if they are only distantly related to each other. Hoffmann's interpretation is consistent with his own theoretical predilections, however, and they lead him to attribute to Rousseau conclusions about international politics that would subvert the whole of his political philosophy.

The essay on Rousseau, brilliant in its own way though profoundly contrary to its subject's philosophy, illustrates the force that theoretical commitments can generate. Such force affects interpretations of the world as well as of other theorists. Writing of international politics in the 1970s, Hoffmann announces the passing of the bipolar world, declares that a world of five major units is emerging, and argues that such a world may lend itself to the moderation and stability enjoyed before and after the French Revolution. But then he had previously declared the bipolar world to be quite moderate and stable also (March 6, 1972, p. 33; March 7, 1972, p. 39; cf. 1968, pp. 343–64).

Changes in expectation are not associated in any consistent way with changes of system. The carelessness with which systemic inferences are drawn is matched by the vagueness with which the system is defined. Having hailed the arrival of a five-power world, Hoffmann immediately adds that the five main actors are not comparable in their capabilities. If we are going to count, we ought to be counting the same things. Hoffmann discovers, however, that two of the main actors are "superpowers"; the other three are not. The number five is reached by adding up different sorts of things. But again that does not really matter, for what the system is, or becomes, depends not on the configuration of power among states but instead on their policies and behavior. This is well demonstrated by his conclusion. Unless the United States begins to pursue proper goals with effective tactics, he says, "we might, at best [or at worst?] have a tripolar world." As ever, the conclusion is reached reductively. The status of other countries, and the character of the international system, are defined in terms of American policy!

States produce their situations. One of course agrees with that statement. But the systems approaches so far examined tend strongly to break off their assessment of causes at that point. Since the weight of systems-level and of unit-level causes may well vary from one system to another, the tendency is an unfortunate one. To say that it would be useful to view international politics from the systems level is not to argue that the system determines the attributes and the behavior of states but rather to keep open the theoretically interesting and practically important question of what, in different systems, the proportionate causal weights of unit-level and of systems-level factors may be.

Hoffmann himself has called for a Copernican revolution in international politics (1959, p. 347). Such a revolution would require looking at international politics from a systems-level perspective. Hoffmann—with his insistence that systems are real, that actors must be aware of them, that theorists' categories must correspond to statesmen's aims—cannot make the revolution he has called for. In the absence of a Copernican revolution, Hoffmann is left with the Ptolemaic solution. Ptolemaic astronomy projected the earth's movement onto the heavenly bodies and compensated for the displacement by geometric ingenuity. Ptolemaic international politics leaves out of its analysis the effects that the overall system may have and then recaptures those effects impressionistically at the level of national attributes and behavior. That is why Hoffmann must proclaim the emergence of a new system whenever a noticeable change occurs within the units that constitute the international system.

Hoffmann's approach does have considerable merit, which the preceding criticisms should not be allowed to obscure. His conception of system and structure captures all of the factors that students of international politics must be concerned with; it conceives of a system as a pattern of relations, of the system as having an overall structure, and of the structure as a collection of elements that influence the behavior of rulers and the operations of states by which the pattern of relations is formed. The failure to resist the temptation to tuck most everything into the structure does, however, make it impossible to use Hoffmann's framework for a system as the basis of a theory of international politics that would identify distinct elements, define different levels of abstraction, try to establish causal relations, and seek to find patterns of recurrent behavior and ranges of expected effects that may be associated with different international systems. His instruction to students of international politics comes perilously close to being this: Remember that any of many factors may affect the relations to states. A knowledge of history and of public affairs will then presumably enable men of intelligence to figure out just what factors may have the most serious effects at a given moment in time.

Hoffmann has not developed a theory but instead has displayed a strong commitment to a particular intellectual approach. This approach gives consistency to his judgments. His commitment to the reality of the international system and his conviction that statesmen must "see" the system correctly in order to act effectively have helped to make his writing vivid. The sensitivity of perception and the sharpness of insight are impressive, but any glimmerings of theory remain crude and confused.

III

Any approach to international politics that is properly called systemic must at least try to infer some expectations about the outcomes of states' behavior and interactions from a knowledge of systems-level elements. For Hoffmann, and especially for Rosecrance, the important explanations are found at the level of states and of statesmen; the systems level thus becomes all product and is not at all productive. Indeed, one is hard pressed to find a systems approach that views structure as a systems-level concept actually having some causal impact. Morton A. Kaplan would seem to be one of the few major theorists who elaborately and consistently takes such a view. Though he calls his attempted theory a "system of action," the distinguishing characteristics of his six systems seem to lie in their organizing principles and in their configurations of power. He seems, moreover, to derive some explanations about outcomes from differences in these elements. Further, his work is usually described as, or praised and condemned for, doing just that. Robert J. Lieber, for example, says in his useful survey of the field that "Kaplan's actual models reflect the assumption that the structure of a complex system tends to determine its characteristic performance" (1972, p. 134). Stanley Hoffmann, believing this, condemns Kaplan for overlooking the diversity of states, for endowing systems with wills of their own, for assuming that systems assign roles to actors, for believing that structures set needs and determine aims, and for neglecting domestic forces (1959, pp. 360–61).

True, in a book that tries to develop a theory of international politics, Kaplan naturally and rightly makes some simplifying assumptions and fails to write at length about national diversities and domestic forces. The important theoretical question, however, is this: How does he define, locate, weigh, and interrelate causal forces that operate in different parts and at different levels of the system? On this question, Lieber's description and Hoffmann's criticisms miss the mark. Let us look at what Kaplan has done.

Although Kaplan makes no claim to having developed a completely deductive theory, the claims he does make are bold enough to leave one breathless. In 1964, reflecting on his work as published seven years earlier, Kaplan claimed that his theory prescribes optimal state behavior under given conditions; predicts behavior given rational, completely informed statesmen; and explains or predicts outcomes as parameters depart from their equilibrium values.* These are extraordinary claims. Unfortunately, the performance does not measure up to them. To say why Kaplan's effort to construct a systems theory of international politics has failed may point the way toward more successful attempts.

---

*See the unpaginated prefaces to the 1957 and 1964 editions. Both prefaces are included in the later edition, which is otherwise identical to the earlier one.

Kaplan examines six systems: namely, balance of power, loose bipolar, tight bipolar, unit veto, universal, and hierarchic.* He then identifies five "variables" that are sufficient for describing the state of each system. They are "the essential rules of the system, the transformation rules, the actor classificatory variables, the capability variables, and the information variables" (1964, p. 9). The relative importance and the interactions of the five variables are not indicated, and, because they are not, Kaplan's systems approach cannot be said to constitute a theory.† One of the five variables, "the essential rules of the system," nevertheless seems to be the weightiest.

Of Kaplan's six systems, the balance-of-power system receives the most attention. It is arbitrarily defined, with an eye on the nineteenth century, as having a minimum of five principal actors.‡ Its rules are the following:

1. Act to increase capabilities but negotiate rather than fight.
2. Fight rather than pass up an opportunity to increase capabilities.
3. Stop fighting rather than eliminate an essential national actor.
4. Act to oppose any coalition or single actor which tends to assume a position of predominance with respect to the rest of the system.
5. Act to constrain actors who subscribe to supranational organizing principles.
6. Permit defeated or constrained essential national actors to re-enter the system as acceptable role partners or act to bring some previously inessential actor within the essential actor classification. Treat all essential actors as acceptable role partners.

On different pages, Kaplan says that the six rules have all of the following characteristics: They are descriptive and prescriptive; they are essential, interdependent, and in equilibrium with one another; and, as prescriptions for the actors, they are inconsistent and contradictory (1964, pp. 9, 25, 52–53). They do indeed have the latter qualities, as William H. Riker has conclusively shown. For reasons that he lays bare, "at some point the participants are necessarily faced with a conflict of rules, in which circumstance they must decide to follow one rule rather than another." Specifically, obedience to rules 1 and 2 under certain conditions will lead to the violation of rule 4 and quite possibly to the violation of rule 3 as well (1962, pp. 171–73).

---

*Though he labels all of them "international," the latter two have political subsystems and thus do not conform to his own definition of an international system (1964, pp. 14, 21, 45).

†On the distinction between a systems approach and a systems theory, see Gregor (1968, p. 425).

‡For an explanation of the arbitrary quality of the definition, see below, p. 118.

Rewriting the rules in the following way makes the source of the difficulty clear.

A. Act as cheaply as possible to increase capabilities (Kaplan's 1 and 2).

B. Protect yourself against others acting according to rule A (Kaplan's 4 and 5).

C. Act to maintain the number of units essential to the system (Kaplan's 3 and 6).

As Kaplan points out, rule A is "egoistic," and rule B is "rational," or, one might better say, commonsensical. Rule C, however, depends for its operation on the separate states being socialized into the system; that is, on their adopting the requirements of the system as the program for their own activity (1964, pp. 23–27). Rules A and B have their counterparts in microeconomic theory: Seek profit by all means permitted, and protect yourself against other firms who are competing against you. If rule C were translated into economic terms, it would have to read: Do not drive any essential firm into bankruptcy. The assumption that firms would conform to such a rule has no place in economic theory, for it is apparent that such a rule would conflict with the assumption that men and firms are profit maximizers. In international politics, a similar conflict is less easily seen. The acceptance of international norms, or the socialization of states to the international system, may of course take place. Kaplan turns this possible result into an assumption of the system.* He turns a dependent variable into an independent one. One may well search for "lawful" regularities in the affairs of states. If some are found, however, the distinction between laws that express a result and rules of action that produce one must be carefully made. Kaplan, like Hoffmann, writes as though actors will produce a given result only if they are motivated to do so. In Kaplan's case this is the more surprising, for he claims to follow general-systems theory, and one of its basic propositions is that systemic constraints modify the effect that a cause would produce in their absence. Kaplan offers no reason for identifying motives and consequences. A nice illustration of what erroneously doing so leads to is found in an essay by one of Kaplan's former students. Misled by a theory, he is surprised to find what he otherwise should have expected—that the Italian city-states in the fourteenth and fifteenth centuries did not comply with Kaplan's rule 1 and rule 4 (Franke, 1968, pp. 427, 436, 439).

Different problems appear in Kaplan's various systems, but the ones I have referred to so far are common to those four of his systems that can be properly be called international.† How do the problems arise? The general answer is that

---

*Weltman (1972) incisively criticizes Kaplan's arbitrary derivation of rules.

†That is, they do not apply to the hierarchical and univeral systems. The rules in the latter are different in kind from those of an international system, for agents exist to apply them (see 1964, pp. 45–50).

Kaplan has failed to develop the concepts that would permit him to bend the recalcitrant materials of international politics to fit the precise and demanding framework of a systems approach. The special demands of a systems approach must be met if the approach is to contain the possibility of developing into a theory rather than remaining merely a taxonomic device that carries with it an awkward vocabulary.

That Kaplan fails to meet these demands is apparent at the outset. He defines a system of action as "a set of variables so related, in contradistinction to its environment, that describable behavioral regularities characterize the internal relationships of the variables to each other and the external relationships of the set of individual variables to combinations of external variables." A system, he adds, "has an identity over time" (1964, p. 4). By this definition, which is not a bad one, he is required, first, to define the system, to indicate the system's environment, and to delineate the boundary between them; and, second, to define the system's structure so that the identity of the system will be distinguishable from the variables within it and from their interactions. These two problems are not solved.

First, Kaplan merges, or confuses, international systems with their environments. Writing of system models, Kaplan has said this: "The transformation rules state the changes that occur in the system as inputs across the boundary of the system that differ from those required for equilibrium move the system either toward instability or toward the stability of a new system" (1969, pp. 212–13). But where is the boundary between an international system and its environment or between the international system and other systems, and what is it that may come in from outside? By Kaplan's definitions, all of the things important for international systems are within them, and yet he writes of the parameters of an international system being "changed by disturbances from outside the system" (1964 preface). What is the environment, and what are the other systems from which disturbances can come?

The reader has to puzzle through an answer for himself, for Kaplan does not describe an environment, draw a boundary, or indicate how some other system coordinate with an international system might be conceived of. Two of his "variables" seem to operate at the systems level. They are the essential rules and the transformation rules. Here Kaplan catches us in a circle. If for the moment we take the essential rules as being consistent, then by Kaplan's assumptions and definitions any given system will remain in equilibrium indefinitely (i.e., be in stable equilibrium) so long as states follow those rules. This is so simply because Kaplan has equated the motivation and behavior of the actors with the results of their actions or with outcomes. The transformation rules come into play only "when environmental conditions are such that changes in characteristic behavior, that is, in the essential rules, are induced" (1964, p. 10). But for any given system, no changes in environmental conditions will occur so long as the actors continue to follow the essential rules. This is so since the term "environmental conditions" here refers to the environment of the states, not to the environment of the system. The environment of the states is, of course, the international system, which remains unchanged so long as states follow the essential rules. That is the circle.

How can the circle be broken? How is change possible? Kaplan mentions that changes may originate in previous states of the system, but in writing of international politics he does not treat this possibility in formal systemic terms. In fact, for him the source of change in international systems lies in the behavior of the actors, specifically in their breaking the essential rules. The states themselves are the sources of "disturbances from outside the system." For Kaplan, then, states in one of their aspects are the international system's environment!* No wonder he has been unable to conceive of the international system in relation to its environment in a useful way or to draw a boundary between them. Kaplan has not been able to meet the first of the requirements mentioned above.

He finds the second requirement—the establishing of the international system's identity—equally troublesome. One sees the difficulty by noticing the other way in which Kaplan views states: not as the environment of an international system but as subsystems of it. The states, being whole systems themselves as well as being subsystems of the international system, can be viewed as the systems in which disturbances originate. Tensions, dysfunctions, destabilizing events must, by Kaplan's definitions, arise from the actors themselves, whether considered as environment or as subsystems. The international system, in Kaplan's words, "tends toward the subsystem dominant pole." He thinks, for example, of his "balance-of-power" system as being "subsystem dominant" because "the essential rules of the 'balance-of-power' international system are subordinate to the rules of the individual national systems" (1964, pp. 17, 125, 129).

Here, as so often, Kaplan's language is loose and imprecise to the point of misleading the reader. On one and the same page, he writes of subsystems sharing dominance and of essential subsystems entering "into an equilibrium somewhat like that of the oligopolistic market" (1964, p. 17). The mind boggles at the thought of subsystems being dominant, let alone sharing dominance. What could subsystems' dominance *be* other than the negation of a systems approach? An oligopolistic market, moreover, is not one in which firms dominate the market but rather one in which, contrary to the notion of dominance, the extent to which firms affect the market and are in turn affected by it is indeterminate. In economics, because the concept of a market as the firms' environment is well defined, the extent of the influence of the market and of the influence of firms can

---

*The point is well developed in Hessler, whose work has also been helpful on a number of other points in this section.

be investigated. In Kaplan, no distinct and operational definition of the environment of states—no definition of such an environment as linked to and yet distinct from the states that form it—is ever developed. He offers, then, no way in which the extent of system's influence and of subsystems' influence can be investigated. He must, therefore, content himself with loose statements about system or subsystems tending toward, or being, dominant.

The consequences of Kaplan's failure to meet the second requirement now unfold. Defining a system as a set of variables so related, etc., requires one to say why a given collection of variables constitutes a set. "Since," as he says, "a system has an identity over time, it is necessary to be able to describe it at various times, that is, to describe its successive states. It is also necessary to be able to locate the variable changes which give rise to different succeeding states" (1964, p. 4). Fine, but the criteria he offers for fixing the identity of a system are weak and incomplete. Obviously one has no system if it is not possible to describe its various states and to specify the variables that produce them. But to say only that leaves aside the prior question of what it is that makes the set a set instead of a mere collection of variables. Kaplan emphasizes the importance of this question rather than answering it. His "models" of each of his systems are not in fact models but are mere collections of variables that are presumptively important for understanding international politics. The variables of a system represent its content. As a different Kaplan, Abraham, points out, "when one system is a model of another they resemble one another in *form* and not in content." Structural properties, he adds, are highly abstract, "for they concern only those features of relations which are wholly independent of what particular things stand in those relations" (1964, pp. 263–64). Morton Kaplan, however, fails even to be concerned with the problem of form. This lack of concern follows naturally from his system-of-action approach. He does not think of different systems in terms of their different structures but instead ranges them "along a scale of integrative activity" (1964, p. 21). This helps to explain his otherwise baffling statement that "theory—in particular, systems theory—permits the integration of *variables* from different disciplines" (1957 preface; my emphasis). Variables in different fields will ordinarily differ in content. Even though substance is different, borrowing across fields is legitimate if the two fields are homologous. It is likeness of form that permits applying theories and concepts across disciplines. In that kind of borrowing lies a possibly important contribution of systems theory. The borrowing of variables, even if possible, in no way advances the intellectual enterprise, for whether variables can be "borrowed" is mainly an empirical question. Because Kaplan has not solved the problem of the identity of a system—the problem of defining its structure or form—he cannot gain one of the important advantages promised by a systems approach, the possibility of applying similar theories to different realms.

Kaplan's failure to establish the identity of a system as distinct both from its environment and from its parts severely limits the matters that his approach can handle. He frequently asks what the effect of the behavior of states on the international system may be. He cannot put the question the other way around, for he has no concept of the system's structure acting as an organizational constraint on the actors, a constraint that would vary in its expected effects from one system to another. Since he cannot say how the system will affect the actors, his explanations or predictions can only be about the system itself—its equilibrium conditions, the extent of its stability, and the likelihood of its transformation (cf. 1964 preface).

Careful explanation of the limits inherent in Kaplan's approach is worthwhile since the points involved are fundamental ones for any systems approach. Making them here will help to sum up and to reinforce what I have already said about systems.

Though claiming to follow a systems approach, Kaplan like so many others fails to distinguish the interaction of units from their arrangement. He puts the relations of states, in the sense of interactions, at the systemic level. This is clearly seen in the way he separates tight bipolar systems from loose ones, with the distinction between them depending on how closely the lines of alliance are drawn (1964, pp. 36–45; cf. below, p. 57–58). On another fundamental point he does appear to avoid reduction from system to unit level, although appearances turn out to be unfortunately deceptive. He declares that his systems deal with any states whatsoever, that at the systems level the particular identities of states are of no account. If, however, the system itself is so vaguely conceived as to offer little if any explanation of the behavior of states, then the answer to the question that is crucial for Kaplan—whether or not states will follow his rules—will depend overwhelmingly on what those states are like! In terms of states' attributes as well as in terms of their interrelations, the approach turns out to be reductionist. Because Kaplan focuses on function and process, he concentrates his attention on the behavior and interaction of states. The propositions he offers are about decision-making units and the rules they follow rather than being about the effect of different international systems on such units (1964, Chapters 5 and 6). Once again an explicitly systemic approach turns out to be reductionist.

Kaplan's method is in fact the classical one of examining the character and the interactions of variables with the aggregate of their interactions taken as a depiction of the system. One can then proceed analytically. If this is indeed true, then those of Kaplan's critics who have found his elaborate constructions and procedures unnecessary are correct. Because their criticism is valid, it can be illustrated in many different ways. I shall take only one: Kaplan's notion of "feedback." The concept is borrowed from cybernetics, wherein it is defined as follows: When we "desire a motion to follow a given pattern the difference between this pattern and the actually performed motion is used as a new input to cause the part regulated to move in such a way as to bring its motion closer to that given by the pattern" (Wiener 1961, pp. 6–7). By such a definition, feedback operates only within an organization; that is, the notion of feedback has no precise, distinct, technical meaning outside of a hierarchic order (Bertalanffy 1968, pp. 42–44; Koestler 1971, p. 204). Kaplan's, and everybody's, favorite example of a thermostat regulating a furnace so as to keep the temperature within a narrow range is consistent with Wiener's definition and with what it entails—a controller and a controlled instrument producing a given result. But in international relations, what corresponds to such notions? Nothing! Kaplan simply uses the word without worrying about its formal appropriateness. The word "feedback" then conveys only that under certain conditions some states are likely to change their policies in response to the moves of other states, whose further moves will in turn be affected by those changes (1964, p. 6). But that thought offers nothing new and entails no distinct concept. The thermostat and the furnace have merged. They are one and the same. There is no notion of a controller separate from the controlled actor.

Sadly, one must agree with Charles McClelland: Kaplan has both popularized systems theory and rendered it mysterious (1970, p. 73) His work is more an approach and a taxonomy than a theory. But the approach is full of puzzles that, because of contradictions and conceptual inadequacies, the reader cannot solve. For the same reasons, the taxonomy is of little use. In summary and in ascending order of importance, the following three difficulties are salient:

1 By identifying his principal system, the balance of power, with the historical condition of contention among five or so great powers, he obscures the fact that balance-of-power theory applies in all situations where two or more units coexist in a self-help system. In new language, Kaplan perpetuates the perennial misconceptions about balance-of-power theory and makes it harder than ever to see that in international politics balance of power is simply a theory about the outcome of units' behavior under conditions of anarchy (cf. below, Chapter 6, part II).

2 One should follow a systems approach only if it seems that systems-level causes operate. One must then carefully keep the attributes and interactions of the system's units out of the definition of its structure. If one does not do this, then no systems-level explanations can be given. One cannot even attempt to say how much the system affects the units. I have indicated above that attributes and interactions creep into Kaplan's work at the systems level. Here, as so often, he is inconsistent. Having explicitly denied attributes a place in the structure, he then smuggles them in through his rules. In his balance-of-power system, relations are apparently not included at the systems level—for example, he does not fall into the common error of describing great-power politics prior to World War I as

being bipolar (1966, pp. 9–10). Yet his loose and tight bipolar systems achieve their special identities precisely through differences in relations, that is, through differences in the characteristics of blocs.

One can scarcely derive a part of the explanation for the formation, the importance, and the durability of blocs or alliances from consideration of the type of system that prevails if systems are themselves differentiated in part according to relational characteristics. In his balance-of-power system, Kaplan follows that logic; in his loose and tight bipolar systems, he does not. Kaplan's confusion on this important point has no doubt helped to perpetuate the prevailing custom of including alliance configurations in the structure of international systems. With distressing frequency, the things we want to explain—the strengths of propensities toward forming alliances, the ease with which they are maintained or changed—get mixed up with what may help to explain them. One must suspect that Kaplan's work, among the first of systemic writings about international politics, bears some responsibility for the widespread confusion.

3 A systems approach is required only if the structure of the system and its interacting units mutually affect each other. A systems approach is successful only if structural effects are clearly defined and displayed. According to Kaplan, the international-political system is an open one. In an open system, the structure of the system may determine outcomes aside from changes in variables and despite the disappearance of some of them and the emergence of others.* Within a given system, different "causes" may produce the same effect; in different systems, the same "causes" may have different consequences. The effect of an organization, in short, may predominate over the attributes and interactions of the elements within it. Short of predominating, a system's structure acts as a constraint on the system's units. It disposes them to behave in certain ways and not in others, and because it does so the system is maintained. If systemic forces are insufficient for these tasks, then the system either dissolves or is transformed. Kaplan, however, does not develop the distinctively systemic component of his system's approach. As is typical of political scientists, the structural concept is weak, or absent, and process and function take over. Kaplan, of course, makes this limitation of his approach explicit by describing international systems as subsystem dominant. A subsystem dominant system is no system at all. Again we have the case of an essentially reductionist approach being labeled systemic.

Students of international politics who claim to follow a systems approach fall into two categories. Some merely use such terms as "system" and "structure" as words of fashion in the ever-developing jargon of the field. Their analyses of

---

*This is the notion of "equifinality," which obtains if the same final state is reached from different initial conditions (Bertalanffy 1968, pp. 131–49).

international events and of the relations of states would be no different if the terms were simply omitted. Others pattern their work on the general-systems model. The presence of systemic effects, however, does not in itself mean that the realm of international politics can be defined as a system in the sense in which that term is used by general-systems theorists. In their sense, a system is a full-blown organization, hierarchically arranged with differentiated parts performing specified functions. The attempt to follow the general-systems model has been a misfortune, for our subject matter does not fit the model closely enough to make the model useful. International politics lacks the articulated order and the hierarchic arrangement that would make a general-systems approach appropriate.

4

Reductionist and Systemic Theories

Chapters 2 and 3 are highly critical. Criticism is a negative task that is supposed to have positive payoffs. To gain them, I shall in this chapter first reflect on the theoretical defects revealed in previous pages and then say what a systems theory of international politics comprises and what it can and cannot accomplish.

I

In one way or another, theories of international politics, whether reductionist or systemic, deal with events at all levels, from the subnational to the supranational. Theories are reductionist or systemic, not according to what they deal with, but according to how they arrange their materials. Reductionist theories explain international outcomes through elements and combinations of elements located at national or subnational levels. That internal forces produce external outcomes is the claim of such theories. $N \longrightarrow X$ is their pattern. The international system, if conceived of at all, is taken to be merely an outcome.

A reductionist theory is a theory about the behavior of parts. Once the theory that explains the behavior of the parts is fashioned, no further effort is required. According to the theories of imperialism examined in Chapter 2, for example, international outcomes are simply the sum of the results produced by the separate states, and the behavior of each of them is explained through its internal characteristics. Hobson's theory, taken as a general one, is a theory about the workings of national economies. Given certain conditions, it explains why demand slackens, why production falls, and why resources are under-employed. From a knowledge of how capitalist economies work, Hobson believed he could infer the external behavior of capitalist states. He made the error of predicting outcomes from attributes. To try to do that amounts to over-looking the difference between these two statements: "He is a troublemaker." "He makes trouble." The second statement does not follow from the first one if the attributes of actors do not uniquely determine outcomes. Just as peacemakers may fail to make peace, so troublemakers may fail to make trouble. From attributes one cannot predict outcomes if outcomes depend on the situations of the actors as well as on their attributes.

Few, it seems, can consistently escape from the belief that international-political outcomes are determined, rather than merely affected, by what states are like. Hobson's error has been made by almost everyone, at least from the nineteenth century onward. In the earlier history of modern great-power politics, all of the states were monarchies, and most of them absolute ones. Was the power-political game played because of international-political imperatives or simply because authoritarian states are power-minded? If the answer to the latter part of the question were "yes," then profound national changes would transform international politics. Such changes began to take place in Europe and America most strikingly in 1789. For some, democracy became the form of the state that would make the world a peaceful one; for others, later, it was socialism that would turn the trick. Not simply war and peace, moreover, but international politics in general was to be understood through study of the states and the statesmen, the elites and the bureaucracies, the subnational and the transnational actors whose behaviors and interactions form the substance of international affairs.

Political scientists, whether traditional or modern in orientation, reify their systems by reducing them to their interacting parts. For two reasons, the lumping of historically minded traditionalists and scientifically oriented modernists together may seem odd. First, the difference in the methods they use obscures the similarity of their methodology, that is, of the logic their inquiries follow. Second, their different descriptions of the objects of their inquiries reinforce the impression that the difference of methods is a difference of methodology. Traditionalists emphasize the structural distinction between domestic and international politics, a distinction that modernists usually deny. The distinction turns on the difference between politics conducted in a condition of settled rules and politics conducted in a condition of anarchy. Raymond Aron, for example, finds the distinctive quality of international politics in "the absence of a tribunal or police force, the right to resort to force, the plurality of autonomous centers of decision, the alternation and continual interplay between peace and war" (1967, p. 192). With this view, contrast J. David Singer's examination of the descriptive, explanatory, and predictive potentialities of two different levels of analysis: the national and the international (1961). In his examination, he fails even to mention the contextual difference between organized politics within states and formally unorganized politics among them. If the contextual difference is overlooked or denied, then the qualitative difference of internal and external politics disappears or never was. And that is indeed the conclusion that modernists reach. The difference between the global system and its subsystems is said to lie not in the anarchy of the former and the formal organization of the latter, but in there being, as Singer puts it, only one international system "on and around the planet Earth" (1969, p. 30). If one believes that, then "the level-of-analysis problem in international relations" is solved by turning the problem into a matter of choice, a choice made according to the investigator's interest (1961, p. 90).

Traditionalists keep harping on the anarchic character of international politics as marking the distinction between internal and external realms, and modernists do not. If we listen to what members of the two camps *say*, the gulf between them is wide. If we look at what members of both camps *do*, methods aside, the gulf narrows and almost disappears. All of them drift to the "subsystem dominant pole." Their attention focuses on the behaving units. They concentrate on finding out who is doing what to produce the outcomes. When Aron and other traditionalists insist that theorists' categories be consonant with actors' motives and perceptions, they are affirming the preeminently behavioral logic that their inquiries follow. Modernists and traditionalists are struck from the same mold. They share the belief that explanations of international-political outcomes can be drawn by examining the actions and interactions of nations and other actors.

The similarity of traditional and modern approaches to the study of international politics is easily shown. Analysts who confine their attention to interacting units, without recognizing that systemic causes are in play, compensate for the omissions by assigning such causes arbitrarily to the level of interacting units and parcelling them out among actors. The effects of relegating systemic causes to the level of interacting units are practical as well as theoretical. Domestic politics are made into matters of direct international concern. This was clearly shown in 1973 and after when détente became something of an issue in American politics. Could détente, some wondered, survive American pressure on Russian political leaders to govern a little more liberally? Hans Morgenthau, not unexpectedly, turned the argument around. American concern with Russia's internal politics he claimed, is not "meddling in the domestic affairs of another country. Rather it reflects the recognition that a stable peace, founded upon a stable balance of power, is predicated upon a common moral framework that expresses the commitment of all the nations concerned to certain basic moral principles, of which the preservation of that balance of power is one" (1974, p. 39). If the international-political outcomes are determined by what states are like, then we must be concerned with, and if necessary do something to change, the internal dispositions of the internationally important ones.

As a policymaker, Secretary of State Henry Kissinger rejected Morgenthau's argument. As a political scientist, however, Kissinger had earlier agreed with Morgenthau in believing that the preservation of peace and the maintenance of international stability depend on the attitudes and the internal characteristics of states. Kissinger defined an international order as "legitimate" if it is accepted by all of the major powers and as "revolutionary" if one or more of them rejects it. In contrast to a legitimate order, a revolutionary order is one in which one or more of the major states refuses to deal with other states according to the conventional rules of the game. The quality of the order depends on the dispositions of the states that constitute it. A legitimate international order tends toward stability and peace; a revolutionary international order, toward instability and war. Revolutionary states make international systems revolutionary; a revolutionary system is one that contains one or more revolutionary states (Kissinger 1957, pp. 316–20; 1964, pp. 1–6, 145–47; 1968, p. 899). The reasoning is circular, and naturally so. Once the system is reduced to its interacting parts, the fate of the system can be determined only by the characteristics of its major units.*

Among political scientists, Morgenthau and Kissinger are considered to be traditionalists—scholars turned toward history and concerned more with policy than with theory and scientific methods. The practice in question, however, is common among social scientists of different orientations. We saw in Chapter 3 that Kaplan's reasoning is Morgenthau's, although Kaplan's vocabulary, borrowed from general-systems theory, has obscured this. Marion Levy, a sociologist who at times writes about international politics, provides another example. He asserts that the "problem foci" of international affairs "are those of the modernization of the relatively non-modernized societies and of the maintenance of stability within (and consequently among) the relatively modernized societies" (1966, p. 734).

Inside-out explanations always produce the results that these examples illustrate. Kissinger's saying that international instability and war are caused by the existence of revolutionary states amounts to saying that wars occur because some states are warlike. And yet revolutionary regimes may obey international rules—or, more simply, tend toward peaceful coexistence—because the pressures of their external situations overwhelm their internally generated aims. Revolutionary international orders are at times stable and peaceful. Conversely, legitimate international orders are at times unstable and war prone. Levy's effort to

---

*What Kissinger learned as a statesman is dramatically different from the conclusions he had reached as a scholar. Statements revealing his new views abound, but one example will suffice. Interviewed while Secretary of State by William F. Buckley, Jr., Kissinger made the following points in three successive paragraphs: "Communist societies are morally, in their internal structure, not acceptable to us. . . ." Though our and their ideologies continue to be incompatible, we can nevertheless make practical and peace-preserving accommodations in our foreign policy. We should, indeed, "avoid creating the illusion that progress on some foreign policy questions . . . means that there has been a change in the domestic structure" (September 13, 1975, p. 5).
The link between internal attributes and external results is not seen as an unbreakable one. Internal conditions and commitments no longer determine the quality of international life.

predict international outcomes from national characteristics leads to similarly unimpressive results. Saying that stable states make for a stable world amounts to no more than saying that order prevails if most states are orderly. But even if every state were stable, the world of states might not be. If each state, being stable, strove only for security and had no designs on its neighbors, all states would nevertheless remain insecure; for the means of security for one state are, in their very existence, the means by which other states are threatened. One cannot infer the condition of international politics from the internal composition of states, nor can one arrive at an understanding of international politics by summing the foreign policies and the external behaviors of states.

Differences across traditional and modern schools are wide enough to obscure their fundamental similarity. The similarity, once seen, is striking: Members of both schools reveal themselves as behavioralists under the skin. Members of both schools offer explanations in terms of behaving units while leaving aside the effect that their situations may have. The full sense of the unity in style of reasoning is conveyed by setting examples from Chapters 2 and 3 alongside those just added. Veblen and Schumpeter explain imperialism and war according to internal social development; Hobson and his vast progeny, by internal economic arrangement. Levy thinks national stability determines international stability. Kaplan declares international politics to be subsystem dominant. Aron says that what the poles of the system are like is more important than how many poles there may be. As scholar, though not as public official, Kissinger identified revolutionary states with international instability and war. Because he agrees with Kissinger as scholar, Morgenthau advises intervention in the domestic affairs of other states in the name of international-political necessity. Rosecrance makes the international system all effect, and not at all cause, and turns his examination of international politics into a "correlating" of internal conditions and international outcomes and a tracing of sequential effects. Many modern students spend much of their time calculating Pearsonian coefficients of correlation. This often amounts to attaching numbers to the kinds of impressionistic associations between internal conditions and international outcomes that traditionalists so frequently offer. International-political studies that conform to the inside-out pattern proceed by correlational logic, whatever the methods used. Scholars who may or may not think of themselves as systems theorists, and formulations that seem to be more scientific or less so, follow the same line of reasoning. They examine international politics in terms of what states are like and how they interact, but not in terms of how they stand in relation to one another. They commit C. F. A. Pantin's "analytic fallacy" by confining their studies to factors that bear on their phenomena without considering that "higher-order configurations may have properties to be studied in their own right" (1968, p. 175).

It is not possible to understand world politics simply by looking inside of states. If the aims, policies, and actions of states become matters of exclusive attention or even of central concern, then we are forced back to the descriptive level; and from simple descriptions no valid generalizations can logically be drawn. We can say what we see, but we cannot know what it may mean. Every time we think that we see something different or new, we will have to designate another unit-level "variable" as its cause. If the situation of actors affects their behavior and influences their interactions, then attempted explanation at the unit level will lead to the infinite proliferation of variables, because at that level no one variable, or set of variables, is sufficient to produce the observed result. So-called variables proliferate wildly when the adopted approach fails to comprehend what is causally important in the subject matter. Variables are added to account for seemingly uncaused effects. What is omitted at the systems level is recaptured—if it is recaptured at all—by attributing characteristics, motives, duties, or whatever to the separate actors. The result observed is turned into a cause, which is then assigned to the actors. There is, however, no logically sound and traceable process by which effects that derive from the system can be attributed to the units. Variables then have to be added subjectively, according to the good or bad judgment of the author. This makes for endless arguments that are doomed to being inconclusive.

In order to take Morgenthau, Kissinger, Levy, and the rest seriously, we would have to believe that no important causes intervene between the aims and actions of states and the results their actions produce. In the history of international relations, however, results achieved seldom correspond to the intentions of actors. Why are they repeatedly thwarted? The apparent answer is that causes not found in their *individual* characters and motives do operate among the actors collectively. Each state arrives at policies and decides on actions according to its own internal processes, but its decisions are shaped by the very presence of other states as well as by interactions with them. When and how internal forces find external expression, if they do, cannot be explained in terms of the interacting parties if the situation in which they act and interact constrains them from some actions, disposes them toward others, and affects the outcomes of their interactions.

If changes in international outcomes are linked directly to changes in actors, how can one account for similarities of outcome that persist or recur even as actors vary? One who believes that he can account for changes in international politics must also ask how continuities can be explained. International politics is sometimes described as the realm of accident and upheaval, of rapid and unpredictable change. Although changes abound, continuities are as impressive, or more so, a proposition that can be illustrated in a number of ways. One who reads the apocryphal book of First Maccabees with events in and after World War I in mind will gain a sense of the continuity that characterizes international politics. Whether in the second century before Christ or in the twentieth century after, Arabs and Jews fought among themselves and over the residues of northern empire, while states outside of the arena warily watched or actively intervened. To illustrate the point more generally, one may cite the famous case of Hobbes experiencing the contemporaneity of Thucydides. Less famous, but equally striking, is the realization by Louis J. Halle of the relevance of Thucydides in the era of nuclear weapons and superpowers (1955, Appendix). In the two world wars of this century, to choose a different type of illustration, the same principal countries lined up against each other, despite the domestic political upheavals that took place in the interwar period. The texture of international politics remains highly constant, patterns recur, and events repeat themselves endlessly. The relations that prevail internationally seldom shift rapidly in type or in quality. They are marked instead by dismaying persistence, a persistence that one must expect so long as none of the competing units is able to convert the anarchic international realm into a hierarchic one.

The enduring anarchic character of international politics accounts for the striking sameness in the quality of international life through the millennia, a statement that will meet with wide assent. Why then do we find such a persistent pull toward reduction? The answer is that usually reduction results not from a scholar's intent but from his errors. The study of interacting units is thought to exhaust the subject, to include all that can be included both at the level of the unit and at the level of the system. Some political scientists claim that a systems perspective draws attention to the relational aspects of international politics. But interacting states have always been the objects of study. Others say that to complete an analysis done in terms of interacting states one need only add consideration of nonstate actors. They may need to be included, but including them will leave us at the unit level or lower. Interactions occur at the level of the units, not at the level of the system. Like the outcome of states' actions, the implications of interactions cannot be known, or intelligently guessed at, without knowledge of the situation within which interactions occur. The sporadic interactions of states may, for example, be more important than the daily conduct of routine business. The fate of states whose economic and touristic relations are sparse may be closely linked. We know that this holds for the United States and the Soviet Union. We could not reach that conclusion by counting transactions and by measuring the interactions that take place. This does not mean that counting and measuring are useless activities. It does mean that conclusions about the condition of international politics cannot be directly inferred from data about the formal or informal relations of states. In fact, we more often proceed in the opposite direction. We say, for example, that the United States and the Soviet

Union, or the United States, the Soviet Union, and China, interact closely because we believe that actions separately taken strongly affect the pair, or the trio, whether or not there are relations to observe and transactions to count. We save ourselves from the absurdity of saying that a low level of observed interactions between or among certain states indicates the unimportance of their relations by falling back on what we already know.

Continuities and repetitions defeat efforts to explain international politics by following the familiar inside-out formula. Think of the various causes of war discovered by students. Governmental forms, economic systems, social institutions, political ideologies: These are but a few examples of where causes have been found. And yet, though causes are specifically assigned, we know that states with every imaginable variation of economic institution, social custom, and political ideology have fought wars. More strikingly still, many different sorts of organizations fight wars, whether those organizations be tribes, petty principalities, empires, nations, or street gangs. If an indicated condition seems to have caused a given war, one must wonder what accounts for the repetition of wars even as their causes vary. Variations in the quality of the units are not linked directly to the outcomes their behaviors produce, nor are variations in patterns of interaction. Many, for example, have claimed that World War I was caused by the interaction of two opposed and closely balanced coalitions. But then many have claimed that World War II was caused by the failure of some states to right an imbalance of power by combining to counter an alliance in being.

II

Nations change in form and in purpose; technological advances are made; weaponry is radically transformed; alliances are forged and disrupted. These are changes within systems, and such changes help to explain variations in international-political outcomes. In Chapter 3 we found that aspiring systems theorists think of such within-system changes as marking shifts from one system to another. Once structure is clearly defined, a task for the next chapter, changes at the level of structure can be kept separate from changes at the level of units. One may wonder, however, whether inadvertent reductions that result in calling unit-level changes structural ones can be remedied by a change of vocabulary. Unfortunately they cannot be. The problem of showing how structural causes produce their effects would be left unsolved.

Low-level explanations are repeatedly defeated, for the similarity and repetition of international outcomes persist despite wide variations in the attributes and in the interactions of the agents that supposedly cause them. How can one account for the disjunction of observed causes and effects? When seeming causes vary more than their supposed effects, we know that causes have been incorrectly or incompletely specified. The repeated failure of attempts to explain inter-national outcomes analytically—that is, through examination of interacting units—strongly signals the need for a systems approach. If the same effects follow from different causes, then constraints must be operating on the independent variables in ways that affect outcomes. One cannot incorporate the constraints by treating them as one or more of the independent variables with all of them at the same level, because the constraints may operate on all of the independent variables and because they do so in different ways as systems change. Because one cannot achieve that incorporation, reduction is not possibly adequate, and an analytic approach must give way to a systemic one. One can believe that some causes of international outcomes are located at the level of the interacting units. Since variations in presumed causes do not correspond very closely to variations in observed outcomes, however, one has to believe that some causes are located at a different level as well. Causes at the level of units and of systems interact, and because they do so explanation at the level of units alone is bound to mislead. If one's approach allows for the handling of both unit-level and systems-level causes, then it can cope with both the changes and the continuities that occur in a system. It can do so, moreover, without proliferating variables and multiplying categories.

From Chapter 1 we know how theories are constructed. To construct a theory we have to abstract from reality, that is, to leave aside most of what we see and experience. Students of international politics have tried to get closer to the reality of international practice and to increase the empirical content of their studies. Natural science, in contrast, has advanced over the millennia by moving away from everyday reality and by fulfilling Conant's previously mentioned aspiration to lower "the degree of the empiricism involved in solving problems." Natural scientists look for simplicities: elemental units and elegant theories about them. Students of international politics complicate their studies and claim to locate more and more variables. The subject matters of the social and natural sci-ences are profoundly different. The difference does not obliterate certain possibilities and necessities. No matter what the subject, we have to bound the domain of our concern, to organize it, to simplify the materials we deal with, to concentrate on central tendencies, and to single out the strongest propelling forces.

From the first part of this chapter, we know that the theory we want to con-struct has to be a systemic one. What will a systems theory of international politics look like? What scope will it have? What will it be able, and unable, to explain?

Theory explains regularities of behavior and leads one to expect that the out-comes produced by interacting units will fall within specified ranges. The behav-ior of states and of statesmen, however, is indeterminate. How can a theory of international politics, which has to comprehend behavior that is indeterminate, possibly be constructed? This is the great unanswered, and many say unanswerable, question of international-political studies. The question cannot be answered by those whose approach is reductionist or behavioral, as we have seen. They try to explain international politics in terms of its principal actors. The dominant behavioral approach to constructing international-political theory proceeds by framing propositions about the behavior, the strategies, and the interactions of states. But propositions at the unit level do not account for the phenomena observed at the systems level. Since the variety of actors and the variations in their actions are not matched by the variety of outcomes, we know that systemic causes are in play. Knowing that, we know further that a systems theory is both needed and possible. To realize the possibility requires conceiving of an international system's structure and showing how it works its effects. We have to bring off the Copernican revolution that others have called for by showing how much of states' actions and interactions, and how much of the outcomes their actions and interactions produce, can be explained by forces that operate at the level of the system, rather than at the level of the units.

What do I mean by *explain*? I mean explain in these senses: to say why the range of expected outcomes falls within certain limits; to say why patterns of behavior recur; to say why events repeat themselves, including events that none or few of the actors may like. The structure of a system acts as a constraining and disposing force, and because it does so systems theories explain and predict continuity within a system. A systems theory shows why changes at the unit level produce less change of outcomes than one would expect in the absence of systemic constraints. A theory of international politics can tell us some things about expected international-political outcomes, about the resilience systems may show in response to the unpredictable acts of a varied set of states, and about the expected effects of systems on states.

A theory has explanatory and predictive power. A theory also has elegance. Elegance in social-science theories means that explanations and predictions will be general. A theory of international politics will, for example, explain why war recurs, and it will indicate some of the conditions that make war more or less likely; but it will not predict the outbreak of particular wars. Within a system, a theory explains continuities. It tells one what to expect and why to expect it. Within a system, a theory explains recurrences and repetitions, not change. At times one is told that structural approaches have proved disappointing, that from the study of structure not much can be learned. This is supposedly so for two reasons. Structure is said to be largely a static concept and nearly an empty one. Though neither point is quite right, both points are suggestive. Structures appear to be static because they often endure for long periods. Even when structures do not change, they are dynamic, not static, in that they alter the behavior of actors and affect the outcome of their interactions. Given a durable structure, it becomes easy to overlook structural effects because they are repeatedly the same. Thus one expects the same broad range of outcomes to result from the actions of states in an anarchic condition. What continues and repeats is surely not less important than what changes. A constancy of structure explains the recurrent patterns and features of international-political life. Is structure nevertheless an empty concept? Pretty much so, and because it is it gains in elegance and power. Structure is certainly no good on detail. Structural concepts, although they lack detailed content, help to explain some big, important, and enduring patterns.

Structures, moreover, may suddenly change. A structural change is a revolution, whether or not violently produced, and it is so because it gives rise to new expectations about the outcomes that will be produced by the acts and interactions of units whose placement in the system varies with changes in structure. Across systems, a theory explains change. A theory of international politics can succeed only if political structures are defined in ways that identify their causal effects and show how those effects vary as structures change. From anarchy one infers broad expectations about the quality of international-political life. Distinguishing between anarchic structures of different type permits somewhat narrower and more precise definitions of expected outcomes.

Consider, for example, the effects on European states of the shift from a multipolar to a bipolar system. So long as European states were the world's great powers, unity among them could only be dreamt of. Politics among the European great powers tended toward the model of a zero-sum game. Each power viewed another's loss as its own gain. Faced with the temptation to cooperate for mutual benefit, each state became wary and was inclined to draw back. When on occasion some of the great powers did move toward cooperation, they did so in order to oppose other powers more strongly. The emergence of the Russian and American superpowers created a situation that permitted wider ranging and more effective cooperation among the states of Western Europe. They became consumers of security, to use an expression common in the days of the League of Nations. For the first time in modern history, the determinants of war and peace lay outside the arena of European states, and the means of their preservation were provided by others. These new circumstances made possible the famous "upgrading of the common interest," a phrase which conveys the thought that all should work together to improve everyone's lot rather than being obsessively concerned with the precise division of benefits. Not all impediments to cooperation were removed, but one important one was—the fear that the greater advantage of one would be translated into military force to be used against the others. Living in the superpowers' shadow, Britain, France, Germany, and Italy quickly saw that war among them would be fruitless and soon began to believe it impossible. Because the security of all of them came to depend ultimately on the policies of others, rather than on their own, unity could effectively be worked for, although not easily achieved.

Once the possibility of war among states disappears, all of them can more freely run the risk of suffering a relative loss. Enterprises more beneficial to some parties than others can be engaged in, partly in the hope for the latter that other activities will reverse the balance of benefits, and partly in the belief that overall the enterprise itself is valuable. Economic gains may be granted by one state to another in exchange for expected political advantages, including the benefit of strengthening the structure of European cooperation. The removal of worries about security among the states of Western Europe does not mean the termination of conflict; it does produce a change in its content. Hard bargaining within the European Economic Community (by France over agricultural policies, for example) indicates that governments do not lose interest in who will gain more and who will gain less. Conflicts of interest remain, but not the expectation that someone will use force to resolve them. Politics among European states became different in quality after World War II because the international system changed from a multipolar to a bipolar one. The limited progress made in economic and other ways toward the unity of Western Europe cannot be understood without considering the effects that followed from the changed structure of international politics. The example helps to show what a theory of international politics can and cannot tell us. It can describe the range of likely outcomes of the actions and interactions of states within a given system and show how the range of expectations varies as systems change. It can tell us what pressures are exerted and what possibilities are posed by systems of different structure, but it cannot tell us just how, and how effectively, the units of a system will respond to those pressures and possibilities.

Structurally we can describe and understand the pressures states are subject to. We cannot predict how they will react to the pressures without knowledge of their internal dispositions. A systems theory explains changes across systems, not within them, and yet international life within a given system is by no means all repetition. Important discontinuities occur. If they occur within a system that endures, their causes are found at the unit level. Because something happens that is outside a theory's purview, a deviation from the expected occurs.

A systems theory of international politics deals with the forces that are in play at the international, and not at the national, level. This question then arises: With both systems-level and unit-level forces in play, how can one construct a theory of international politics without simultaneously constructing a theory of foreign policy? The question is exactly like asking how an economic theory of markets can be written in the absence of a theory of the firm. The answer is "very easily." Market theory is a structural theory showing how firms are pressed by market forces to do certain things in certain ways. Whether and how well they will do them varies from firm to firm, with variations depending on their different internal organization and management. An international-political theory does not imply or require a theory of foreign policy any more than a market theory implies or requires a theory of the firm. Systems theories, whether political or economic, are theories that explain how the organization of a realm acts as a constraining and disposing force on the interacting units within it. Such theories tell us about the forces the units are subject to. From them, we can infer some things about the expected behavior and fate of the units: namely, how they will have to compete with and adjust to one another if they are to survive and flourish. To the extent that dynamics of a system limit the freedom of its units, their behavior and the outcomes of their behavior become predictable. How do w₂ expect firms to respond to differently structured markets, and states to differently structured international-political systems? These theoretical questions require us to take firms as firms, and states as states, without paying attention to differences among them. The questions are then answered by reference to the placement of the units in their system and not by reference to their internal qualities. Systems theories explain why different units behave similarly and, despite their variations, produce outcomes that fall within expected ranges. Conversely, theories at the unit level tell us why different units behave differently despite their similar placement in a system. A theory about foreign policy is a theory at the national level. It leads to expectations about the responses that dissimilar polities will make to external pressures. A theory of international politics bears on the foreign policies of nations while claiming to explain only certain aspects of them. It can tell us what international conditions national policies have to cope with. To think that a theory of international politics can in itself say how the coping is likely to be done is the opposite of the reductionist error.

The theory, like the story, of international politics is written in terms of the great powers of an era. This is the fashion among political scientists as among historians, but fashion does not reveal the reason lying behind the habit. In international politics, as in any self-help system, the units of greatest capability set the scene of action for others as well as for themselves. In systems theory, structure is a generative notion; and the structure of a system is generated by the interactions of its principal parts. Theories that apply to self-help systems are written in terms of the systems' principal parts. It would be as ridiculous to construct a theory of international politics based on Malaysia and Costa Rica as it would be to construct an economic theory of oligopolistic competition based on the minor firms in a sector of an economy. The fates of all the states and of all the firms in a system are affected much more by the acts and the interactions of the major ones than of the minor ones. At the turn of the century, one who was concerned with the prospects for international politics as a system, and for large and small nations within it, did not concentrate attention on the foreign and military policies of Switzerland, Denmark, and Norway, but rather on those of Britain and Germany, of Russia and France. To focus on great powers is not to lose sight of lesser ones. Concern with the latter's fate requires paying most attention to the former. Concern with international politics as a system requires concentration on the states that make the most difference. A general theory of international politics is necessarily based on the great powers. The theory once written also applies to lesser states that interact insofar as their interactions are insulated from the intervention of the great powers of a system, whether by the relative indifference of the latter or by difficulties of communication and transportation.

III

In a systems theory, some part of the explanation of behaviors and outcomes is found in the system's structure. A political structure is akin to a field of forces in physics: Interactions within a field have properties different from those they would have if they occurred outside of it, and as the field affects the objects, so the objects affect the field. How can one give clear and useful political meaning to such a concept as structure? How do structures work their effects? In considering structures as causes, it is useful to draw a distinction between two definitions.

The term "structure" is now a social-science favorite. As such, its meaning has become all inclusive. In meaning everything, it has ceased to mean anything in particular. Its casual and vacuous uses aside, the term has two important meanings. First, it may designate a compensating device that works to produce a uniformity of outcomes despite the variety of inputs. Bodily organs keep variations within tolerable ranges despite changes of condition. One's liver, for example, keeps the blood-sugar level within a certain range despite the variety of food and drink ingested. Similarly, negative and progressive income taxes narrow disparities of income despite variations in people's skill, energy, and luck. Because such structures bring leveling processes into play, those who experience the leveling effects need be aware neither of the structure nor of how its effects are produced. Structures of this sort are agents or contrivances that work within systems. They are structures of the sort that political scientists usually have in mind. They do share one quality with structures as I shall define them: They work to keep outcomes within narrow ranges. They differ in being designed by nature or man to operate for particular purposes within larger systems. When referring to such devices, I use terms such as agent, agency, and compensating device. I use the word "structure" only in its second sense.

In the second sense structure designates a set of constraining conditions. Such a structure acts as a selector, but it cannot be seen, examined, and observed at work as livers and income taxes can be. Freely formed economic markets and international-political structures are selectors, but they are not agents. Because structures select by rewarding some behaviors and punishing others, outcomes cannot be inferred from intentions and behaviors. This is simple logic that everyone will understand. What is not so simple is to say just what it is politically that disjoins behavior and result. Structures are causes, but they are not causes in the sense meant by saying that A causes X and B causes Y. X and Y are different outcomes produced by different actions or agents. A and B are stronger, faster, earlier, or weightier than X and Y. By observing the values of variables, by calculating their covariance, and by tracing sequences, such causes are fixed.* Because A and B are different, they produce different effects. In contrast, structures limit and mold agents and agencies and point them in ways that tend toward a common quality of outcomes even though the efforts and aims of agents and agencies vary. Structures do not work their effects directly. Structures do not act as agents and agencies do. How then can structural forces be understood? How can one think of structural causes as being more than vague social propensities or ill-defined political tendencies?

Agents and agencies act; systems as wholes do not. But the actions of agents and agencies are affected by the system's structure. In itself a structure does not directly lead to one outcome rather than another. Structure affects behavior within the system, but does so indirectly. The effects are produced in two ways: through socialization of the actors and through competition among them. These two pervasive processes occur in international politics as they do in societies of all sorts. Because they are fundamental processes, I shall risk stating the obvious by explaining each of them in elementary terms.

Consider the process of socialization in the simplest case of a pair of persons, or for that matter of firms or of states. A influences B. B, made different by A's influence, influences A. As Mary Parker Follett, an organization theorist, put it: "A's own activity enters into the stimulus which is causing his activity" (1941, p. 194). This is an example of the familiar structural-functional logic by which consequences become causes (cf. Stinchcombe, 1968, pp. 80–101). B's attributes and actions are affected by A, and vice versa. Each is not just influencing the other; both are being influenced by the situation their interaction creates. Extending the example makes the logic clearer. George and Martha, the principal characters in Edward Albee's play, *Who's Afraid of Virginia Woolf?*, through their behavior and interaction create a condition that neither can control by individual acts and decisions. In a profound study of Albee's play, Paul Watzlawick and his associates show that George's and Martha's activities cannot be understood without considering the system that emerges from their interactions. They put it this way:

---

*A variable, contrary to political-science usage, is not just anything that varies. It is a concept that takes different values, a concept developed as part of a highly simplified model of some part of the world. Recall Chapter 1.

> That which is George or Martha, individually, does not explain what is com-
> pounded between them, nor how. To break this whole into individual
> personality traits . . . is essentially to separate them from each other, to deny
> that their behaviors have special meaning in the context of this interaction—
> that in fact the pattern of the interaction perpetuates these (1967, p. 156).

The behavior of the pair cannot be apprehended by taking a unilateral view of
either member. The behavior of the pair cannot, moreover, be resolved into a set
of two-way relations because each element of behavior that contributes to the
interaction is itself shaped by their being a pair. They have become parts of a
system. To say simply that George and Martha are interacting, with the action of
one eliciting a response from the other, obscures the circularity of their interactions. Each acts and reacts to the other. Stimulus and response are part of the
story. But also the two of them act together in a game, which—no less because
they have "devised" it—motivates and shapes their behavior. Each is playing a
game, *and* they are playing the game together. They react to each other and to the
tensions their interactions produce.

These are descriptions and examples of what we all know and experience.
One may firmly intend to end an argument, may announce the intention, may
insist on it, and yet may be carried along by the argument. One may firmly predict one's action and yet be led to act in ways that surprise oneself as well as
others. Years ago, Gustave Le Bon said this about the effect of the group on the
individual:

> The most striking peculiarity presented by a psychological crowd is the
> following: Whoever be the individuals that compose it, however like or unlike
> be their mode of life, their occupations, their character, or their intelligence, the
> fact that they have been transformed into a crowd puts them in possession of a
> sort of collective mind which makes them feel, think, and act in a manner quite
> different from that in which each individual of them would feel, think, and act
> were he in a state of isolation (1896, pp. 29–30).

We do not cease to be ourselves when situations strongly affect us, but we
become ourselves and something else as well. We become different, but we cannot say that any agent or agency caused us to do so.

Pairs and crowds provide microcosmic and transitory examples of the
socialization that takes place in organizations and in societies on larger scales and
over longer periods. Nobody tells all of the teenagers in a given school or town to
dress alike, but most of them do. They do so, indeed, despite the fact that many
people—their parents—are ordinarily telling them not to. In spontaneous and
informal ways, societies establish norms of behavior. A group's opinion controls
its members. Heroes and leaders emerge and are emulated. Praise for behavior
that conforms to group norms reinforces them. Socialization brings members of a

group into conformity with its norms. Some members of the group will find this repressive and incline toward deviant behavior. Ridicule may bring deviants into line or cause them to leave the group. Either way the group's homogeneity is preserved. In various ways, societies establish norms and encourage conformity. Socialization reduces variety. The differences of society's members are greater than the differences in their observed behavior. The persistent characteristics of group behavior result in one part from the qualities of its members. They result in another part from the characteristics of the society their interactions produce.

The first way in which structures work their effects is through a process of socialization that limits and molds behavior. The second way is through competition. In social sectors that are loosely organized or segmented, socialization takes place within segments and competition takes place among them. Socialization encourages similarities of attributes and of behavior. So does competition. Competition generates an order, the units of which adjust their relations through their autonomous decisions and acts. Adam Smith published *The Wealth of Nations* in 1776. He did not claim to explain economic behavior and outcomes only from then onward. He did not develop a theory that applies only to the economic activities of those who read, understand, and follow his book. His economic theory applies wherever indicated conditions prevail, and it applies aside from the state of producers' and consumers' knowledge.* This is so because the theory Smith fashioned deals with structural constraints. Insofar as selection rules, results can be predicted whether or not one knows the actors' intentions and whether or not they understand structural constraints. Consider an example. Suppose I plan to open a shoe store. Where should I put it? I might notice that shoe stores tend to cluster. Following common political-science reasoning, I would infer either that towns pass laws regulating the location of shoe stores or that shoe-store owners are familiar with the location theory of economists, which tells them generally how to locate their stores in order to catch the attention of the largest number of shoppers. Neither inference is justified. Following common economic reasoning, I would say that market conditions reward those who wittingly or not place their stores in the right places and punish those who do not. Behaviors are selected for their consequences. Individual entrepreneurs need not know how to increase their chances of turning a profit. They can blunder along, if they wish to, and rely on the market selector to sort out the ones who happen to operate intelligently from those who do not.

Firms are assumed to be maximizing units. In practice, some of them may not even be trying to maximize anything. Others may be trying, but their ineptitude may make this hard to discern. Competitive systems are regulated, so to speak, by the "rationality" of the more successful competitors. What does

---

*In saying that the theory applies, I leave aside the question of the theory's validity.

rationality mean? It means only that some do better than others—whether through intelligence, skill, hard work, or dumb luck. They succeed in providing a wanted good or service more attractively and more cheaply than others do. Either their competitors emulate them or they fall by the wayside. The demand for their product shrinks, their profits fall, and ultimately they go bankrupt. To break this unwanted chain of events, they must change their ways. And thus the units that survive come to look like one another. Patterns are formed in the location of firms, in their organization, in their modes of production, in the design of their products, and in their marketing methods. The orderliness is in the outcomes and not necessarily in the inputs. Those who survive share certain characteristics. Those who go bankrupt lack them. Competition spurs the actors to accommodate their ways to the socially most acceptable and successful practices. Socialization and competition are two aspects of a process by which the variety of behaviors and of outcomes is reduced.

Where selection according to consequences rules, patterns emerge and endure without anyone arranging the parts to form patterns or striving to maintain them. The acts and the relations of parties may be regulated through the accommodations they mutually make. Order may prevail without an orderer; adjustments may be made without an adjuster; tasks may be allocated without an allocator. The mayor of New York City does not 'phone the truck gardeners of southern New Jersey and tell them to grow more tomatoes next year because too few were recently supplied. Supply and demand are more sensitively and reliably adjusted through the self-interested responses of numerous buyers and sellers than they are by mayors' instructions. An example of a somewhat different sort is provided by considering Montesquieu's response when presented with a scheme for an ideal society. "Who," he is said to have asked, "will empty the chamber pots?" As an equivalent question, we might ask: Who will collect the trash? The buyers of the trash-collecting service want to buy the service cheaply. The sellers want to sell their service dearly. What happens? Cities take steps to make the trash detail more attractive: cleaner and simpler through moves toward automation, and socially more acceptable through increasing the status of the job, for example, by providing classy uniforms for the workers. Insofar as trash collecting remains unattractive, society pays more in relation to the talents required than it does for other services. The real society becomes hard to distinguish from the ideal.

IV

Different structures may cause the same outcomes to occur even as units and interactions vary. Thus throughout a market the price of any good or service is uniform if many firms compete, if a few oligopolists engage in collusive pricing, or if the government controls prices. Perfect competition, complete collusion, absolute control: These different causes produce identical results. From uniformity of outcomes one cannot infer that the attributes and the interactions of the parts of a system have remained constant. Structure may determine outcomes aside from changes at the level of the units and aside from the disappearance of some of them and the emergence of others. Different "causes" may produce the same effects; the same "causes" may have different consequences. Unless one knows how a realm is organized, one can hardly tell the causes from the effects.

The effect of an organization may predominate over the attributes and the interactions of the elements within it. A system that is independent of initial conditions is said to display equifinality. If it does, *"the system is then its own best explanation*, and the study of its present organization the appropriate methodology" (Watzlawick, *et al.*, 1967, p. 129; cf. p. 32). If structure influences without determining, then one must ask how and to what extent the structure of a realm accounts for outcomes and how and to what extent the units account for outcomes. Structure has to be studied in its own right as do units. To claim to be following a systems approach or to be constructing a systems theory requires one to show how system and unit levels can be distinctly defined. Failure to mark and preserve the distinction between structure, on the one hand, and units and processes, on the other, makes it impossible to disentangle causes of different sorts and to distinguish between causes and effects. Blurring the distinction between the different levels of a system has, I believe, been the major impediment to the development of theories about international politics. The next chapter shows how to define political structures in a way that makes the construction of a systems theory possible.

5

Political Structures

We learned in Chapters 2, 3, and 4 that international-political outcomes cannot be explained reductively. We found in Chapter 3 that even avowedly systemic approaches mingle and confuse systems-level with unit-level causes. Reflecting on theories that follow the general-systems model, we concluded at once that international politics does not fit the model closely enough to make the model useful and that only through some sort of systems theory can international politics be understood. To be a success, such a theory has to show how international politics can be conceived of as a domain distinct from the economic, social, and other international domains that one may conceive of. To mark international-political systems off from other international systems, and to distinguish systems-level from unit-level forces, requires showing how political structures are generated and how they affect, and are affected by, the units of the system. How can we conceive of international politics as a distinct system? What is it that intervenes between interacting units and the results that their acts and interactions produce? To answer these questions, this chapter first examines the concept of social structure and then defines structure as a concept appropriate for national and for international politics.

I

A system is composed of a structure and of interacting units. The structure is the system-wide component that makes it possible to think of the system as a whole. The problem, unsolved by the systems theorists considered in Chapter 3, is to contrive a definition of structure free of the attributes and the interactions of units. Definitions of structure must leave aside, or abstract from, the characteristics of units, their behavior, and their interactions. Why must those obviously important matters be omitted? They must be omitted so that we can distinquish between variables at the level of the units and variables at the level of the system.

The problem is to develop theoretically useful concepts to replace the vague and varying systemic notions that are customarily employed—notions such as environment, situation, context, and milieu. Structure is a useful concept if it gives clear and fixed meaning to such vague and varying terms.

We know what we have to omit from any definition of structure if the definition is to be useful theoretically. Abstracting from the attributes of units means leaving aside questions about the kinds of political leaders, social and economic institutions, and ideological commitments states may have. Abstracting from relations means leaving aside questions about the cultural, economic, political, and military interactions of states. To say what is to be left out does not indicate what is to be put in. The negative point is important nevertheless because the instruction to omit attributes is often violated and the instruction to omit interactions almost always goes unobserved. But if attributes and interactions are omitted, what is left? The question is answered by considering the double meaning of the term "relation." As S. F. Nadel points out, ordinary language obscures a distinction that is important in theory. "Relation" is used to mean both the interaction of units and the positions they occupy vis-à-vis each other (1957, pp. 8–11). To define a structure requires ignoring how units relate with one another (how they interact) and concentrating on how they stand in relation to one another (how they are arranged or positioned). Interactions, as I have insisted, take place at the level of the units. How units stand in relation to one another, the way they are arranged or positioned, is not a property of the units. The arrangement of units is a property of the system.

By leaving aside the personality of actors, their behavior, and their interactions, one arrives at a purely positional picture of society. Three propositions follow from this. First, structures may endure while personality, behavior, and interactions vary widely. Structure is sharply distinguished from actions and interactions. Second, a structural definition applies to realms of widely different substance so long as the arrangement of parts is similar (cf. Nadel, pp. 104–109). Third, because this is so, theories developed for one realm may with some modification be applicable to other realms as well.

A structure is defined by the arrangement of its parts. Only changes of arrangement are structural changes. A system is composed of a structure and of interacting parts. Both the structure and the parts are concepts, related to, but not identical with, real agents and agencies. Structure is not something we see. The anthropologist Meyer Fortes put this well. "When we describe structure," he said, "we are in the realm of grammar and syntax, not of the spoken word. We discern structure in the 'concrete reality' of social events only by virtue of having first established structure by abstraction from 'concrete reality' " (Fortes 1949, p. 56). Since structure is an abstraction, it cannot be defined by enumerating material characteristics of the system. It must instead be defined by the arrangement of the system's parts and by the principle of that arrangement.

This is an uncommon way to think of political systems, although structural notions are familiar enough to anthropologists, to economists, and even to political scientists who deal not with political systems in general but with such of their parts as political parties and bureaucracies. In defining structures, anthropologists do not ask about the habits and the values of the chiefs and the Indians; economists do not ask about the organization and the efficiency of particular firms and the exchanges among them; and political scientists do not ask about the personalities and the interests of the individuals occupying various offices. They leave aside the qualities, the motives, and the interactions of the actors, not because those matters are uninteresting or unimportant, but because they want to know how the qualities, the motives, and the interactions of tribal units are affected by tribal structure, how decisions of firms are influenced by their market, and how people's behavior is molded by the offices they hold.

II

The concept of structure is based on the fact that units differently juxtaposed and combined behave differently and in interacting produce different outcomes. I first want to show how internal political structure can be defined. In a book on international-political theory, domestic political structure has to be examined in order to draw a distinction between expectations about behavior and outcomes in the internal and external realms. Moreover, considering domestic political structure now will make the elusive international-political structure easier to catch later on.

Structure defines the arrangement, or the ordering, of the parts of a system. Structure is not a collection of political institutions but rather the arrangement of them. How is the arrangement defined? The constitution of a state describes some parts of the arrangement, but political structures as they develop are not identical with formal constitutions. In defining structures, the first question to answer is this: What is the principle by which the parts are arranged?

Domestic politics is hierarchically ordered. The units—institutions and agencies—stand vis-à-vis each other in relations of super- and subordination. The ordering principle of a system gives the first, and basic, bit of information about how the parts of a realm are related to each other. In a polity the hierarchy of offices is by no means completely articulated, nor are all ambiguities about relations of super- and subordination removed. Nevertheless, political actors are formally differentiated according to the degrees of their authority, and their distinct functions are specified. By "specified" I do not mean that the law of the land fully describes the duties that different agencies perform, but only that broad agreement prevails on the tasks that various parts of a government are to undertake and on the extent of the power they legitimately wield. Thus Congress supplies the military forces; the President commands them. Congress makes the laws; the executive branch enforces them; agencies administer laws; judges inter- pret them. Such specification of roles and differentiation of functions is found in any state, the more fully so as the state is more highly developed. The specifica- tion of functions of formally differentiated parts gives the second bit of structural information. This second part of the definition adds some content to the struc- ture, but only enough to say more fully how the units stand in relation to one another. The roles and the functions of the British Prime Minister and Par- liament, for example, differ from those of the American President and Congress. When offices are juxtaposed and functions are combined in different ways, dif- ferent behaviors and outcomes result, as I shall shortly show.

The placement of units in relation to one another is not fully defined by a system's ordering principle and by the formal differentiation of its parts. The standing of the units also changes with changes in their relative capabilities. In the performance of their functions, agencies may gain capabilities or lose them. The relation of Prime Minister to Parliament and of President to Congress depends on, and varies with, their relative capabilities. The third part of the definition of structure acknowledges that even while specified functions remain unchanged, units come to stand in different relation to each other through changes in relative capability.

A domestic political structure is thus defined, first, according to the principle by which it is ordered; second, by specification of the functions of formally dif- ferentiated units; and third, by the distribution of capabilities across those units. Structure is a highly abstract notion, but the definition of structure does not abstract from everything. To do so would be to leave everything aside and to include nothing at all. The three-part definition of structure includes only what is required to show how the units of the system are positioned or arranged. Every- thing else is omitted. Concern for tradition and culture, analysis of the character and personality of political actors, consideration of the conflictive and accommo- dative processes of politics, description of the making and execution of policy— all such matters are left aside. Their omission does not imply their unimportance. They are omitted because we want to figure out the expected effects of structure on process and of process on structure. That can be done only if structure and process are distinctly defined.

Political structures shape political processes, as can best be seen by com- paring different governmental systems. In Britain and America legislative and executive offices are differently juxtaposed and combined. In England they are fused; in America they are separated and in many ways placed in opposition to each other. Differences in the distribution of power and authority among formal and informal agencies affect the chief executives' power and help to account for persistent differences in their performance. I have shown elsewhere how struc- tural differences explain contrasts in the patterns of British and American political behavior. Repeating a few points in summary form will make preceding definitional statements politically concrete. I shall take just political leadership as an example and concentrate more on Britain than on America so as to be able to go into some small amount of detail (1967a; I draw mainly on Chapters 3 and 11).

Prime Ministers have been described, at least since the late nineteenth century, as gaining ever more power to the point where one should no longer refer to parliamentary or even to cabinet government. The Prime Minister alone now carries the day, or so one is told. One must then wonder why these increasingly strong Prime Ministers react so slowly to events, do the same ineffective things over and over again, and in general govern so weakly. The answers are not found in the different personalities of Prime Ministers, for the patterns I refer to embrace all of them and extend backward to the 1860s, that is, to the time when the discipline of parties began to emerge as a strong feature of British governance. The formal powers of Prime Ministers appear to be ample, and yet their behavior is more closely constrained than that of American Presidents. The constraints are found in the structure of British government, especially in the relation of leader to party. Two points are of major importance: the way leaders are recruited and the effect of their having to manage their parties so carefully.

In both countries, directly or indirectly, the effective choice of a chief executive lies between the leaders of two major parties. How do they become the two from whom the choice is made? An MP becomes leader of his party or Prime Minister by long service in Parliament, by proving his ability in successive steps up the ministerial ladder, and by displaying the qualities that the House of Commons deems important. The members of the two major parliamentary parties determine who will rise to the highest office. They select the person who will lead their party when it is out of power and become Prime Minister when it is triumphant. The MP who would be Prime Minister must satisfy his first constituents, the members of his party who sit in the Commons, that he would be competent and, according to the lights of the party, safe and reliable in office. They will look for someone who has shown over the years that he will displease few of his fellow MPs. Given no limits on length of service as Prime Minister, MPs will, moreover, be reluctant to support a younger person, whose successful candidacy might block the road to the highest office for decades.

Like most countries of settled political institutions, the British apprentice their rulers. The system by which Britain apprentices her rulers is more likely than America's quite different system to produce not only older chief executives but also ones who are safer and surer. Since the Second Reform Act, in 1867, Britain has had 20 Prime Ministers. Their average age in office is 62 years. Their average service in Parliament prior to becoming Prime Minister is 28 years, during which time they served their apprenticeships in various high Cabinet posts. In England the one way of attaining the highest office is to climb the ministerial ladder.* Since the Civil War, America has had 22 Presidents. Their average age in office is 56 years.† Since Congress is not a direct route to executive preferment, it is pointless to compare congressional with parliamentary service. It is, however, safe and significant to say that the Presidency draws on a wider field of experience, occasionally—as with Grant and Eisenhower—on a field not political at all.

The British mode of recruitment creates a condition that serves as a gross restraint on executive power. The Prime Minister, insofar as he has great powers, is likely to be of an age and experience, a worldly wisdom if you like, that makes his exercising them with force and vigor improbable. If it is true that England muddles through, here is part of the explanation, a bigger part than the oft-cited national character to which ideological commitment and programmatic politics are supposedly alien.

The limitations that come to bear on Prime Ministers in the very process by which they are selected are as important as they are subtle, elusive, and generally overlooked. These qualities also characterize the limitations that derive from the Prime Minister's relation to his party and to Parliament, where his strength is often thought to be greatest. The situation in the two countries can be put as follows: The President can lead but has trouble getting his party to follow; the Prime Minister has the followers but on condition that he not be too far in front of, or to the side of, his party, which makes it difficult for him to lead. The requisite art for a Prime Minister is to manage the party in ways that avoid the defiance of the many or the rebellion of the few, if those few are important, rather than to levy penalties after rebellion has occurred. Most often the Prime Minister's worry is less that some members will defy him than that his real and effective support will dwindle in the years between general elections, as happened to Churchill and Macmillan in their last governments, and even more obviously to Eden and Heath. It is wrong to see the parliamentary party as a brake on the government only when the party is split and the Prime Minister faces an unruly faction, for a party is never monolithic. A well-managed party will appear to be almost passively obedient, but the managerial arts are difficult to master. The effective Prime Minister or party leader moves in ways that avoid dissent, if possible, by anticipating it. Concessions are made; issues are postponed and at times evaded entirely. If we think of the two parties as disciplined armies marching obediently at their leaders' commands, we not only ignore much important history but we also overlook the infinite care and calculation that goes into getting

---

*The exception, which does not disprove the rule, is Ramsay MacDonald, who, absent from the wartime coalition and with his party not previously in power, had never served in a ministerial position.

†All calculations as of July 1978.

groups, be they armies, football teams, or political parties, to act in concert. The Prime Minister can ordinarily count on his party to support him, but only within limits that are set in part by the party members collectively. The Prime Minister can only ask for what his party will give. He cannot say: "The trade unions must be disciplined." He cannot say: "The relations of labor and management must be recast." He cannot say: "Industry must be rationalized." He cannot make such statements, even if he believes them. He can give a bold lead only if he is sure that his party will come around without a major faction splitting off. But by the time a Prime Minister is sure of that, any lead given is no longer a bold one. One can be a bold Prime Minister only at the cost of being a bad party manager. "A Party has to be managed, and he who can manage it best, will probably be its best leader. The subordinate task of legislation and of executive government may well fall into the inferior hands of less astute practitioners."* Such were the reflections of Anthony Trollope on the career of Sir Timothy Beeswax, a party manager of near magical skills (1880, III, 169; cf. I, 216). The roles of leader of the country and manager of a party easily come into conflict. In the absence of formal checks and balances of the American sort, the party that would act can do so. Because the party in power acts on the word of its leader, the leader must be cautious about the words he chooses to utter.

The leadership problem coupled with the apprenticeship factor goes far to describe the texture of British politics. The Prime Minister must preserve the unity of his party, for it is not possible for him to perpetuate his rule by constructing a series of majorities whose composition varies from issue to issue. Prime Ministers must be, and must take pains to remain, acceptable to their parliamentary parties. By the political system within which he operates, the Prime Minister is impelled to seek the support of his entire party, at the cost of considerably reducing his freedom of action. He is constrained to crawl along cautiously, to let situations develop until the near necessity of decision blunts inclinations to quarrel about just what the decision should be. Leadership characteristics are built into the system. The typical Prime Minister is a weak national leader but an expert party manager—characteristics that he ordinarily must have in order to gain office and retain it.

In contrast, consider Presidents. Because their tenure does not depend on securing majority support in Congress, because they can be defeated on policies and still remain in office, and because obstruction is an ordinary and accepted part of the system, they are encouraged to ask for what at the moment may well

---

*In some respects a century brings little change. Despite the many harsh comments made about Callaghan by Crossman, Wilson, and others, Crossman thought of him as "easily the most accomplished politician in the Labour Party"; and apparently because of that distinction, Callaghan gained Wilson's help in succeeding him as Prime Minister (1977, III, 627–28 *et passim*).

not be granted. Presidents are expected to educate and inform, to explain that the legislation Congress refuses to pass is actually what the interest of the country requires; they may, indeed, ask for more than they want, hoping that the half-loaf they often get will conform roughly to their private estimate of need. The gap between promise and performance, between presidential request and congressional acquiescence is thus often illusory. Prime Ministers get all that they ask, and yet major social and economic legislation in Britain is ordinarily a long time maturing. Presidents ask for much that they do not get, and yet the pace of reform is not slower, the flexibility and response of American government are not less, than those of Great Britain.

Appearances are often deceptive. Prime Ministers are thought to be strong leaders because they are in public so ineffectively opposed. The fusion of powers, however, tempts the Prime Minister to place his concern for the unity of the party above his regard for the public interest and in rendering the party responsible in the eyes of the voter makes the government unresponsive to the needs of the nation. "A public man is responsible," as a character in one of Disraeli's novels once said, "and a responsible man is a slave" (1880, p. 156). To be clearly responsible is to be highly visible. In America, the congressional show detracts in some measure from the attention the President receives; in Britain, the public concentrates its gaze with single-minded intensity on the Prime Minister. Fairly or not, he is praised or blamed for the good or ill health of the polity. Responsibility is concentrated rather than diffused. The leader who is responsible then has to husband his power; the onus for the risky policy that fails to come off falls entirely on him.

Americans, accustomed to rule by strong Presidents, naturally think only in terms of limits that are institutionally imposed and overlook the structural constraints on British government. Indeed in the two countries, the term "leadership" has different political meanings: in the United States, that strong men occupy the Presidency; in Britain, that the will of the Prime Minister becomes the law of the land. To say that the will of the leader becomes law should not be taken to mean that the system is one of strong leadership in the American sense; instead everything depends on the leader's identity and on the forces that shape his decisions. The British system goes far to ensure that the leader is moderate and will behave with propriety. This is not seen by simply observing political processes. One has first to relate political structure to process, to consider the ways in which political offices and institutions are juxtaposed and combined. Power is concentrated in the hands of the Prime Minister and yet with great, though informal, checks against its impetuous use: the apprentice system by which parliamentarians rise to office; the subtle restraints of party that work upon the Prime Minister; the habit, institutionally encouraged, of moving slowly with events and of postponing changes in policy until their necessity is widely accepted.

The endurance of patterns over the decades is striking. Think of the Prime Ministers Britain has known since the turn of the century. They are Balfour, Campbell-Bannerman, Asquith, Lloyd George, Bonar Law, Baldwin, Mac-Donald, Chamberlain, Churchill, Attlee, Eden, Macmillan, Home, Wilson, Heath, and Callaghan. Two failed to fit the pattern—Lloyd George and Winston Churchill. Both had long sat in the Commons. Both had worked their ways up the ladder. They had served their apprenticeships, but doing so had not tamed them. In normal times each of them appeared unreliable at best, and perhaps downright dangerous, to fractions of their parties large enough to deny them the highest office. Back benchers in large number thought of them as being unlikely to balance the interests and convictions of various groups within the party, to calculate nicely whose services and support merited higher or lower ministerial positions, and to show a gentlemanly respect for the opinions of others even when they were thought to be ill-founded. A few comments on Winston Churchill will show what I mean. Member of Parliament since 1900 and the holder of more ministerial posts than any politician in British history, he was richly qualified for the highest office. But he had been a maverick for most of his political life. A Conservative at the outset of his political career, he became a Liberal in 1906 and did not return to the Conservative fold until the middle 1920s. In the 1930s, he was at odds with his party on great matters of state policy, first on Indian and then on European affairs. Nothing less than a crisis big enough to turn his party liabilities into national assets could elevate him to the highest office. The events required to raise him to prime ministerial office, by virtue of their exceptional quality, cause the normal practice to stand out more clearly. Accidents do occur, but it takes great crises to produce them. To pull someone from outside the normal lines of succession is not easily done.

Political structure produces a similarity in process and performance so long as a structure endures. Similarity is not uniformity. Structure operates as a cause, but it is not the only cause in play. How can one know whether observed effects are caused by the structure of national politics rather than by a changing cast of political characters, by variations of nonpolitical circumstances, and,by a host of other factors? How can one separate structural from other causes? One does it by extending the comparative method that I have just used. Look, for example, at British political behavior where structure differs. Contrast the behavior of the Labour movement with that of the Parliamentary Labour Party. In the Labour movement, where power is checked and balanced, the practice of politics, especially when the party is out of power, is strikingly similar to the political conduct that prevails in America. In the face of conflict and open dissension, the leaders of the party are stimulated actually to lead, to explore the ground and try to work out compromises, to set a line of policy, to exhort and persuade, to threaten and cajole, to inform and educate, all with the hope that the parts of the party—the National Executive Committee, the trade unions, and the constituency parties, as well as the Members of Parliament—can be brought to follow the leader.

Within a country one can identify the effects of structure by noticing *differences* of behavior in differently structured parts of the polity. From one country to another, one can identify the effects of structure by noticing *similarities* of behavior in polities of similar structure. Thus Chihiro Hosoya's description of the behavior of Prime Ministers in postwar Japan's parliamentary system exactly fits British Prime Ministers (1974, pp. 366–69). Despite cultural and other differences, similar structures produce similar effects.

III

I defined domestic political structures first by the principle according to which they are organized or ordered, second by the differentiation of units and the specification of their functions, and third by the distribution of capabilities across units. Let us see how the three terms of the definition apply to international politics.

1. ORDERING PRINCIPLES

Structural questions are questions about the arrangement of the parts of a system. The parts of domestic political systems stand in relations of super- and subordination. Some are entitled to command; others are required to obey. Domestic systems are centralized and hierarchic. The parts of international-political systems stand in relations of coordination. Formally, each is the equal of all the others. None is entitled to command; none is required to obey. International systems are decentralized and anarchic. The ordering principles of the two structures are distinctly different, indeed, contrary to each other. Domestic political structures have governmental institutions and offices as their concrete counterparts. International politics, in contrast, has been called "politics in the absence of government" (Fox 1959, p. 35). International organizations do exist, and in ever-growing numbers. Supranational agents able to act effectively, however, either themselves acquire some of the attributes and capabilities of states, as did the medieval papacy in the era of Innocent III, or they soon reveal their inability to act in important ways except with the support, or at least the acquiescence, of the principal states concerned with the matters at hand. Whatever elements of authority emerge internationally are barely once removed from the capability that provides the foundation for the appearance of those elements. Authority quickly reduces to a particular expression of capability. In the absence of agents with system-wide authority, formal relations of super- and subordination fail to develop.

The first term of a structural definition states the principle by which the system is ordered. Structure is an organizational concept. The prominent characteristic of international politics, however, seems to be the lack of order and of organization. How can one think of international politics as being any kind of an order at all? The anarchy of politics internationally is often referred to. If structure is an organizational concept, the terms "structure" and "anarchy" seem to be in contradiction. If international politics is "politics in the absence of government," what are we in the presence of? In looking for international structure, one is brought face to face with the invisible, an uncomfortable position to be in.

The problem is this: how to conceive of an order without an orderer and of organizational effects where formal organization is lacking. Because these are difficult questions, I shall answer them through analogy with microeconomic theory. Reasoning by analogy is helpful where one can move from a domain for which theory is well developed to one where it is not. Reasoning by analogy is permissible where different domains are structurally similar.

Classical economic theory, developed by Adam Smith and his followers, is microtheory. Political scientists tend to think that microtheory is theory about small-scale matters, a usage that ill accords with its established meaning. The term "micro" in economic theory indicates the way in which the theory is constructed rather than the scope of the matters it pertains to. Microeconomic theory describes how an order is spontaneously formed from the self-interested acts and interactions of individual units—in this case, persons and firms. The theory then turns upon the two central concepts of the economic units and of the market. Economic units and economic markets are concepts, not descriptive realities or concrete entities. This must be emphasized since from the early eighteenth century to the present, from the sociologist Auguste Comte to the psychologist George Katona, economic theory has been faulted because its assumptions fail to correspond with realities (Martineau 1853, II, 51–53; Katona 1953). Unrealistically, economic theorists conceive of an economy operating in isolation from its society and polity. Unrealistically, economists assume that the economic world is the whole of the world. Unrealistically, economists think of the acting unit, the famous "economic man," as a single-minded profit maximizer. They single out one aspect of man and leave aside the wondrous variety of human life. As any moderately sensible economist knows, "economic man" does not exist. Anyone who asks businessmen how they make their decisions will find that the assumption that men are economic maximizers grossly distorts their characters. The assumption that men behave as economic men, which is known to be false as a descriptive statement, turns out to be useful in the construction of theory.

Markets are the second major concept invented by microeconomic theorists. Two general questions must be asked about markets: How are they formed? How do they work? The answer to the first question is this: The market of a decentralized economy is individualist in origin, spontaneously generated, and unintended. The market arises out of the activities of separate units—persons and firms—whose aims and efforts are directed not toward creating an order but rather toward fulfilling their own internally defined interests by whatever means they can muster. The individual unit acts for itself. From the coaction of like units emerges a structure that affects and constrains all of them. Once formed, a market becomes a force in itself, and a force that the constitutive units acting singly or in small numbers cannot control. Instead, in lesser or greater degree as market conditions vary, the creators become the creatures of the market that their activity gave rise to. Adam Smith's great achievement was to show how self-interested, greed-driven actions may produce good social outcomes if only political and social conditions permit free competition. If a laissez-faire economy is harmonious, it is so because the intentions of actors do *not* correspond with the outcomes their actions produce. What intervenes between the actors and the objects of their action in order to thwart their purposes? To account for the unexpectedly favorable outcomes of selfish acts, the concept of a market is brought into play. Each unit seeks its own good; the result of a number of units simultaneously doing so transcends the motives and the aims of the separate units. Each would like to work less hard and price his product higher. Taken together, all have to work harder and price their products lower. Each firm seeks to increase its profit; the result of many firms doing so drives the profit rate downward. Each man seeks his own end, and, in doing so, produces a result that was no part of his intention. Out of the mean ambition of its members, the greater good of society is produced.

The market is a cause interposed between the economic actors and the results they produce. It conditions their calculations, their behaviors, and their interactions. It is not an agent in the sense of A being the agent that produces outcome X. Rather it is a structural cause. A market constrains the units that comprise it from taking certain actions and disposes them toward taking others. The market, created by self-directed interacting economic units, selects behaviors according to their consequences (cf. Chapter 4, part III). The market rewards some with high profits and assigns others to bankruptcy. Since a market is not an institution or an agent in any concrete or palpable sense, such statements become impressive only if they can be reliably inferred from a theory as part of a set of more elaborate expectations. They can be. Microeconomic theory explains how an economy operates and why certain effects are to be expected. It generates numerous "if-then" statements that can more or less easily be checked. Consider, for example, the following simple but important propositions. If the money demand for a commodity rises, then so will its price. If price rises, then so will profits. If profits rise, then capital will be attracted and production will increase. If production increases, then price will fall to the level that returns profits to the producers of the commodity at the prevailing rate. This sequence of statements could be extended and refined, but to do so would not serve my purpose. I want to point out that although the stated expectations are now commonplace, they could not be arrived at by economists working in a pre-theoretic era. All of the statements are, of course, made at an appropriate level of generality. They require an "other things being equal" stipulation. They apply, as do statements inferred from any theory, only to the extent that the conditions contemplated by the theory obtain. They are idealizations, and so they are never fully borne out in practice. Many things—social customs, political interventions—will in fact interfere with the theoretically predicted outcomes. Though interferences have to be allowed for, it is nevertheless extraordinarily useful to know what to expect in general.

International-political systems, like economic markets, are formed by the coaction of self-regarding units. International structures are defined in terms of the primary political units of an era, be they city states, empires, or nations. Structures emerge from the coexistence of states. No state intends to participate in the formation of a structure by which it and others will be constrained. International-political systems, like economic markets, are individualist in origin, spontaneously generated, and unintended. In both systems, structures are formed by the coaction of their units. Whether those units live, prosper, or die depends on their own efforts. Both systems are formed and maintained on a principle of self-help that applies to the units. To say that the two realms are structurally similar is not to proclaim their identity. Economically, the self-help principle applies within governmentally contrived limits. Market economies are hedged about in ways that channel energies constructively. One may think of pure food-and-drug standards, antitrust laws, securities and exchange regulations, laws against shooting a competitor, and rules forbidding false claims in advertising. International politics is more nearly a realm in which anything goes. International politics is structurally similar to a market economy insofar as the self-help principle is allowed to operate in the latter.

In a microtheory, whether of international politics or of economics, the motivation of the actors is assumed rather than realistically described. I assume that states seek to ensure their survival. The assumption is a radical simplification made for the sake of constructing a theory. The question to ask of the assumption, as ever, is not whether it is true but whether it is the most sensible and useful one that can be made. Whether it is a useful assumption depends on whether a theory based on the assumption can be contrived, a theory from which important consequences not otherwise obvious can be inferred. Whether it is a sensible assumption can be directly discussed.

Beyond the survival motive, the aims of states may be endlessly varied; they may range from the ambition to conquer the world to the desire merely to be left alone. Survival is a prerequisite to achieving any goals that states may have, other than the goal of promoting their own disappearance as political entities. The survival motive is taken as the ground of action in a world where the security of states is not assured, rather than as a realistic description of the impulse that lies behind every act of state. The assumption allows for the fact that no state always acts exclusively to ensure its survival. It allows for the fact that some states may persistently seek goals that they value more highly than survival; they may, for example, prefer amalgamation with other states to their own survival in form. It allows for the fact that in pursuit of its security no state will act with perfect knowledge and wisdom—if indeed we could know what those terms might mean. Some systems have high requirements for their functioning. Traffic will not flow if most, but not all, people drive on the proper side of the road. If necessary, strong measures have to be taken to ensure that everyone does so. Other systems have medium requirements. Elevators in skyscrapers are planned so that they can handle the passenger load if most people take express elevators for the longer runs and locals only for the shorter ones. But if some people choose locals for long runs because the speed of the express makes them dizzy, the system will not break down. To keep it going, most, but not all, people have to act as expected. Some systems, market economies and international politics among them, make still lower demands. Traffic systems are designed on the knowledge that the system's requirements will be enforced. Elevators are planned with extra capacity to allow for human vagaries. Competitive economic and international-political systems work differently. Out of the interactions of their parts they develop structures that reward or punish behavior that conforms more or less nearly to what is required of one who wishes to succeed in the system. Recall my description of the constraints of the British parliamentary system. Why should a would-be Prime Minister not strike out on a bold course of his own? Why not behave in ways markedly different from those of typical British political leaders? Anyone can, of course, and some who aspire to become Prime Ministers do so. They rarely come to the top. Except in deepest crisis, the system selects others to hold the highest office. One may behave as one likes to. Patterns of behavior nevertheless emerge, and they derive from the structural constraints of the system.

Actors may perceive the structure that constrains them and understand how it serves to reward some kinds of behavior and to penalize others. But then again they either may not see it or, seeing it, may for any of many reasons fail to conform their actions to the patterns that are most often rewarded and least often punished. To say that "the structure selects" means simply that those who conform to accepted and successful practices more often rise to the top and are likelier to stay there. The game one has to win is defined by the structure that determines the kind of player who is likely to prosper.

Where selection according to behavior occurs, no enforced standard of behavior is required for the system to operate, although either system may work better if some standards are enforced or accepted. Internationally, the environment of states' action, or the structure of their system, is set by the fact that some states prefer survival over other ends obtainable in the short run and act with relative efficiency to achieve that end. States may alter their behavior because of the structure they form through interaction with other states. But in what ways and why? To answer these questions we must complete the definition of international structure.

2. THE CHARACTER OF THE UNITS

The second term in the definition of domestic political structure specifies the functions performed by differentiated units. Hierarchy entails relations of super- and subordination among a system's parts, and that implies their differentiation. In defining domestic political structure the second term, like the first and third, is needed because each term points to a possible source of structural variation. The states that are the units of international-political systems are not formally differentiated by the functions they perform. Anarchy entails relations of coordination among a system's units, and that implies their sameness. The second term is not needed in defining international-political structure, because so long as anarchy endures, states remain like units. International structures vary only through a change of organizing principle or, failing that, through variations in the capabilities of units. Nevertheless I shall discuss these like units here, because it is by their interactions that international-political structures are generated.

Two questions arise: Why should states be taken as the units of the system? Given a wide variety of states, how can one call them "like units"? Questioning the choice of states as the primary units of international-political systems became popular in the 1960s and '70s as it was at the turn of the century. Once one understands what is logically involved, the issue is easily resolved. Those who question the state-centric view do so for two main reasons. First, states are not the only actors of importance on the international scene. Second, states are declining in importance, and other actors are gaining, or so it is said. Neither reason is cogent, as the following discussion shows.

States are not and never have been the only international actors. But then structures are defined not by all of the actors that flourish within them but by the major ones. In defining a system's structure one chooses one or some of the infinitely many objects comprising the system and defines its structure in terms of them. For international-political systems, as for any system, one must first decide which units to take as being the parts of the system. Here the economic analogy will help again. The structure of a market is defined by the number of firms competing. If many roughly equal firms contend, a condition of perfect competition is approximated. If a few firms dominate the market, competition is said to be oligopolistic even though many smaller firms may also be in the field. But we are told that definitions of this sort cannot be applied to international politics because of the interpenetration of states, because of their inability to control the environment of their action, and because rising multinational corporations and other nonstate actors are difficult to regulate and may rival some states in influence. The importance of nonstate actors and the extent of transnational activities are obvious. The conclusion that the state-centric conception of international politics is made obsolete by them does not follow. That economists and economically minded political scientists have thought that it does is ironic. The irony lies in the fact that all of the reasons given for scrapping the state-centric concept can be restated more strongly and applied to firms. Firms competing with numerous others have no hope of controlling their market, and oligopolistic firms constantly struggle with imperfect success to do so. Firms interpenetrate, merge, and buy each other up at a merry pace. Moreover, firms are constantly threatened and regulated by, shall we say, "nonfirm" actors. Some governments encourage concentration; others work to prevent it. The market structure of parts of an economy may move from a wider to a narrower competition or may move in the opposite direction, but whatever the extent and the frequency of change, market structures, generated by the interaction of firms, are defined in terms of them.

Just as economists define markets in terms of firms, so I define international-political structures in terms of states. If Charles P. Kindleberger were right in saying that "the nation-state is just about through as an economic unit" (1969, p. 207), then the structure of international politics would have to be redefined. That would be necessary because economic capabilities cannot be separated from the other capabilities of states. The distinction frequently drawn between matters of high and low politics is misplaced. States use economic means for military and political ends; and military and political means for the achievement of economic interests.

An amended version of Kindleberger's statement may hold: Some states may be nearly washed up as economic entities, and others not. That poses no problem for international-political theory since international politics is mostly about inequalities anyway. So long as the major states are the major actors, the structure of international politics is defined in terms of them. That theoretical statement is of course borne out in practice. States set the scene in which they, along with nonstate actors, stage their dramas or carry on their humdrum affairs. Though they may choose to interfere little in the affairs of nonstate actors for long periods of time, states nevertheless set the terms of the intercourse, whether by passively permitting informal rules to develop or by actively intervening to change rules that no longer suit them. When the crunch comes, states remake the rules by which other actors operate. Indeed, one may be struck by the ability of weak states to impede the operation of strong international corporations and by the attention the latter pay to the wishes of the former.

It is important to consider the nature of transnational movements, the extent of their penetration, and the conditions that make it harder or easier for states to control them (see Chapter 7). But the adequate study of these matters, like others, requires finding or developing an adequate approach to the study of international politics. Two points should be made about latter-day transnational studies. First, students of transnational phenomena have developed no distinct theory of their subject matter or of international politics in general. They have drawn on existing theories, whether economic or political. Second, that they have developed no distinct theory is quite proper, for a theory that denies the central role of states will be needed only if nonstate actors develop to the point of rivaling or surpassing the great powers, not just a few of the minor ones. They show no sign of doing that.

The study of transnational movements deals with important factual questions, which theories can help one to cope with. But the help will not be gained if it is thought that nonstate actors call the state-centric view of the world into question. To say that major states maintain their central importance is not to say that other actors of some importance do not exist. The "state-centric" phrase suggests something about the system's structure. Transnational movements are among the processes that go on within it. That the state-centric view is so often questioned merely reflects the difficulty political scientists have in keeping the distinction between structures and processes clearly and constantly in mind.

States are the units whose interactions form the structure of international-political systems. They will long remain so. The death rate among states is remarkably low. Few states die; many firms do. Who is likely to be around 100 years from now—the United States, the Soviet Union, France, Egypt, Thailand, and Uganda? Or Ford, IBM, Shell, Unilever, and Massey-Ferguson? I would bet on the states, perhaps even on Uganda. But what does it mean to refer to the 150-odd states of today's world, which certainly form a motley collection, as being "like units"? Many students of international politics are bothered by the description. To call states "like units" is to say that each state is like all other states in being an autonomous political unit. It is another way of saying that states are sovereign. But sovereignty is also a bothersome concept. Many believe, as the anthropologist M. G. Smith has said, that "in a system of sovereign states no state is sovereign."* The error lies in identifying the sovereignty of states with

---

*Smith should know better. Translated into terms that he has himself so effectively used, to say that states are sovereign is to say that they are segments of a plural society (1966, p. 122; cf. 1956).

their ability to do as they wish. To say that states are sovereign is not to say that they can do as they please, that they are free of others' influence, that they are able to get what they want. Sovereign states may be hardpressed all around, constrained to act in ways they would like to avoid, and able to do hardly anything just as they would like to. The sovereignty of states has never entailed their insulation from the effects of other states' actions. To be sovereign and to be dependent are not contradictory conditions. Sovereign states have seldom led free and easy lives. What then is sovereignty? To say that a state is sovereign means that it decides for itself how it will cope with its internal and external problems, including whether or not to seek assistance from others and in doing so to limit its freedom by making commitments to them. States develop their own strategies, chart their own courses, make their own decisions about how to meet whatever needs they experience and whatever desires they develop. It is no more contradictory to say that sovereign states are always constrained and often tightly so than it is to say that free individuals often make decisions under the heavy pressure of events.

Each state, like every other state, is a sovereign political entity. And yet the differences across states, from Costa Rica to the Soviet Union, from Gambia to the United States, are immense. States are alike, and they are also different. So are corporations, apples, universities, and people. Whenever we put two or more objects in the same category, we are saying that they are alike not in all respects but in some. No two objects in this world are identical, yet they can often be usefully compared and combined. "You can't add apples and oranges" is an old saying that seems to be especially popular among salesmen who do not want you to compare their wares with others. But we all know that the trick of adding dissimilar objects is to express the result in terms of a category that comprises them. Three apples plus four oranges equals seven pieces of fruit. The only interesting question is whether the category that classifies objects according to their common qualities is useful. One can add up a large number of widely varied objects and say that one has eight million things, but seldom need one do that.

States vary widely in size, wealth, power, and form. And yet variations in these and in other respects are variations among like units. In what way are they like units? How can they be placed in a single category? States are alike in the tasks that they face, though not in their abilities to perform them. The differences are of capability, not of function. States perform or try to perform tasks, most of which are common to all of them; the ends they aspire to are similar. Each state duplicates the activities of other states at least to a considerable extent. Each state has its agencies for making, executing, and interpreting laws and regulations, for raising revenues, and for defending itself. Each state supplies out of its own resources and by its own means most of the food, clothing, housing, transportation, and amenities consumed and used by its citizens. All states, except the smallest ones, do much more of their business at home than abroad. One has to be impressed with the functional similarity of states and, now more than ever before, with the similar lines their development follows. From the rich to the poor states, from the old to the new ones, nearly all of them take a larger hand in matters of economic regulation, of education, health, and housing, of culture and the arts, and so on almost endlessly. The increase of the activities of states is a strong and strikingly uniform international trend. The functions of states are similar, and distinctions among them arise principally from their varied capabilities. National politics consists of differentiated units performing specified functions. International politics consists of like units duplicating one another's activities.

3. THE DISTRIBUTION OF CAPABILITIES

The parts of a hierarchic system are related to one another in ways that are determined both by their functional differentiation and by the extent of their capabilities. The units of an anarchic system are functionally undifferentiated. The units of such an order are then distinguished primarily by their greater or lesser capabilities for performing similar tasks. This states formally what students of international politics have long noticed. The great powers of an era have always been marked off from others by practitioners and theorists alike. Students of national government make such distinctions as that between parliamentary and presidential systems; governmental systems differ in form. Students of international politics make distinctions between international-political systems only according to the number of their great powers. The structure of a system changes with changes in the distribution of capabilities across the system's units. And changes in structure change expectations about how the units of the system will behave and about the outcomes their interactions will produce. Domestically, the differentiated parts of a system may perform similar tasks. We know from observing the American government that executives sometimes legislate and legislatures sometimes execute. Internationally, like units sometimes perform different tasks. Why they do so, and how the likelihood of their doing so varies with their capabilities, are matters treated at length in the last three chapters. Meanwhile, two problems should be considered.

The first problem is this: Capability tells us something about units. Defining structure partly in terms of the distribution of capabilities seems to violate my instruction to keep unit attributes out of structural definitions. As I remarked earlier, structure is a highly but not entirely abstract concept. The maximum of abstraction allows a minimum of content, and that minimum is what is needed to enable one to say how the units stand in relation to one another. States are differently placed by their power. And yet one may wonder why only *capability* is included in the third part of the definition, and not such characteristics as ideology, form of government, peacefulness, bellicosity, or whatever. The answer is this: Power is estimated by comparing the capabilities of a number of units. Although capabilities are attributes of units, the distribution of capabilities across units is not. The distribution of capabilities is not a unit attribute, but rather a system-wide concept. Again, the parallel with market theory is exact. Both firms and states are like units. Through all of their variations in form, firms share certain qualities: They are self-regarding units that, within governmentally imposed limits, decide for themselves how to cope with their environment and just how to work for their ends. Variation of structure is introduced, not through differences in the character and function of units, but only through distinctions made among them according to their capabilities.

The second problem is this: Though relations defined in terms of interactions must be excluded from structural definitions, relations defined in terms of groupings of states do seem to tell us something about how states are placed in the system. Why not specify how states stand in relation to one another by considering the alliances they form? Would doing so not be comparable to defining national political structures partly in terms of how presidents and prime ministers are related to other political agents? It would not be. Nationally as internationally, structural definitions deal with the relation of agents and agencies in terms of the organization of realms and not in terms of the accommodations and conflicts that may occur within them or the groupings that may now and then form. Parts of a government may draw together or pull apart, may oppose each other or cooperate in greater or lesser degree. These are the relations that form and dissolve within a system rather than structural alterations that mark a change from one system to another. This is made clear by an example that runs nicely parallel to the case of alliances. Distinguishing systems of political parties according to their number is common. A multiparty system changes if, say, eight parties become two, but not if two groupings of the eight form merely for the occasion of fighting an election. By the same logic, an international-political system in which three or more great powers have split into two alliances remains a multipolar system—structurally distinct from a bipolar system, a system in which no third power is able to challenge the top two. In defining market structure, information about the particular quality of firms is not called for, nor is information about their interactions, short of the point at which the formal merger of firms significantly reduces their number. In the definition of market structure, firms are not identified and their interactions are not described. To take the qualities of firms and the nature of their interactions as being parts of market structure would be to say that whether a sector of an economy is oligopolistic or not depends on how the firms are organized internally and how they deal with one another, rather than simply on how many major firms coexist. Market structure is defined by counting firms; international-political structure, by counting states. In the counting, distinctions are made only according to capabilities.

In defining international-political structures we take states with whatever traditions, habits, objectives, desires, and forms of government they may have. We do not ask whether states are revolutionary or legitimate, authoritarian or democratic, ideological or pragmatic. We abstract from every attribute of states except their capabilities. Nor in thinking about structure do we ask about the relations of states—their feelings of friendship and hostility, their diplomatic exchanges, the alliances they form, and the extent of the contacts and exchanges among them. We ask what range of expectations arises merely from looking at the type of order that prevails among them and at the distribution of capabilities within that order. We abstract from any particular qualities of states and from all of their concrete connections. What emerges is a positional picture, a general description of the ordered overall arrangement of a society written in terms of the placement of units rather than in terms of their qualities.

IV

I have now defined the two essential elements of a systems theory of international politics—the structure of the system and its interacting units. In doing so I have broken sharply away from common approaches. As we have seen, some scholars who attempt systems approaches to international politics conceive of a system as being the product of its interacting parts, but they fail to consider whether anything at the systems level affects those parts. Other systems theorists, like students of international politics in general, mention at times that the effects of the international environment must be allowed for; but they pass over the question of how this is to be done and quickly return their attention to the level of interacting units. Most students, whether or not they claim to follow a systems approach, think of international politics in the way Fig. 5.1 suggests. $N_{1,2,3}$ are states internally generating their external effects. $X_{1,2,3}$ are states acting externally and interacting with each other. No systemic force or factor shows up in the picture.

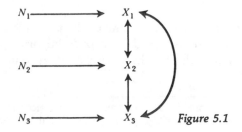

Figure 5.1

Because systemic effects are evident, international politics should be seen as in Fig. 5.2. The circle represents the structure of an international-political system. As the arrows indicate, it affects both the interactions of states and their attributes.* Although structure as an organizational concept has proved elusive, its meaning can be explained simply. While states retain their autonomy, each stands in a specifiable relation to the others. They form some sort of an order. We can use the term "organization" to cover this preinstitutional condition if we think of an organization as simply a constraint, in the manner of W. Ross Ashby (1956, p. 131). Because states constrain and limit each other, international politics can be viewed in rudimentary organizational terms. Structure is the concept that makes it possible to say what the expected organizational effects are and how structures and units interact and affect each other.

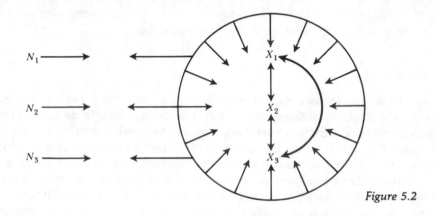

Figure 5.2

Thinking of structure as I have defined it solves the problem of separating changes at the level of the units from changes at the level of the system. If one is concerned with the different expected effects of different systems, one must be able to distinguish changes of systems from changes within them, something that would-be systems theorists have found exceedingly difficult to do. A three-part definition of structure enables one to discriminate between those types of changes:

- Structures are defined, first, according to the principle by which a system is ordered. Systems are transformed if one ordering principle replaces another. To move from an anarchic to a hierarchic realm is to move from one system to another.

---

*No essentials are omitted from Fig. 5.2, but some complications are. A full picture would include, for example, coalitions possibly forming on the right-hand side.

- Structures are defined, second, by the specification of functions of differentiated units. Hierarchic systems change if functions are differently defined and allotted. For anarchic systems, the criterion of systems change derived from the second part of the definition drops out since the system is composed of like units.

- Structures are defined, third, by the distribution of capabilities across units. Changes in this distribution are changes of system whether the system be an anarchic or a hierarchic one.

6

Anarchic Orders and Balances of Power

Two tasks remain: first, to examine the characteristics of anarchy and the expectations about outcomes associated with anarchic realms; second, to examine the ways in which expectations vary as the structure of an anarchic system changes through changes in the distribution of capabilities across nations. The second task, undertaken in Chapters 7, 8, and 9, requires comparing different international systems. The first, which I now turn to, is best accomplished by drawing some comparisons between behavior and outcomes in anarchic and hierarchic realms.

I

1. VIOLENCE AT HOME AND ABROAD

The state among states, it is often said, conducts its affairs in the brooding shadow of violence. Because some states may at any time use force, all states must be prepared to do so—or live at the mercy of their militarily more vigorous neighbors. Among states, the state of nature is a state of war. This is meant not in the sense that war constantly occurs but in the sense that, with each state deciding for itself whether or not to use force, war may at any time break out. Whether in the family, the community, or the world at large, contact without at least occasional conflict is inconceivable; and the hope that in the absence of an agent to manage or to manipulate conflicting parties the use of force will always be avoided cannot be realistically entertained. Among men as among states, anarchy, or the absence of government, is associated with the occurrence of violence.

    The threat of violence and the recurrent use of force are said to distinguish international from national affairs. But in the history of the world surely most rulers have had to bear in mind that their subjects might use force to resist or overthrow them. If the absence of government is associated with the threat of violence, so also is its presence. A haphazard list of national tragedies illustrates the point all too well. The most destructive wars of the hundred years following the defeat of Napoleon took place not among states but *within* them. Estimates of deaths in China's Taiping Rebellion, which began in 1851 and lasted 13 years, range as high as 20 million. In the American Civil War some 600 thousand people lost their lives. In more recent history, forced collectivization and Stalin's purges eliminated five million Russians, and Hitler exterminated six million Jews. In some Latin American countries, coups d'états and rebellions have been normal features of national life. Between 1948 and 1957, for example, 200 thousand Colombians were killed in civil strife. In the middle 1970s most inhabitants of Idi Amin's Uganda must have felt their lives becoming nasty, brutish, and short, quite as in Thomas Hobbes's state of nature. If such cases constitute aberrations, they are uncomfortably common ones. We easily lose sight of the fact that struggles to achieve and maintain power, to establish order, and to contrive a kind of justice within states, may be bloodier than wars among them.

If anarchy is identified with chaos, destruction, and death, then the distinction between anarchy and government does not tell us much. Which is more precarious: the life of a state among states, or of a government in relation to its subjects? The answer varies with time and place. Among some states at some times, the actual or expected occurrence of violence is low. Within some states at some times, the actual or expected occurrence of violence is high. The use of force, or the constant fear of its use, are not sufficient grounds for distinguishing international from domestic affairs. If the possible and the actual use of force mark both national and international orders, then no durable distinction between the two realms can be drawn in terms of the use or the nonuse of force. No human order is proof against violence.

To discover qualitative differences between internal and external affairs one must look for a criterion other than the occurrence of violence. The distinction between international and national realms of politics is not found in the use or the nonuse of force but in their different structures. But if the dangers of being violently attacked are greater, say, in taking an evening stroll through downtown Detroit than they are in picnicking along the French and German border, what practical difference does the difference of structure make? Nationally as internationally, contact generates conflict and at times issues in violence. The difference between national and international politics lies not in the use of force but in the different modes of organization for doing something about it. A government, ruling by some standard of legitimacy, arrogates to itself the right to use force—that is, to apply a variety of sanctions to control the use of force by its subjects. If some use private force, others may appeal to the government. A government has no monopoly on the use of force, as is all too evident. An effective government, however, has a monopoly on the *legitimate* use of force, and legitimate here means that public agents are organized to prevent and to counter the private use of force. Citizens need not prepare to defend themselves. Public agencies do that. A national system is not one of self-help. The international system is.

2. INTERDEPENDENCE AND INTEGRATION

The political significance of interdependence varies depending on whether a realm is organized, with relations of authority specified and established, or remains formally unorganized. Insofar as a realm is formally organized, its units are free to specialize, to pursue their own interests without concern for developing the means of maintaining their identity and preserving their security in the presence of others. They are free to specialize because they have no reason to fear the increased interdependence that goes with specialization. If those who specialize most benefit most, then competition in specialization ensues. Goods are manufactured, grain is produced, law and order are maintained, commerce is conducted, and financial services are provided by people who ever more narrowly specialize. In simple economic terms, the cobbler depends on the tailor for his pants and the tailor on the cobbler for his shoes, and each would be ill-clad without the services of the other. In simple political terms, Kansas depends on Washington for protection and regulation and Washington depends on Kansas for beef and wheat. In saying that in such situations interdependence is close, one need not maintain that the one part could not learn to live without the other. One need only say that the cost of breaking the interdependent relation would be high. Persons and institutions depend heavily on one another because of the different tasks they perform and the different goods they produce and exchange. The parts of a polity bind themselves together by their differences (cf. Durkheim 1893, p. 212).

Differences between national and international structures are reflected in the ways the units of each system define their ends and develop the means for reaching them. In anarchic realms, like units coact. In hierarchic realms, unlike units interact. In an anarchic realm, the units are functionally similar and tend to remain so. Like units work to maintain a measure of independence and may even strive for autarchy. In a hierarchic realm, the units are differentiated, and they tend to increase the extent of their specialization. Differentiated units become closely interdependent, the more closely so as their specialization proceeds. Because of the difference of structure, interdependence within and interdependence among nations are two distinct concepts. So as to follow the logicians' admonition to keep a single meaning for a given term throughout one's discourse, I shall use "integration" to describe the condition within nations and "interdependence" to describe the condition among them.

Although states are like units functionally, they differ vastly in their capabilities. Out of such differences something of a division of labor develops (see Chapter 9). The division of labor across nations, however, is slight in comparison with the highly articulated division of labor within them. Integration draws the parts of a nation closely together. Interdependence among nations leaves them loosely connected. Although the integration of nations is often talked about, it seldom takes place. Nations could mutually enrich themselves by further dividing not just the labor that goes into the production of goods but also some of the other tasks they perform, such as political management and military defense. Why does their integration not take place? The structure of international politics limits the cooperation of states in two ways.

In a self-help system each of the units spends a portion of its effort, not in forwarding its own good, but in providing the means of protecting itself against others. Specialization in a system of divided labor works to everyone's advantage, though not equally so. Inequality in the expected distribution of the increased product works strongly against extension of the division of labor internationally. When faced with the possibility of cooperating for mutual gain, states that feel insecure must ask how the gain will be divided. They are compelled to ask not "Will both of us gain?" but "Who will gain more?" If an expected gain is to be divided, say, in the ratio of two to one, one state may use its disproportionate gain to implement a policy intended to damage or destroy the other. Even the prospect of large absolute gains for both parties does not elicit their cooperation so long as each fears how the other will use its increased capabilities. Notice that the impediments to collaboration may not lie in the character and the immediate intention of either party. Instead, the condition of insecurity—at the least, the uncertainty of each about the other's future intentions and actions—works against their cooperation.

In any self-help system, units worry about their survival, and the worry conditions their behavior. Oligopolistic markets limit the cooperation of firms in much the way that international-political structures limit the cooperation of states. Within rules laid down by governments, whether firms survive and prosper depends on their own efforts. Firms need not protect themselves physically against assaults from other firms. They are free to concentrate on their economic interests. As economic entities, however, they live in a self-help world. All want to increase profits. If they run undue risks in the effort to do so, they must expect to suffer the consequences. As William Fellner says, it is "impossible to maximize joint gains without the collusive handling of all relevant variables." And this can be accomplished only by "complete disarmament of the firms in relation to each other." But firms cannot sensibly disarm even to increase their profits. This statement qualifies, rather than contradicts, the assumption that firms aim at maximum profits. To maximize profits tomorrow as well as today, firms first have to survive. Pooling all resources implies, again as Fellner puts it, "discounting the future possibilities of all participating firms" (1949, p. 35). But the future cannot be discounted. The relative strength of firms changes over time in ways that cannot be foreseen. Firms are constrained to strike a compromise between maximizing their profits and minimizing the danger of their own demise. Each of two firms may be better off if one of them accepts compensation from the other in return for withdrawing from some part of the market. But a firm that accepts smaller markets in exchange for larger profits will be gravely disadvantaged if, for example, a price war should break out as part of a renewed struggle for markets. If possible, one must resist accepting smaller markets in return for larger profits (pp. 132, 217–18). "It is," Fellner insists, "not advisable to disarm in relation to one's rivals" (p. 199). Why not? Because "the potentiality of renewed warfare always exists" (p. 177). Fellner's reasoning is much like the reasoning that led Lenin to believe that capitalist countries would never be able to cooperate for their mutual enrichment in one vast imperialist enterprise. Like nations, oligopolistic firms must be more concerned with relative strength than with absolute advantage.

A state worries about a division of possible gains that may favor others more than itself. That is the first way in which the structure of international politics limits the cooperation of states. A state also worries lest it become dependent on others through cooperative endeavors and exchanges of goods and services. That is the second way in which the structure of international politics limits the cooperation of states. The more a state specializes, the more it relies on others to supply the materials and goods that it is not producing. The larger a state's imports and exports, the more it depends on others. The world's well-being would be increased if an ever more elaborate division of labor were developed, but states would thereby place themselves in situations of ever closer interdependence. Some states may not resist that. For small and ill-endowed states the costs of doing so are excessively high. But states that can resist becoming ever more enmeshed with others ordinarily do so in either or both of two ways. States that are heavily dependent, or closely interdependent, worry about securing that which they depend on. The high interdependence of states means that the states in question experience, or are subject to, the common vulnerability that high interdependence entails. Like other organizations, states seek to control what they depend on or to lessen the extent of their dependency. This simple thought explains quite a bit of the behavior of states: their imperial thrusts to widen the scope of their control and their autarchic strivings toward greater self-sufficiency.

Structures encourage certain behaviors and penalize those who do not respond to the encouragement. Nationally, many lament the extreme development of the division of labor, a development that results in the allocation of ever narrower tasks to individuals. And yet specialization proceeds, and its extent is a measure of the development of societies. In a formally organized realm a premium is put on each unit's being able to specialize in order to increase its value to others in a system of divided labor. The domestic imperative is "specialize"! Internationally, many lament the resources states spend unproductively for their own defense and the opportunities they miss to enhance the welfare of their people through cooperation with other states. And yet the ways of states change little. In an unorganized realm each unit's incentive is to put itself in a position to be able to take care of itself since no one else can be counted on to do so. The international imperative is "take care of yourself"! Some leaders of nations may understand that the well-being of all of them would increase through their participation in a fuller division of labor. But to act on the idea would be to act on a domestic imperative, an imperative that does not run internationally. What one might want to do in the absence of structural constraints is different from what one is encouraged to do in their presence. States do not willingly place themselves in situations of increased dependence. In a self-help system, considerations of security subordinate economic gain to political interest.

What each state does for itself is much like what all of the others are doing. They are denied the advantages that a full division of labor, political as well as economic, would provide. Defense spending, moreover, is unproductive for all and unavoidable for most. Rather than increased well-being, their reward is in the maintenance of their autonomy. States compete, but not by contributing their individual efforts to the joint production of goods for their mutual benefit. Here is a second big difference between international-political and economic systems, one which is discussed in part I, section 4, of the next chapter.

3. STRUCTURES AND STRATEGIES

That motives and outcomes may well be disjoined should now be easily seen. Structures cause actions to have consequences they were not intended to have. Surely most of the actors will notice that, and at least some of them will be able to figure out why. They may develop a pretty good sense of just how structures work their effects. Will they not then be able to achieve their original ends by appropriately adjusting their strategies? Unfortunately, they often cannot. To show why this is so I shall give only a few examples; once the point is made, the reader will easily think of others.

If shortage of a commodity is expected, all are collectively better off if they buy less of it in order to moderate price increases and to distribute shortages equitably. But because some will be better off if they lay in extra supplies quickly, all have a strong incentive to do so. If one expects others to make a run on a bank, one's prudent course is to run faster than they do even while knowing that if few others run, the bank will remain solvent, and if many run, it will fail. In such cases, pursuit of individual interest produces collective results that nobody

wants, yet individuals by behaving differently will hurt themselves without alter-
ing outcomes. These two much used examples establish the main point. Some
courses of action I cannot sensibly follow unless you do too, and you and I cannot sensibly follow them unless we are pretty sure that many others will as well.
Let us go more deeply into the problem by considering two further examples in
some detail.

Each of many persons may choose to drive a private car rather than take a
train. Cars offer flexibility in scheduling and in choice of destination; yet at times,
in bad weather for example, railway passenger service is a much wanted convenience. Each of many persons may shop in supermarkets rather than at corner
grocery stores. The stocks of supermarkets are larger, and their prices lower; yet
at times the corner grocery store, offering, say, credit and delivery service, is a
much wanted convenience. The result of most people usually driving their own
cars and shopping at supermarkets is to reduce passenger service and to decrease
the number of corner grocery stores. These results may not be what most people
want. They may be willing to pay to prevent services from disappearing. And yet
individuals can do nothing to affect the outcomes. Increased patronage *would* do
it, but not increased patronage by me and the few others I might persuade to follow my example.

We may well notice that our behavior produces unwanted outcomes, but we
are also likely to see that such instances as these are examples of what Alfred E.
Kahn describes as "large" changes that are brought about by the accumulation of
"small" decisions. In such situations people are victims of the "tyranny of small
decisions," a phrase suggesting that "if one hundred consumers choose option x,
and this causes the market to make decision X (where X equals 100 x), it is not
necessarily true that those same consumers would have voted for that outcome if
that large decision had ever been presented for their explicit consideration" (Kahn
1966, p. 523). If the market does not present the large question for decision, then
individuals are doomed to making decisions that are sensible within their narrow
contexts even though they know all the while that in making such decisions they
are bringing about a result that most of them do not want. Either that or they
organize to overcome some of the effects of the market by changing its structure—for example, by bringing consumer units roughly up to the size of the units
that are making producers' decisions. This nicely makes the point: So long as one
leaves the structure unaffected it is not possible for changes in the intentions and
the actions of particular actors to produce desirable outcomes or to avoid
undesirable ones. Structures may be changed, as just mentioned, by changing the
distribution of capabilities across units. Structures may also be changed by
imposing requirements where previously people had to decide for themselves. If
some merchants sell on Sunday, others may have to do so in order to remain
competitive even though most prefer a six-day week. Most are able to do as they

please only if all are required to keep comparable hours. The only remedies for strong structural effects are structural changes.

Structural constraints cannot be wished away, although many fail to understand this. In every age and place, the units of self-help systems—nations, corporations, or whatever—are told that the greater good, along with their own, requires them to act for the sake of the system and not for their own narrowly defined advantage. In the 1950s, as fear of the world's destruction in nuclear war grew, some concluded that the alternative to world destruction was world disarmament. In the 1970s, with the rapid growth of population, poverty, and pollution, some concluded, as one political scientist put it, that "states must meet the needs of the political ecosystem in its global dimensions or court annihilation" (Sterling 1974, p. 336). The international interest must be served; and if that means anything at all, it means that national interests are subordinate to it. The problems are found at the global level. Solutions to the problems continue to depend on national policies. What are the conditions that would make nations more or less willing to obey the injunctions that are so often laid on them? How can they resolve the tension between pursuing their own interests and acting for the sake of the system? No one has shown how that can be done, although many wring their hands and plead for rational behavior. The very problem, however, is that rational behavior, given structural constraints, does not lead to the wanted results. With each country constrained to take care of itself, no one can take care of the system.*

A strong sense of peril and doom may lead to a clear definition of ends that must be achieved. Their achievement is not thereby made possible. The possibility of effective action depends on the ability to provide necessary means. It depends even more so on the existence of conditions that permit nations and other organizations to follow appropriate policies and strategies. World-shaking problems cry for global solutions, but there is no global agency to provide them. Necessities do not create possibilities. Wishing that final causes were efficient ones does not make them so.

Great tasks can be accomplished only by agents of great capability. That is why states, and especially the major ones, are called on to do what is necessary for the world's survival. But states have to do whatever they think necessary for their own preservation, since no one can be relied on to do it for them. Why the advice to place the international interest above national interests is meaningless can be explained precisely in terms of the distinction between micro- and macro-

---

*Put differently, states face a "prisoners' dilemma." If each of two parties follows his own interest, both end up worse off than if each acted to achieve joint interests. For thorough examination of the logic of such situations, see Snyder and Diesing 1977; for brief and suggestive international applications, see Jervis, January 1978.

theories. Among economists the distinction is well understood. Among political scientists it is not. As I have explained, a microeconomic theory is a theory of the market built up from assumptions about the behavior of individuals. The theory shows how the actions and interactions of the units form and affect the market and how the market in turn affects them. A macrotheory is a theory about the national economy built on supply, income, and demand as systemwide aggregates. The theory shows how these and other aggregates are interconnected and indicates how changes in one or some of them affect others and the performance of the economy. In economics, both micro- and macrotheories deal with large realms. The difference between them is found not in the size of the objects of study, but in the way the objects of study are approached and the theory to explain them is constructed. A macrotheory of international politics would show how the international system is moved by system-wide aggregates. One can imagine what some of them might be—amount of world GNP, amount of world imports and exports, of deaths in war, of everybody's defense spending, and of migration, for example. The theory would look something like a macroeconomic theory in the style of John Maynard Keynes, although it is hard to see how the international aggregates would make much sense and how changes in one or some of them would produce changes in others. I am not saying that such a theory cannot be constructed, but only that I cannot see how to do it in any way that might be useful. The decisive point, anyway, is that a macrotheory of international politics would lack the practical implications of macroeconomic theory. National governments can manipulate system-wide economic variables. No agencies with comparable capabilities exist internationally. Who would act on the possibilities of adjustment that a macrotheory of international politics might reveal? Even were such a theory available, we would still be stuck with nations as the only agents capable of acting to solve global problems. We would still have to revert to a micropolitical approach in order to examine the conditions that make benign and effective action by states separately and collectively more or less likely.

Some have hoped that changes in the awareness and purpose, in the organization and ideology, of states would change the quality of international life. Over the centuries states have changed in many ways, but the quality of international life has remained much the same. States may seek reasonable and worthy ends, but they cannot figure out how to reach them. The problem is not in their stupidity or ill will, although one does not want to claim that those qualities are lacking. The depth of the difficulty is not understood until one realizes that intelligence and goodwill cannot discover and act on adequate programs. Early in this century Winston Churchill observed that the British-German naval race promised disaster *and* that Britain had no realistic choice other than to run it. States facing global problems are like individual consumers trapped by the "tyranny of small decisions." States, like consumers, can get out of the trap only by changing the structure of their field of activity. The message bears repeating: The only remedy for a strong structural effect is a structural change.

4. THE VIRTUES OF ANARCHY

To achieve their objectives and maintain their security, units in a condition of anarchy—be they people, corporations, states, or whatever—must rely on the means they can generate and the arrangements they can make for themselves. Self-help is necessarily the principle of action in an anarchic order. A self-help situation is one of high risk—of bankruptcy in the economic realm and of war in a world of free states. It is also one in which organizational costs are low. Within an economy or within an international order, risks may be avoided or lessened by moving from a situation of coordinate action to one of super- and subordination, that is, by erecting agencies with effective authority and extending a system of rules. Government emerges where the functions of regulation and management themselves become distinct and specialized tasks. The costs of maintaining a hierarchic order are frequently ignored by those who deplore its absence. Organizations have at least two aims: to get something done and to maintain themselves as organizations. Many of their activities are directed toward the second purpose. The leaders of organizations, and political leaders preeminently, are not masters of the matters their organizations deal with. They have become leaders not by being experts on one thing or another but by excelling in the organizational arts— in maintaining control of a group's members, in eliciting predictable and satisfactory efforts from them, in holding a group together. In making political decisions, the first and most important concern is not to achieve the aims the members of an organization may have but to secure the continuity and health of the organization itself (cf. Diesing 1962, pp. 198–204; Downs 1967, pp. 262–70).

Along with the advantages of hierarchic orders go the costs. In hierarchic orders, moreover, the means of control become an object of struggle. Substantive issues become entwined with efforts to influence or control the controllers. The hierarchic ordering of politics adds one to the already numerous objects of struggle, and the object added is at a new order of magnitude.

If the risks of war are unbearably high, can they be reduced by organizing to manage the affairs of nations? At a minimum, management requires controlling the military forces that are at the disposal of states. Within nations, organizations have to work to maintain themselves. As organizations, nations, in working to maintain themselves, sometimes have to use force against dissident elements and areas. As hierarchical systems, governments nationally or globally are disrupted by the defection of major parts. In a society of states with little coherence, attempts at world government would founder on the inability of an emerging central authority to mobilize the resources needed to create and maintain the unity of the system by regulating and managing its parts. The prospect of world government would be an invitation to prepare for world civil war. This calls to mind Milovan Djilas's reminiscence of World War II. According to him, he and many Russian soldiers in their wartime discussions came to believe that human struggles would acquire their ultimate bitterness if all men were subject to the same social system, "for the system would be untenable as such and various sects would undertake the reckless destruction of the human race for the sake of its greater 'happiness' " (1962, p. 50). States cannot entrust managerial powers to a central agency unless that agency is able to protect its client states. The more powerful the clients and the more the power of each of them appears as a threat to the others, the greater the power lodged in the center must be. The greater the power of the center, the stronger the incentive for states to engage in a struggle to control it.

States, like people, are insecure in proportion to the extent of their freedom. If freedom is wanted, insecurity must be accepted. Organizations that establish relations of authority and control may increase security as they decrease freedom. If might does not make right, whether among people or states, then some institution or agency has intervened to lift them out of nature's realm. The more influential the agency, the stronger the desire to control it becomes. In contrast, units in an anarchic order act for their own sakes and not for the sake of preserving an organization and furthering their fortunes within it. Force is used for one's own interest. In the absence of organization, people or states are free to leave one another alone. Even when they do not do so, they are better able, in the absence of the politics of the organization, to concentrate on the politics of the problem and to aim for a minimum agreement that will permit their separate existence rather than a maximum agreement for the sake of maintaining unity. If might decides, then bloody struggles over right can more easily be avoided.

Nationally, the force of a government is exercised in the name of right and justice. Internationally, the force of a state is employed for the sake of its own protection and advantage. Rebels challenge a government's claim to authority; they question the rightfulness of its rule. Wars among states cannot settle questions of authority and right; they can only determine the allocation of gains and losses among contenders and settle for a time the question of who is the stronger. Nationally, relations of authority are established. Internationally, only relations of strength result. Nationally, private force used against a government threatens the political system. Force used by a state—a public body—is, from the international perspective, the private use of force; but there is no government to overthrow and no governmental apparatus to capture. Short of a drive toward world hegemony, the private use of force does not threaten the system of international politics, only some of its members. War pits some states against others in a struggle among similarly constituted entities. The power of the strong may deter the weak from asserting their claims, not because the weak recognize a kind of rightfulness of rule on the part of the strong, but simply because it is not sensible to tangle with them. Conversely, the weak may enjoy considerable freedom of action if they are so far removed in their capabilities from the strong that the latter are not much bothered by their actions or much concerned by marginal increases in their capabilities.

National politics is the realm of authority, of administration, and of law. International politics is the realm of power, of struggle, and of accommodation. The international realm is preeminently a political one. The national realm is variously described as being hierarchic, vertical, centralized, heterogeneous, directed, and contrived; the international realm, as being anarchic, horizontal, decentralized, homogeneous, undirected, and mutually adaptive. The more centralized the order, the nearer to the top the locus of decisions ascends. Internationally, decisions are made at the bottom level, there being scarcely any other. In the vertical horizontal dichotomy, international structures assume the prone position. Adjustments are made internationally, but they are made without a formal or authoritative adjuster. Adjustment and accommodation proceed by mutual adaptation (cf. Barnard 1948, pp. 148 52; Polanyi 1941, pp. 428 56). Action and reaction, and reaction to the reaction, proceed by a piecemeal process. The parties feel each other out, so to speak, and define a situation simultaneously with its development. Among coordinate units, adjustment is achieved and accommodations arrived at by the exchange of "considerations," in a condition, as Chester Barnard put it, "in which the duty of command and the desire to obey are essentially absent" (pp. 150–51). Where the contest is over considerations, the parties seek to maintain or improve their positions by maneuvering, by bargaining, or by fighting. The manner and intensity of the competition is determined by the desires and the abilities of parties that are at once separate and interacting.

Whether or not by force, each state plots the course it thinks will best serve its interests. If force is used by one state or its use is expected, the recourse of other states is to use force or be prepared to use it singly or in combination. No appeal can be made to a higher entity clothed with the authority and equipped with the ability to act on its own initiative. Under such conditions the possibility that force will be used by one or another of the parties looms always as a threat in the background. In politics force is said to be the *ultima ratio*. In international politics force serves, not only as the *ultima ratio*, but indeed as the first and constant one. To limit force to being the *ultima ratio* of politics implies, in the words of Ortega y Gasset, "the previous submission of force to methods of reason" (quoted in Johnson 1966, p. 13). The constant possibility that force will be used limits manipulations, moderates demands, and serves as an incentive for the settlement of disputes. One who knows that pressing too hard may lead to war has strong reason to consider whether possible gains are worth the risks entailed. The threat of force internationally is comparable to the role of the strike in labor and management bargaining. "The few strikes that take place are in a sense," as Livernash has said, "the cost of the strike option which produces settlements in the large mass of negotiations" (1963, p. 430). Even if workers seldom strike, their doing so is always a possibility. The possibility of industrial disputes leading to long and costly strikes encourages labor and management to face difficult issues, to try to understand each other's problems, and to work hard to find accommodations. The possibility that conflicts among nations may lead to long and costly wars has similarly sobering effects.

5. ANARCHY AND HIERARCHY

I have described anarchies and hierarchies as though every political order were of one type or the other. Many, and I suppose most, political scientists who write of structures allow for a greater, and sometimes for a bewildering, variety of types. Anarchy is seen as one end of a continuum whose other end is marked by the presence of a legitimate and competent government. International politics is then described as being flecked with particles of government and alloyed with elements of community—supranational organizations whether universal or regional, alliances, multinational corporations, networks of trade, and what not. International-political systems are thought of as being more or less anarchic.

Those who view the world as a modified anarchy do so, it seems, for two reasons. First, anarchy is taken to mean not just the absence of government but also the presence of disorder and chaos. Since world politics, although not reliably peaceful, falls short of unrelieved chaos, students are inclined to see a lessening of anarchy in each outbreak of peace. Since world politics, although not formally organized, is not entirely without institutions and orderly procedures, students are inclined to see a lessening of anarchy when alliances form, when transactions across national borders increase, and when international agencies multiply. Such views confuse structure with process, and I have drawn attention to that error often enough.

Second, the two simple categories of anarchy and hierarchy do not seem to accommodate the infinite social variety our senses record. Why insist on reducing the types of structure to two instead of allowing for a greater variety? Anarchies are ordered by the juxtaposition of similar units, but those similar units are not identical. Some specialization by function develops among them. Hierarchies are ordered by the social division of labor among units specializing in different tasks, but the resemblance of units does not vanish. Much duplication of effort continues. All societies are organized segmentally or hierarchically in greater or lesser degree. Why not, then, define additional social types according to the mixture of organizing principles they embody? One might conceive of some societies approaching the purely anarchic, of others approaching the purely hierarchic, and of still others reflecting specified mixes of the two organizational types. In anarchies the exact likeness of units and the determination of relations by capability alone would describe a realm wholly of politics and power with none of the interaction of units guided by administration and conditioned by authority. In hierarchies the complete differentiation of parts and the full specification of their functions would produce a realm wholly of authority and administration with none of the interaction of parts affected by politics and power. Although such pure orders do not exist, to distinguish realms by their organizing principles is nevertheless proper and important.

Increasing the number of categories would bring the classification of societies closer to reality. But that would be to move away from a theory claiming explanatory power to a less theoretical system promising greater descriptive accuracy. One who wishes to explain rather than to describe should resist moving in that direction if resistance is reasonable. Is it? What does one gain by insisting on two types when admitting three or four would still be to simplify boldly? One gains clarity and economy of concepts. A new concept should be introduced only to cover matters that existing concepts do not reach. If some societies are neither anarchic nor hierarchic, if their structures are defined by some third ordering principle, then we would have to define a third system.* All societies are mixed. Elements in them represent both of the ordering principles. That does not mean that some societies are ordered according to a third principle. Usually one can easily identify the principle by which a society is ordered. The appearance of anarchic sectors within hierarchies does not alter and should not obscure the ordering principle of the larger system, for those sectors are anarchic only within limits. The attributes and behavior of the units populating those sectors within the larger system differ, moreover, from what they would be and how they would behave outside of it. Firms in oligopolistic markets again are perfect examples of this. They struggle against one another, but because they need not prepare to defend themselves physically, they can afford to specialize and to participate more fully in the division of economic labor than states can. Nor do the states that populate an anarchic world find it impossible to work with one another, to make agreements limiting their arms, and to cooperate in establishing organizations. Hierarchic elements within international structures limit and restrain the

---

*Emile Durkheim's depiction of solidary and mechanical societies still provides the best explication of the two ordering principles, and his logic in limiting the types of society to two continues to be compelling despite the efforts of his many critics to overthrow it (see esp. 1893). I shall discuss the problem at some length in a future work.

exercise of sovereignty but only in ways strongly conditioned by the anarchy of the larger system. The anarchy of that order strongly affects the likelihood of cooperation, the extent of arms agreements, and the jurisdiction of international organizations.

But what about borderline cases, societies that are neither clearly anarchic nor clearly hierarchic? Do they not represent a third type? To say that there are borderline cases is not to say that at the border a third type of system appears. All categories have borders, and if we have any categories at all, we have borderline cases. Clarity of concepts does not eliminate difficulties of classification. Was China from the 1920s to the 1940s a hierarchic or an anarchic realm? Nominally a nation, China looked more like a number of separate states existing alongside one another. Mao Tse-tung in 1930, like Bolshevik leaders earlier, thought that striking a revolutionary spark would "start a prairie fire." Revolutionary flames would spread across China, if not throughout the world. Because the interdependence of China's provinces, like the interdependence of nations, was insufficiently close, the flames failed to spread. So nearly autonomous were China's provinces that the effects of war in one part of the country were only weakly registered in other parts. Battles in the Hunan hills, far from sparking a national revolution, were hardly noticed in neighboring provinces. The interaction of largely self-sufficient provinces was slight and sporadic. Dependent neither on one another economically nor on the nation's center politically, they were not subject to the close interdependence characteristic of organized and integrated polities.

As a practical matter, observers may disagree in their answers to such questions as just when did China break down into anarchy, or whether the countries of Western Europe are slowly becoming one state or stubbornly remaining nine. The point of theoretical importance is that our expectations about the fate of those areas differ widely depending on which answer to the structural question becomes the right one. Structures defined according to two distinct ordering principles help to explain important aspects of social and political behavior. That is shown in various ways in the following pages. This section has explained why two, and only two, types of structure are needed to cover societies of all sorts.

II

How can a theory of international politics be constructed? Just as any theory must be. As Chapters 1 and 4 explain, first, one must conceive of international politics as a bounded realm or domain; second, one must discover some law-like regularities within it; and third, one must develop a way of explaining the observed regularities. The first of these was accomplished in Chapter 5. Chapter 6 so far has shown how political structures account for some recurrent aspects of the behavior of states and for certain repeated and enduring patterns. Wherever agents and agencies are coupled by force and competition rather than by authority and law, we expect to find such behaviors and outcomes. They are closely identified with the approach to politics suggested by the rubric, *Realpolitik*. The elements of *Realpolitik*, exhaustively listed, are these: The ruler's, and later the state's, interest provides the spring of action; the necessities of policy arise from the unregulated competition of states; calculation based on these necessities can discover the policies that will best serve a state's interests; success is the ultimate test of policy, and success is defined as preserving and strengthening the state. Ever since Machiavelli, interest and necessity—and *raison d'état*, the phrase that comprehends them—have remained the key concepts of *Realpolitik*. From Machiavelli through Meinecke and Morgenthau the elements of the approach and the reasoning remain constant. Machiavelli stands so clearly as the exponent of *Realpolitik* that one easily slips into thinking that he developed the closely associated idea of balance of power as well. Although he did not, his conviction that politics can be explained in its own terms established the ground on which balance-of-power theory can be built.

Realpolitik indicates the methods by which foreign policy is conducted and provides a rationale for them. Structural constraints explain why the methods are repeatedly used despite differences in the persons and states who use them. Balance-of-power theory purports to explain the result that such methods produce. Rather, that is what the theory should do. If there is any distinctively political theory of international politics, balance-of-power theory is it. And yet one cannot find a statement of the theory that is generally accepted. Carefully surveying the copious balance-of-power literature, Ernst Haas discovered eight distinct meanings of the term, and Martin Wight found nine (1953, 1966). Hans Morgenthau, in his profound historical and analytic treatment of the subject, makes use of four different definitions (1973). Balance of power is seen by some as being akin to a law of nature; by others, as simply an outrage. Some view it as a guide to statesmen; others as a cloak that disguises their imperialist policies. Some believe that a balance of power is the best guarantee of the security of states and the peace of the world; others, that it has ruined states by causing most of the wars they have fought.*

To believe that one can cut through such confusion may seem quixotic. I shall nevertheless try. It will help to hark back to several basic propositions about theory. (1) A theory contains at least one theoretical assumption. Such assumptions are not factual. One therefore cannot legitimately ask if they are true, but

---

*Along with the explication of balance-of-power theory in the pages that follow, the reader may wish to consult a historical study of balance-of-power politics in practice. The best brief work is Wight (1973).

only if they are useful. (2) Theories must be evaluated in terms of what they claim to explain. Balance-of-power theory claims to explain the results of states' actions, under given conditions, and those results may not be foreshadowed in any of the actors' motives or be contained as objectives in their policies. (3) Theory, as a general explanatory system, cannot account for particularities.

Most of the confusions in balance-of-power theory, and criticisms of it, derive from misunderstanding these three points. A balance-of-power theory, properly stated, begins with assumptions about states: They are unitary actors who, at a minimum, seek their own preservation and, at a maximum, drive for universal domination. States, or those who act for them, try in more or less sensible ways to use the means available in order to achieve the ends in view. Those means fall into two categories: internal efforts (moves to increase economic capability, to increase military strength, to develop clever strategies) and external efforts (moves to strengthen and enlarge one's own alliance or to weaken and shrink an opposing one). The external game of alignment and realignment requires three or more players, and it is usually said that balance-of-power systems require at least that number. The statement is false, for in a two-power system the politics of balance continue, but the way to compensate for an incipient external disequilibrium is primarily by intensifying one's internal efforts. To the assumptions of the theory we then add the condition for its operation: that two or more states coexist in a self-help system, one with no superior agent to come to the aid of states that may be weakening or to deny to any of them the use of whatever instruments they think will serve their purposes. The theory, then, is built up from the assumed motivations of states and the actions that correspond to them. It describes the constraints that arise from the system that those actions produce, and it indicates the expected outcome: namely, the formation of balances of power. Balance-of-power theory is microtheory precisely in the economist's sense. The system, like a market in economics, is made by the actions and interactions of its units, and the theory is based on assumptions about their behavior.

A self-help system is one in which those who do not help themselves, or who do so less effectively than others, will fail to prosper, will lay themselves open to dangers, will suffer. Fear of such unwanted consequences stimulates states to behave in ways that tend toward the creation of balances of power. Notice that the theory requires no assumptions of rationality or of constancy of will on the part of all of the actors. The theory says simply that if some do relatively well, others will emulate them or fall by the wayside. Obviously, the system won't work if all states lose interest in preserving themselves. It will, however, continue to work if some states do, while others do not, choose to lose their political identities, say, through amalgamation. Nor need it be assumed that all of the competing states are striving relentlessly to increase their power. The possibility that force may be used by some states to weaken or destroy others does, however, make it difficult for them to break out of the competitive system.

The meaning and importance of the theory are made clear by examining prevalent misconceptions of it. Recall our first proposition about theory. A theory contains assumptions that are theoretical, not factual. One of the most common misunderstandings of balance-of-power theory centers on this point. The theory is criticized because its assumptions are erroneous. The following statement can stand for a host of others:

> If nations were in fact unchanging units with no permanent ties to each other, and if all were motivated primarily by a drive to maximize their power, except for a single balancer whose aim was to prevent any nation from achieving preponderant power, a balance of power might in fact result. But we have seen that these assumptions are not correct, and since the assumptions of the theory are wrong, the conclusions are also in error (Organski 1968, p. 292).

The author's incidental error is that he has compounded a sentence some parts of which are loosely stated assumptions of the theory, and other parts not. His basic error lies in misunderstanding what an assumption is. From previous discussion, we know that assumptions are neither true nor false and that they are essential for the construction of theory. We can freely admit that states are in fact not unitary, purposive actors. States pursue many goals, which are often vaguely formulated and inconsistent. They fluctuate with the changing currents of domestic politics, are prey to the vagaries of a shifting cast of political leaders, and are influenced by the outcomes of bureaucratic struggles. But all of this has always been known, and it tells us nothing about the merits of balance-of-power theory.

A further confusion relates to our second proposition about theory. Balance-of-power theory claims to explain a result (the recurrent formation of balances of power), which may not accord with the intentions of any of the units whose actions combine to produce that result. To contrive and maintain a balance may be the aim of one or more states, but then again it may not be. According to the theory, balances of power tend to form whether some or all states consciously aim to establish and maintain a balance, or whether some or all states aim for universal domination.* Yet many, and perhaps most, statements of balance-of-power theory attribute the maintenance of a balance to the separate states as a motive. David Hume, in his classic essay "Of the Balance of Power," offers "the maxim of preserving the balance of power" as a constant rule of prudent politics (1742, pp. 142–44). So it may be, but it has proved to be an unfortunately short

---

*Looking at states over a wide span of time and space, Dowty concludes that in no case were shifts in alliances produced "by considerations of an overall balance of power" (1969, p. 95).

step from the belief that a high regard for preserving a balance is at the heart of wise statesmanship to the belief that states must follow the maxim if a balance of power is to be maintained. This is apparent in the first of Morgenthau's four definitions of the term: namely, "a policy aimed at a certain state of affairs." The reasoning then easily becomes tautological. If a balance of power is to be maintained, the policies of states must aim to uphold it. If a balance of power is in fact maintained, we can conclude that their aim was accurate. If a balance of power is not produced, we can say that the theory's assumption is erroneous. Finally, and this completes the drift toward the reification of a concept, if the purpose of states is to uphold a balance, the purpose of the balance is "to maintain the stability of the system without destroying the multiplicity of the elements composing it." Reification has obviously occurred where one reads, for example, of the balance operating "successfully" and of the difficulty that nations have in applying it (1973, pp. 167–74, 202–207).

Reification is often merely the loose use of language or the employment of metaphor to make one's prose more pleasing. In this case, however, the theory has been drastically distorted, and not only by introducing the notion that if a balance is to be formed, somebody must want it and must work for it. The further distortion of the theory arises when rules are derived from the results of states' actions and then illogically prescribed to the actors as duties. A possible effect is turned into a necessary cause in the form of a stipulated rule. Thus, it is said, "the balance of power" can "impose its restraints upon the power aspirations of nations" only if they first "restrain themselves by accepting the system of the balance of power as the common framework of their endeavors." Only if states recognize "the same rules of the game" and play "for the same limited stakes" can the balance of power fulfill "its functions for international stability and national independence" (Morgenthau 1973, pp. 219–20).

The closely related errors that fall under our second proposition about theory are, as we have seen, twin traits of the field of international politics: namely, to assume a necessary correspondence of motive and result and to infer rules for the actors from the observed results of their action. What has gone wrong can be made clear by recalling the economic analogy (Chapter 5, part III, 1). In a purely competitive economy, everyone's striving to make a profit drives the profit rate downward. Let the competition continue long enough under static conditions, and everyone's profit will be zero. To infer from that result that everyone, or anyone, is seeking to minimize profit, and that the competitors must adopt that goal as a rule in order for the system to work, would be absurd. And yet in international politics one frequently finds that rules inferred from the results of the interactions of states are prescribed to the actors and are said to be a condition of the system's maintenance. Such errors, often made, are also often pointed out, though seemingly to no avail. S. F. Nadel has put the matter simply:

"an orderliness abstracted from behaviour cannot guide behaviour" (Nadel 1957, p. 148; cf. Durkheim 1893, pp. 366, 418; Shubik 1959, pp. 11, 32).

Analytic reasoning applied where a systems approach is needed leads to the laying down of all sorts of conditions as prerequisites to balances of power forming and tending toward equilibrium and as general preconditions of world stability and peace. Some require that the number of great powers exceed two; others that a major power be willing to play the role of balancer. Some require that military technology not change radically or rapidly; others that the major states abide by arbitrarily specified rules. But balances of power form in the absence of the "necessary" conditions, and since 1945 the world has been stable, and the world of major powers remarkably peaceful, even though international conditions have not conformed to theorists' stipulations. Balance-of-power politics prevail wherever two, and only two, requirements are met: that the order be anarchic and that it be populated by units wishing to survive.

For those who believe that if a result is to be produced, someone, or everyone, must want it and must work for it, it follows that explanation turns ultimately on what the separate states are like. If that is true, then theories at the national level, or lower, will sufficiently explain international politics. If, for example, the equilibrium of a balance is maintained through states abiding by rules, then one needs an explanation of how agreement on the rules is achieved and maintained. One does not need a balance-of-power theory, for balances would result from a certain kind of behavior explained perhaps by a theory about national psychology or bureaucratic politics. A balance-of-power theory could not be constructed because it would have nothing to explain. If the good or bad motives of states result in their maintaining balances or disrupting them, then the notion of a balance of power becomes merely a framework organizing one's account of what happened, and that is indeed its customary use. A construction that starts out to be a theory ends up as a set of categories. Categories then multiply rapidly to cover events that the embryo theory had not contemplated. The quest for explanatory power turns into a search for descriptive adequacy.

Finally, and related to our third proposition about theory in general, balance-of-power theory is often criticized because it does not explain the particular policies of states. True, the theory does not tell us why state X made a certain move last Tuesday. To expect it to do so would be like expecting the theory of universal gravitation to explain the wayward path of a falling leaf. A theory at one level of generality cannot answer questions about matters at a different level of generality. Failure to notice this is one error on which the criticism rests. Another is to mistake a theory of international politics for a theory of foreign policy. Confusion about the explanatory claims made by a properly stated balance-of-power theory is rooted in the uncertainty of the distinction drawn between national and international politics or in the denials that the distinction should be made. For those who deny the distinction, for those who devise explanations that are entirely in terms of interacting units, explanations of international politics *are* explanations of foreign policy, and explanations of foreign policy *are* explanations of international politics. Others mix their explanatory claims and confuse the problem of understanding international politics with the problem of understanding foreign policy. Morgenthau, for example, believes that problems of predicting foreign policy and of developing theories about it make international-political theories difficult, if not impossible, to contrive (1970b, pp. 253–58). But the difficulties of explaining foreign policy work against contriving theories of international politics only if the latter reduces to the former. Graham Allison betrays a similar confusion. His three "models" purport to offer alternative approaches to the study of international politics. Only model I, however, is an approach to the study of international politics. Models II and III are approaches to the study of foreign policy. Offering the bureaucratic-politics approach as an alternative to the state-as-an-actor approach is like saying that a theory of the firm is an alternative to a theory of the market, a mistake no competent economist would make (1971; cf. Allison and Halperin 1972). If Morgenthau and Allison were economists and their thinking continued to follow the same pattern, they would have to argue that the uncertainties of corporate policy work against the development of market theory. They have confused and merged two quite different matters.*

Any theory covers some matters and leaves other matters aside. Balance-of-power theory is a theory about the results produced by the uncoordinated actions of states. The theory makes assumptions about the interests and motives of states, rather than explaining them. What it does explain are the constraints that confine all states. The clear perception of constraints provides many clues to the expected reactions of states, but by itself the theory cannot explain those reactions. They depend not only on international constraints but also on the characteristics of states. How will a particular state react? To answer that question we need not only a theory of the market, so to speak, but also a theory about the firms that compose it. What will a state have to react to? Balance-of-power theory can give general and useful answers to that question. The theory explains why a certain similarity of behavior is expected from similarly situated states. The expected behavior is similar, not identical. To explain the expected differences in national responses, a theory would have to show how the different internal structures of states affect their external policies and actions. A theory of

---

*The confusion is widespread and runs both ways. Thus Herbert Simon thinks the goal of classical economic theorists is unattainable because he wrongly believes that they were trying "to predict the behavior of rational man without making an empirical investigation of his psychological properties" (1957, p. 199).

foreign policy would not predict the detailed content of policy but instead would lead to different expectations about the tendencies and styles of different countries' policies. Because the national and the international levels are linked, theories of both types, if they are any good, tell us some things, but not the same things, about behavior and outcomes at both levels (cf. the second parts of Chapters 4 and 5).

III

In the previous chapter, I constructed a systems theory of international politics. In this chapter, I have stated balance-of-power theory as a further development of that theory. In the next three chapters, I shall refine the theory by showing how expectations vary with changes in the structure of international systems. At this point I pause to ask how good the theory so far developed is.

Before subjecting a theory to tests, one asks whether the theory is internally consistent and whether it tells us some things of interest that we would not know in its absence. That the theory meets those requirements does not mean that it can survive tests. Many people prefer tests that, if flunked, falsify a theory. Some people, following Karl Popper (1934, Chapter 1), insist that theories are tested only by attempting to falsify them. Confirmations do not count because, among other reasons, confirming cases may be offered as proof while consciously or not cases likely to confound the theory are avoided. This difficulty, I suggest later, is lessened by choosing hard cases—situations, for example, in which parties have strong reasons to behave contrary to the predictions of one's theory. Confirmations are also rejected because numerous tests that appear to confirm a theory are negated by one falsifying instance. The conception of theory presented in Chapter 1, however, opens the possibility of devising tests that confirm. If a theory depicts a domain, and displays its organization and the connections among its parts, then we can compare features of the observed domain with the picture the theory has limned (cf. Harris 1970). We can ask whether expected behaviors and outcomes are repeatedly found where the conditions contemplated by the theory obtain.

Structural theories, moreover, gain plausibility if similarities of behavior are observed across realms that are different in substance but similar in structure, and if differences of behavior are observed where realms are similar in substance but different in structure. This special advantage is won: International-political theory gains credibility from the confirmation of certain theories in economics, sociology, anthropology, and other such nonpolitical fields.

Testing theories, of course, always means inferring expectations, or hypotheses, from them and testing those expectations. Testing theories is a difficult and subtle task, made so by the interdependence of fact and theory, by the elusive relation between reality and theory as an instrument for its apprehension. Questions of truth and falsity are somehow involved, but so are questions of usefulness and uselessness. In the end, one sticks with the theory that reveals most, even if its validity is suspect. I shall say more about the acceptance and rejection of theories elsewhere. Here I say only enough to make the relevance of a few examples of theory testing clear. Others can then easily be thought of. Many are provided in the first part of this chapter and in all parts of the next three, although I have not always labeled them as tests or put them in testable form.

Tests are easy to think up, once one has a theory to test, but they are hard to carry through. Given the difficulty of testing any theory, and the added difficulty of testing theories in such nonexperimental fields as international politics, we should exploit all of the ways of testing I have mentioned—by trying to falsify, by devising hard confirmatory tests, by comparing features of the real and the theoretical worlds, by comparing behaviors in realms of similar and of different structure. Any good theory raises many expectations. Multiplying hypotheses and varying tests are all the more important because the results of testing theories are necessarily problematic. That a single hypothesis appears to hold true may not be very impressive. A theory becomes plausible if many hypotheses inferred from it are successfully subjected to tests.

Knowing a little bit more about testing, we can now ask whether expectations drawn from our theory can survive subjection to tests. What will some of the expectations be? Two that are closely related arise in the above discussion. According to the theory, balances of power recurrently form, and states tend to emulate the successful policies of others. Can these expectations be subjected to tests? In principle, the answer is "yes." Within a given arena and over a number of years, we should find the military power of weaker and smaller states or groupings of states growing more rapidly, or shrinking more slowly, than that of stronger and larger ones. And we should find widespread imitation among competing states. In practice, to check such expectations against historical observations is difficult.

Two problems are paramount. First, though balance-of-power theory offers some predictions, the predictions are indeterminate. Because only a loosely defined and inconstant condition of balance is predicted, it is difficult to say that any given distribution of power falsifies the theory. The theory, moreover, does not lead one to expect that emulation among states will proceed to the point where competitors become identical. What will be imitated, and how quickly and closely? Because the theory does not give precise answers, falsification again is difficult. Second, although states may be disposed to react to international constraints and incentives in accordance with the theory's expectations, the policies and actions of states are also shaped by their internal conditions. The failure of balances to form, and the failure of some states to conform to the successful practices of other states, can too easily be explained away by pointing to effects produced by forces that lie outside of the theory's purview.

In the absence of theoretical refinements that fix expectations with certainty and in detail, what can we do? As I have just suggested, and as the sixth rule for testing theories set forth in Chapter 1 urges, we should make tests ever more difficult. If we observe outcomes that the theory leads us to expect even though strong forces work against them, the theory will begin to command belief. To confirm the theory one should not look mainly to the eighteenth-century heyday of the balance of power when great powers in convenient numbers interacted and were presumably able to adjust to a shifting distribution of power by changing partners with a grace made possible by the absence of ideological and other cleavages. Instead, one should seek confirmation through observation of difficult cases. One should, for example, look for instances of states allying, in accordance with the expectations the theory gives rise to, even though they have strong reasons not to cooperate with one another. The alliance of France and Russia, made formal in 1894, is one such instance (see Chapter 8, part I). One should, for example, look for instances of states making internal efforts to strengthen themselves, however distasteful or difficult such efforts might be. The United States and the Soviet Union following World War II provide such instances: the United States by rearming despite having demonstrated a strong wish not to by dismantling the most powerful military machine the world had ever known; the Soviet Union by maintaining about three million men under arms while striving to acquire a costly new military technology despite the terrible destruction she had suffered in war.

These examples tend to confirm the theory. We find states forming balances of power whether or not they wish to. They also show the difficulties of testing. Germany and Austria-Hungary formed their Dual Alliance in 1879. Since detailed inferences cannot be drawn from the theory, we cannot say just when other states are expected to counter this move. France and Russia waited until 1894. Does this show the theory false by suggesting that states may or may not be brought into balance? We should neither quickly conclude that it does nor lightly chalk the delayed response off to "friction." Instead, we should examine diplomacy and policy in the 15-year interval to see whether the theory serves to explain and broadly predict the actions and reactions of states and to see whether the delay is out of accord with the theory. Careful judgment is needed. For this, historians' accounts serve better than the historical summary I might provide.

The theory leads us to expect states to behave in ways that result in balances forming. To infer that expectation from the theory is not impressive if balancing is a universal pattern of political behavior, as is sometimes claimed. It is not. Whether political actors balance each other or climb on the bandwagon depends on the system's structure. Political parties, when choosing their presidential candidates, dramatically illustrate both points. When nomination time approaches and no one is established as the party's strong favorite, a number of would-be leaders contend. Some of them form coalitions to check the progress of others. The maneuvering and balancing of would-be leaders when the party lacks one is like the external behavior of states. But this is the pattern only during the leaderless period. As soon as someone looks like the winner, nearly all jump on the bandwagon rather than continuing to build coalitions intended to prevent anyone from winning the prize of power. Bandwagoning, not balancing, becomes the characteristic behavior.*

Bandwagoning and balancing behavior are in sharp contrast. Internally, losing candidates throw in their lots with the winner. Everyone wants someone to win; the members of a party want a leader established even while they disagree on who it should be. In a competition for the position of leader, bandwagoning is sensible behavior where gains are possible even for the losers and where losing does not place their security in jeopardy. Externally, states work harder to increase their own strength, or they combine with others, if they are falling behind. In a competition for the position of leader, balancing is sensible behavior where the victory of one coalition over another leaves weaker members of the winning coalition at the mercy of the stronger ones. Nobody wants anyone else to win; none of the great powers wants one of their number to emerge as the leader.

If two coalitions form and one of them weakens, perhaps because of the political disorder of a member, we expect the extent of the other coalition's military preparation to slacken or its unity to lessen. The classic example of the latter effect is the breaking apart of a war-winning coalition in or just after the moment of victory. We do not expect the strong to combine with the strong in order to increase the extent of their power over others, but rather to square off and look for allies who might help them. In anarchy, security is the highest end. Only if survival is assured can states safely seek such other goals as tranquility, profit, and power. Because power is a means and not an end, states prefer to join the weaker of two coalitions. They cannot let power, a possibly useful means, become the end they pursue. The goal the system encourages them to seek is security. Increased power may or may not serve that end. Given two coalitions, for example, the greater success of one in drawing members to it may tempt the other to risk preventive war, hoping for victory through surprise before disparities widen. If states wished to maximize power, they would join the stronger side, and we would see not balances forming but a world hegemony forged. This does not happen because balancing, not bandwagoning, is the behavior induced by the system. The first concern of states is not to maximize power but to maintain their positions in the system.

---

*Stephen Van Evera suggested using "bandwagoning" to serve as the opposite of "balancing."

Secondary states, if they are free to choose, flock to the weaker side; for it is the stronger side that threatens them. On the weaker side, they are both more appreciated and safer, provided, of course, that the coalition they join achieves enough defensive or deterrent strength to dissuade adversaries from attacking. Thus Thucydides records that in the Peloponnesian War the lesser city states of Greece cast the stronger Athens as the tyrant and the weaker Sparta as their liberator (circa 400 B.C., Book v, Chapter 17). According to Werner Jaeger, Thucydides thought this "perfectly natural in the circumstances," but saw "that the parts of tyrant and liberator did not correspond with any permanent moral quality in these states but were simply masks which would one day be interchanged to the astonishment of the beholder when the balance of power was altered" (1939, I, 397). This shows a nice sense of how the placement of states affects their behavior and even colors their characters. It also supports the proposition that states balance power rather than maximize it. States can seldom afford to make maximizing power their goal. International politics is too serious a business for that.

The theory depicts international politics as a competitive realm. Do states develop the characteristics that competitors are expected to display? The question poses another test for the theory. The fate of each state depends on its responses to what other states do. The possibility that conflict will be conducted by force leads to competition in the arts and the instruments of force. Competition produces a tendency toward the sameness of the competitors. Thus Bismarck's startling victories over Austria in 1866 and over France in 1870 quickly led the major continental powers (and Japan) to imitate the Prussian military staff system, and the failure of Britain and the United States to follow the pattern simply indicated that they were outside the immediate arena of competition. Contending states imitate the military innovations contrived by the country of greatest capability and ingenuity. And so the weapons of major contenders, and even their strategies, begin to look much the same all over the world. Thus at the turn of the century Admiral Alfred von Tirpitz argued successfully for building a battleship fleet on the grounds that Germany could challenge Britian at sea only with a naval doctrine and weapons similar to hers (Art 1973, p. 16).

The effects of competition are not confined narrowly to the military realm. Socialization to the system should also occur. Does it? Again, because we can almost always find confirming examples if we look hard, we try to find cases that are unlikely to lend credence to the theory. One should look for instances of states conforming to common international practices even though for internal reasons they would prefer not to. The behavior of the Soviet Union in its early years is one such instance. The Bolsheviks in the early years of their power preached international revolution and flouted the conventions of diplomacy. They were saying, in effect, "we will not be socialized to this system." The attitude was well expressed by Trotsky, who, when asked what he would do as foreign minister, replied, "I will issue some revolutionary proclamations to the peoples and then close up the joint" (quoted in Von Laue 1963, p. 235). In a competitive arena, however, one party may need the assistance of others. Refusal to play the political game may risk one's own destruction. The pressures of competition were rapidly felt and reflected in the Soviet Union's diplomacy. Thus Lenin, sending foreign minister Chicherin to the Genoa Conference of 1922, bade him farewell with this caution: "Avoid big words" (quoted in Moore 1950, p. 204). Chicherin, who personified the carefully tailored traditional diplomat rather than the simply uniformed revolutionary, was to refrain from inflammatory rhetoric for the sake of working deals. These he successfully completed with that other pariah power and ideological enemy, Germany.

The close juxtaposition of states promotes their sameness through the disadvantages that arise from a failure to conform to successful practices. It is this "sameness," an effect of the system, that is so often attributed to the acceptance of so-called rules of state behavior. Chiliastic rulers occasionally come to power. In power, most of them quickly change their ways. They can refuse to do so, and yet hope to survive, only if they rule countries little affected by the competition of states. The socialization of nonconformist states proceeds at a pace that is set by the extent of their involvement in the system. And that is another testable statement.

The theory leads to many expectations about behaviors and outcomes. From the theory, one predicts that states will engage in balancing behavior, whether or not balanced power is the end of their acts. From the theory, one predicts a strong tendency toward balance in the system. The expectation is not that a balance, once achieved, will be maintained, but that a balance, once disrupted, will be restored in one way or another. Balances of power recurrently form. Since the theory depicts international politics as a competitive system, one predicts more specifically that states will display characteristics common to competitors: namely, that they will imitate each other and become socialized to their system. In this chapter, I have suggested ways of making these propositions more specific and concrete so as to test them. In remaining chapters, as the theory is elaborated and refined, additional testable propositions will appear.

7

Structural Causes and Economic Effects

Chapter 6 compared national and international systems and showed how behavior and outcomes vary from one system to another. Chapters 7, 8, and 9 compare different international systems and show how behavior and outcomes vary in systems whose ordering principles endure but whose structures vary through changes in the distribution of capabilities across states. The question posed in this chapter is whether we should prefer larger or smaller numbers of great powers. Part I carries the theory further. Part II moves from theory to practice.*

I

1. COUNTING POLES AND MEASURING POWER

How should we count poles, and how can we measure power? These questions must be answered in order to identify variations of structure. Almost everyone agrees that at some time since the war the world was bipolar. Few seem to believe that it remains so. For years Walter Lippmann wrote of the bipolar world as being perpetually in the process of rapidly passing away (e.g., 1950 and 1963). Many others now carry on the tradition he so firmly established. To reach the conclusion that bipolarity is passing, or past, requires some odd counting. The inclination to count in funny ways is rooted in the desire to arrive at a particular answer. Scholars feel a strong affection for the balance-of-power world of Metternich and Bismarck, on which many of their theoretical notions rest. That was a world in which five or so great powers manipulated their neighbors and maneuvered for advantage. Great powers were once defined according to their capabilities. Students of international politics now seem to look at other conditions. The ability or inability of states to solve problems is said to raise or lower their rankings. The

---

*Some parts of this chapter and the next one were written as a study of interdependence for the Department of State, whose views may differ from mine.

relations of states may be examined instead of their capabilities, and since the former are always multilateral, the world is said to be multipolar. Thus the dissolution of blocs was said to signal the end of bipolarity even though to infer bipolarity from the existence of blocs in itself confuses the relations with the capabilities of states. The world was never bipolar because two blocs opposed each other, but because of the preeminence of bloc leaders.

In addition to confusion about what to count, one often finds that those who try to identify great powers by gauging their capabilities make their measurements strangely. Of all the ways of playing the numbers game the favorite is probably this: to separate the economic, military, and political capabilities of nations in gauging their ability to act. Henry Kissinger, for example, while Secretary of State, observed that although militarily "there are two superpowers," economically "there are at least five major groupings." Power is no longer "homogeneous." Throughout history, he added, "military, economic, and political potential were closely related. To be powerful a nation had to be strong in all categories." This is no longer so. "Military muscle does not guarantee political influence. Economic giants can be militarily weak, and military strength may not be able to obscure economic weakness. Countries can exert political influence even when they have neither military nor economic strength" (October 10, 1973, p. 7). If the different capabilities of a nation no longer reinforce each other, one can focus on a nation's strengths and overlook its weaknesses. Nations are then said to be superpowers even though they have only some of the previously required characteristics. China has more than 800 million people; Japan has a strong economy; Western Europe has the population and the resources and lacks only political existence. As commonly, the wanted number of great powers is reached by projecting the future into the present. When Europe unites . . . ; if Japan's economy continues to grow . . . ; once China's industrious people have developed their resources. . . . And then, although the imagined future lies some decades ahead, we hear that the world is no longer bipolar. A further variant is to infer another country's status from our policy toward it (cf. my comments on Hoffmann, above, Chapter 3, part II). Thus Nixon, when he was President, slipped easily from talking of China's becoming a superpower to conferring superpower status on her. In one of the statements that smoothed the route to Peking, he accomplished this in two paragraphs (August 5, 1971, p. 16). And the headlines of various news stories before, during, and after his visit confirmed China's new rank. This was the greatest act of creation since Adam and Eve, and a true illustration of the superpower status of the United States. A country becomes a superpower if we treat it like one. We create other states in our image.

Many of those who have recently hailed the world's return to multipolarity have not unexpectedly done so because they confuse structure and process. How are capabilities distributed? What are the likely results of a given distribution?

These are distinct questions. The difficulty of counting poles is rooted in the failure to observe the distinction. A systems theory requires one to define structures partly by the distribution of capabilities across units. States, because they are in a self-help system, have to use their combined capabilities in order to serve their interests. The economic, military, and other capabilities of nations cannot be sectored and separately weighed. States are not placed in the top rank because they excel in one way or another. Their rank depends on how they score on *all* of the following items: size of population and territory, resource endowment, economic capability, military strength, political stability and competence. States spend a lot of time estimating one another's capabilities, especially their abilities to do harm. States have different combinations of capabilities which are difficult to measure and compare, the more so since the weight to be assigned to different items changes with time. We should not be surprised if wrong answers are sometimes arrived at. Prussia startled most foreigners, and most Prussians, by the speed and extent of her victories over Austria in 1866 and over France in 1870. Ranking states, however, does not require predicting their success in war or in other endeavors. We need only rank them roughly by capability. Any ranking at times involves difficulties of comparison and uncertainties about where to draw lines. Historically, despite the difficulties, one finds general agreement about who the great powers of a period are, with occasional doubt about marginal cases. The recent inordinate difficulty of counting great powers arose not from problems of measurement but from confusion about how polarities should be defined.

Counting the great powers of an era is about as difficult, or as easy, as saying how many major firms populate an oligopolistic sector of an economy. The question is an empirical one, and common sense can answer it. Economists agree that, even when the total number of firms in a sector is large, their interactions can be understood, though not fully predicted, through theories about oligopoly if the number of consequential firms reduces to a small number by virtue of the preeminence of a few of them. International politics can be viewed in the same way. The 150-odd states in the world appear to form a system of fairly large numbers. Given the inequality of nations, however, the number of consequential states is small. From the Treaty of Westphalia to the present, eight major states at most have sought to coexist peacefully or have contended for mastery. Viewed as the politics of the powerful, international politics can be studied in terms of the logic of small-number systems.

2. THE VIRTUES OF INEQUALITY

The logic of small-number systems applies internationally because of the imbalance of capabilities between each of the few larger states and the many smaller ones. This imbalance of power is a danger to weak states. It may also be a danger to strong ones. An imbalance of power, by feeding the ambition of some states to extend their control, may tempt them to dangerously adventurous activity. Safety for all states, one may conclude, depends on the maintenance of a balance among them. Ideally, in this view, the rough equality of states gives each of them the ability to fend for itself. Equality may then also be viewed as a morally desirable condition. Each of the states within the arena of balance will have at least a modest ability to maintain its integrity. Inequality, moreover, violates one's sense of justice and leads to national resentments that are in many ways troublesome. On such grounds, one may prefer systems having large numbers of great powers. Inequality, however, is inherent in the state system; it cannot be removed. At the pinnacle of power, no more than small numbers of states have ever coexisted as approximate equals; in relation to them, other states have always been of lesser moment.

The bothersome qualities of the inevitable inequality of states should not cause one to overlook its virtues. In an economy, in a polity, or in the world at large, extreme equality is associated with instability. To draw a domestic analogy: Where individualism is extreme, where society is atomistic, and where secondary organizations are lacking, governments tend either to break down into anarchy or to become highly centralized and despotic. Under conditions of extreme equality, the prospect of oscillation between those two poles was well described by de Tocqueville; it was illustrated by Hobbes; and its avoidance was earnestly sought by the authors of the *Federalist Papers*. In a collection of equals, any impulse ripples through the whole society. Lack of secondary groups with some cohesion and continuity of commitment, for example, turns elections into auctions with each party in its promises tempted to bid up the others. The presence of social and economic groups, which inevitably will not all be equal, makes for less volatility in society. Such durable propositions of political theory are lost sight of by those who believe that the larger the number of consequential states the more surely major wars will be prevented, the survival of states secured, and domination by one of them avoided (Deutsch and Singer 1964). Carried to its logical conclusion, this argument must mean that tranquility would prevail in a world of many states, all of them approximate equals in power. I reach a different conclusion. The inequality of states, though it provides no guarantee, at least makes peace and stability possible.

3. THE CHARACTER OF SMALL-NUMBER SYSTEMS

How do small- and large-number systems differ? I shall answer this question first by economic analogy. From perfect to duopolistic competition, market structures are the same in being individualistic in origin, spontaneous in generation, and homogeneous in composition. Variation of structure is introduced not by differences in the attributes and functions of units but only by distinctions among them according to capability. Because this is so, number becomes a factor of high explanatory power. Different results follow from significant variation in the number of producers. Among thousands of wheat farmers the effect of any one farmer on the market is negligible. As a wheat farmer I see the market as a tyrannical force scarcely affected by my own action. Subject to general and impersonal pressures, I am driven inward, making decisions in terms of my own enterprise. As one among thousands, I must define my goals in terms of myself. I think of the return on my own effort, with calculations, if any, made in terms of expected changes in price. Price is determined by the market and is not affected by how much I offer for sale. I therefore work to raise production and lower costs without considering the plans of competitors. If price falls and I along with others wish to maintain gross income, self-interest dictates that we all boost production. This works against our collective interest by driving prices still lower. Boosting production brings bad results, and yet any other course of action pursued individually will bring even worse ones. This is another example of the tyranny of small decisions, a tyranny to be overcome only by governments legislating such structural changes as those introduced in America by the Agricultural Adjustment Act of 1936.

The independent variables are everybody's decisions about how much to produce. Since anybody's decision makes only an infinitesimal difference in the total that all will produce, the independent variables are inaccessible to those in the market. The sensible pursuit of individual interest makes all of the producers worse off. But because nobody's decision makes a noticeable difference in the outcome, the competition leads neither to the conflict that comes when parties believe that by influencing others they can improve their own lots nor to efforts to strike accommodations. One wheat farmer is free of the control of any other wheat farmer—is free of the pressures that develop when one's plans and activities may affect, and in turn be affected by, the calculations and operations of particular others. Unable to affect the market, each farmer is free to ignore competitors. Because the market dominates, farmers individually have to consider only how to plan and conduct their own operations. The economist, who would explain outcomes, looks at the market; the actors look to themselves.

Given perfect competition, the individual producer is free of tactical constraints and subject only to strategic ones. Given small numbers of major competitors, the individual producer is subject to a combination of both. Large firms are not dominated by impersonal market forces unalterable by their own actions. They are therefore not free to make their internal dispositions or set their external policies without regard for the effects their acts will have on other firms in the field. Because the market does not uniquely determine outcomes, all are impelled both to watch their competitors and to try to manipulate the market.

Each firm or farm, large or small, pursues its interest. To say only that much is not very interesting. It is like saying that both the Ford Motor Company and the individual wheat farmer seek to maximize expected returns. That tells us only what we already knew. From an assumed interest, no useful inferences can be made unless we can figure out what actions are required for its successful pursuit. How interests are appropriately pursued depends on the structure of the market in which one's enterprise is located. Similarly, to say that a state seeks its own preservation or pursues its national interest becomes interesting only if we can figure out what the national interest requires a country to do. States, especially the big ones, are like major corporations. They are at once limited by their situations and able to act to affect them. They have to react to the actions of others whose actions may be changed by the reaction. As in an oligopolistic market, the outcome is indeterminate. Both the situation and the actors exercise influence, but neither controls. By comparing nations and corporations, the elusive notion of the national interest is made clear. By assumption, economic actors seek to maximize expected returns, and states strive to secure their survival. Major firms are in a self-help situation, with their survival depending on their own efforts within limits established by law. Insofar as they are in a self-help situation, survival outranks profit as a goal, since survival is a prerequisite to the achievement of other ends. This corollary attaches to the economists' basic assumption whenever the situation of firms enables them to influence both the market and one another. Relative gains may be more important than absolute ones because one's gain measured against that of others affects the ability to shift for oneself. The interest of firms so placed requires them to put the imperatives of survival ahead of other aims.

Similarly, to say that a country acts according to its national interest means that, having examined its security requirements, it tries to meet them. That is simple; it is also important. Entailed in the concept of national interest is the notion that diplomatic and military moves must at times be carefully planned lest the survival of the state be in jeopardy. The appropriate state action is calculated according to the situation in which the state finds itself. Great powers, like large firms, have always had to allow for the reactions of others. Each state chooses its own policies. To choose effectively requires considering the ends of the state in relation to its situation. How do the problems of states, and the likely fate of their systems, change as the number of great powers varies? The number of great powers is always small, but not always the same. For the sake of stability, peacefulness, and the management of collective affairs, should we prefer some such number as ten, or five, or what?

4. WHY SMALLER IS MORE BEAUTIFUL THAN SMALL

What is best, and for what purposes—numbers that are small or still smaller? Again, I shall first look for economic answers. Economic stability increases as oligopolistic sectors narrow.* Other effects also follow. The likelihood of price wars lessens; the affairs of the competitors become more orderly because they can more easily be managed. These effects follow from a decline in the number of major competitors for nine main reasons. The first two show how one characteristic of firms—their size—promotes sectoral stability. The remaining seven show how variations in market structure affect behavior, how problems become easier or harder to solve as the number of those who participate in efforts to solve them varies. The basic proposition is this: As collusion and bargaining become easier, the fortunes of firms and the orderliness of their markets are promoted; and collusion and bargaining become easier as the number of parties declines. I shall state the points briefly, since their major implications are obvious, and then develop some of them further when considering political cases.

(i) Economists agree that more than any other factor relative size determines the survival of firms. Firms that are large in comparison to most others in their field find many ways of taking care of themselves—of protecting themselves against other large firms, of mounting research and development programs that enable them to keep pace with others' innovations, of amassing capital and generating borrowing power that enables them to ride through recessions.

(ii) Stability is further promoted by the difficulty newcomers have in competing with large and experienced firms operating in established markets. Oligopolistic sectors are most stable when barriers to entry are high. The larger the investment needed to compete with established firms, the more difficult entry becomes. Fewer firms means bigger ones, and bigger firms means higher barriers to entry. If the barriers are sufficiently high, few are likely to try to jump over them and fewer still to succeed.

(iii) The costs of bargaining increase at an accelerating rate as the number of parties becomes larger. As numbers increase each has to bargain with more others. Complications accelerate rapidly. The number of possible two-way relations within a group is given by the formula

$$\frac{(n-1)\,n}{2},$$

where n is the number of parties. Thus with three parties, three different pairs may form; with six, fifteen; with ten, forty-five.

(iv) As a group grows, each member has less incentive to bear the costs of bargaining. Each member of a pair expects to get about one-half of the benefits of a bargain made; each member of a trio, about one-third, and so on.

---

*A system is stable as long as its structure endures. In self-help systems, a structure endures as long as there is no consequential change in the number of principal units. For further discussion, see Chapter 8, part I.

(v) As a group shrinks, each remaining member acquires a larger stake in the system and has more incentive to help to maintain it.

(vi) The expected costs of enforcing agreements, and of collecting the gains they offer, increase disproportionately as the group becomes larger.

(vii) The diversity of parties increases the difficulty of reaching agreements, and expected diversity increases as numbers grow.

(viii) Because the effects of an agreement and the desirability of maintaining or amending it change over time, surveillance of all parties by each of them is called for. The problem of surveillance increases more than proportionately to the increase of numbers . . .

(ix) and so does the difficulty of predicting and detecting deals that other parties may make to one's own disadvantage.

These nine points strongly argue that smaller is better than small. Smaller systems are more stable, and their members are better able to manage affairs for their mutual benefit. Stable systems are self-reinforcing, moreover, because understanding others' behavior, making agreements with them, and policing the agreements become easier through continued experience. (Various of the above points are made by Bain 1956, Baumol 1952, Buchanan and Tullock 1962, Diesing 1962, Fellner 1949, Olson 1965, Shubik 1959, Simmel 1902, Stigler 1964, Williamson 1965).

I should emphasize two limitations of the argument so far made. First, to say that smaller is better is not to say that two, the smallest number possible in a self-help system, is best of all. We have not yet considered whether, say, five-member systems have advantages that outweigh those of still smaller ones. Second, smaller is better for specified ends, and they may not be ends that everyone seeks. Take stability as an example. Firms are interested in their survival; for them, stability has a high value. Over the years, larger firms perform better than smaller ones; that is, they make higher profits. Consumers' interests, however, may be better served if old firms feel the stimulation that comes from being constantly threatened by new ones. The narrowing of competition is better for the firms that survive; a wider competition may be better for the economy. The system-wide view may differ from that of the participants. Henry J. Kaiser would have wanted stability in the automobile industry only after Kaiser-Frazer became an established firm. Internationally, especially with present-day weapons, stability appears as an important end if the existing system offers the best hope for peaceful coexistence among great powers. If it provides other benefits as well, then stability is all the more wanted. Even so, it will not be everyone's highest value. One may believe that a bipolar world is best as a system and yet prefer a world with a larger number of powers. The unity of Europe, for example, or the ascendance of one's own country, may rank higher as goals than stability and peace.

In the economic realm, harmony is defined in terms of the quality and price of products, while their producers may be constantly in jeopardy. Harmony is taken to be not only consistent with, but also in part dependent on, the periodic disappearance of some of the constituent units of the system, only to have them replaced by others. In a system of economic competition, it is desirable that the inefficient be driven to the wall. Each firm seeks to promote its own interest, but the constructive results of competition transcend the interests of the separate units. Firms that are proficient survive, while others, less skillfully managed, go bankrupt. The disappearance of the inefficient, forced by the operation of the system, is a condition for the good performance of the economy. In international politics "efficiency" has little system-wide meaning. The producers, not the products, are of paramount concern. Two states competing for the favor of third parties may be led by the competition to provide more and better political, economic, and military goods and services for consumption by some part of the world. The competition, however, serves chiefly as incentive for each of the states to promote its own interest. Benefits others may gain are mainly by products of this. Economic systems are judged more by the quantity and quality of their products than by the fate of the producers. International-political systems are judged more by the fate of the units than by the quantity and quality of their products.

Although the constructive purpose of economic competition is easily seen, it is hard to argue that states are better off because of the political competition they engage in. In the age of Social Darwinism, the invigoration of states that was thought to result from competition among them was applauded. The triumph of the strong was an indication of virtue; if the weak succumbed, it was because of their vices. Internationally, discord is said to prevail because we are no longer content that the system be perpetuated but are necessarily obsessed with the fate of the units that compose it. Differences in the incidence of destruction and "death" do not account for the reluctance to refer to international politics as a harmonious realm, while competitive economies are often so described. Instead, one may say that the standards of performance now applied to international-political systems are higher, or at least widely different. As John Maynard Keynes once remarked, those who believe that unhampered processes of natural selection lead to progress do not "count the cost of the struggle" (1926, p. 37). In international politics, we often count nothing but the costs of the struggle.

Internationally, if an aggressive state becomes strong or a strong state becomes aggressive, other states will presumably suffer. The death rate among states, however, is remarkably low. I can think of only four states that have met involuntary ends in the last half-century—Estonia, Latvia, Lithuania, and Tibet.

In the international system few states lose their lives; in a freely competitive economy many firms do. Economically, large numbers of competitors are wanted because free competition makes them try harder to supply what consumers want at good prices. To lessen their efforts places their survival in jeopardy. Big-number systems are stable if high death rates are matched by high birth rates. Internationally, large numbers of great powers are not wanted because we care more about the fate of states than about the efficiency with which they compete. Economists deplore small-number systems because they favor producers at the expense of consumers. What is deplored economically is just what is wanted politically. Rather than compare large- and small-number systems, I therefore compare international systems with few and with still fewer great powers.

II

How do the relations of nations vary as systems change? To answer that question, and to refine the theory further, I shall consider economic interdependence now and military interdependence in Chapter 8.

In a self-help system, interdependence tends to loosen as the number of parties declines, and as it does so the system becomes more orderly and peaceful. As with other international-political concepts, interdependence looks different when viewed in the light of our theory. Many seem to believe that a growing closeness of interdependence improves the chances of peace. But close interdependence means closeness of contact and raises the prospect of occasional conflict. The fiercest civil wars and the bloodiest international ones are fought within arenas populated by highly similar people whose affairs are closely knit. It is impossible to get a war going unless the potential participants are somehow linked. Interdependent states whose relations remain unregulated must experience conflict and will occasionally fall into violence. If interdependence grows at a pace that exceeds the development of central control, then interdependence hastens the occasion for war.

I am inclined to be sanguine because I believe that interdependence is low in the present bipolar system as compared to the previous multipolar one. The opposite belief, now commonly held, rests on four claims. First, the world of the nation state has given way to a world in which nations are no longer consistently and generally the most important of actors, with their standings and their fates determined mainly by their varied capabilities. Nonstate actors, multinational corporations prominent among them, grow in importance and become ever harder for states to control. Second, some countries have recently increased their capabilities more than America and Russia have done, thus reducing the margin of superiority. Status and fate are anyway more and more disjoined from capability; military power no longer brings political control. Third, common problems can be solved only through the common efforts of a number, often a large number, of states. We shall all suffocate or sink into the sludge unless the polluters of the air and the sea are effectively regulated. We shall all starve if population continues to explode as in a chain reaction. We may all be blown up if nuclear weapons continue to spread. The four p's—pollution, poverty, population, and proliferation—pose problems so pressing that national interest must be subordinated to collective need. Fourth, nations have become so closely interdependent that all are tightly constrained. States steadily become more entangled in one another's affairs. They become more and more dependent on resources that lie outside of their borders.

These four points assert that great powers are no longer clearly set off from others. If that is true, then my definition of international structure has become inappropriate. We have seen that the first point is grossly misleading: Though multinational corporations are neither politically insignificant nor easily controlled, they do not call the international system's structure into question. The second and third points are examined in the next two chapters. The fourth I now turn to.

1. INTERDEPENDENCE AS SENSITIVITY

"Interdependence" is the catchword of the day. As is the way with catchwords, the term usually goes undefined. We all supposedly experience it, and thus we know what it is. As the introduction to an *International Economic Report of the President* put it: "The fact and character of worldwide economic interdependence has been established in the past decade with leaders of all sectors of society and with most of the people of the world" (CIEP, March 1976, p. 1). But "interdependence" is a concept before it is a fact, and unless the concept is defined, we cannot intelligibly discuss what the present condition of interdependence is, whether it has been increasing, and what its political implications may be. I shall first examine the conception of interdependence that is common: interdependence as sensitivity. I shall then offer a more useful definition of the term: interdependence as mutual vulnerability (cf. Waltz 1970).

As now used, "interdependence" describes a condition in which anything that happens anywhere in the world may affect somebody, or everybody, elsewhere. To say that interdependence is close and rapidly growing closer is to suggest that the impact of developments anywhere on the globe are rapidly registered in a variety of far-flung places. This is essentially an economist's definition. In some ways that is not surprising. Interdependence has been discussed largely in economic terms. The discussion has been led by Americans, whose ranks include nine-tenths of the world's living economists (Strange 1971, p. 223). Economists understandably give meaning to interdependence by defining it in market terms.

Producers and consumers may or may not form a market. How does one know when they do? By noticing whether changes in the cost of production, in the price of goods, and in the quality of products in some places respond to similar changes elsewhere. Parties that respond sensitively are closely interdependent. Thus Richard Cooper defines interdependence as "quick responsiveness to differential earning opportunities resulting in a sharp reduction in differences in factor rewards" (1968, p. 152).

This notion of interdependence calls to mind the freely interacting, self-adjusting markets described by liberal economists of the nineteenth century. Because England, by far the leading state, pursued a policy of free trade from the repeal of the Corn Laws in 1846 onward; because American borders were open to the free flow of people and capital; because the fragmented states of the German, Italian, and East European areas lacked the political ability to control economic movements whether within or beyond their boundaries; because no state had the knowledge and the instruments that permitted the exercise of economic control as fully before the First World War as after it: For these reasons among others the late nineteenth and the early twentieth centuries were, in the phrase of Asa Briggs, "the *belle époque* of interdependence" (1968, p. 47). Capital and labor moved freely, goods less so, and all moved in volumes that are immense when measured against domestic populations and products and when compared to present-day movements (see Appendix Tables I, II, and III at the rear of the book). For much of the century beginning with Napoleon's defeat, "the Atlantic Community of Nations" could be viewed "as a single economy made up of interdependent regions," with national boundaries disregarded (Thomas 1961, pp. 9–15).

So much did earlier economic activities sprawl across national boundaries that commentators on public affairs, whatever their ideological commitments, shared the belief that interdependence—developing rapidly, taking new forms, and drawing people closer together—was making those boundaries ever more porous and thus lowering their political as well as their economic significance. In the *Communist Manifesto*, Marx and Engels optimistically expressed the conviction that the development of a world market, by making economic conditions uniform across nations, was fast eliminating their differences and antagonisms (see above, p. 23). Nikolai Bukharin, in a book written in 1915 and published two years later with Lenin's imprimatur, inferred from the large and rapidly increasing movement of people, commodities, goods, money, and capital that "the various countries have become knitted" closely together and that "an ever-thickening network of international interdependence was being created" (1917, pp. 25, 41–42). Liberal publicist Norman Angell, in *The Great Illusion*, the most influential tract of the early 1900s, summed up a century of liberal economists' conviction that economic interests are personal and universal, rather than national and particular, and persuaded many that spurious political interests were fast being subdued by real economic interests in a world becoming ever more prosperous and peaceful. They were right about the unusual extent of interdependence, but wrong about its likely effects.

Old-fashioned liberals, those whose beliefs were rooted politically in John Locke and economically in Adam Smith, thought in global terms. From their standpoint, to speak of a world economy made sense. If economic adjustments were left to the market worldwide, everyone's interests would be best served in the long run. In the economists' view the uneven distribution of capabilities across nations could be ignored. It is not so surprising that earlier commentators overlooked the distorting effects of inequalities and wrote of a world economy as though it were all of a piece. Yet even for the good old days, that economic view was distorted. From E. H. Chamberlin and Joan Robinson onward, economists have been aware of the difference between "monopolistic" and perfect competition. To think of interdependence in simple market terms is appropriate where economic units interact without their mutual adjustment being affected by the ability of some of them to use their superior capabilities to influence the market or by the intervention of government. All economies work within orders that are politically contrived and maintained. One cannot understand an economy or explain its workings without consideration of the rules that are politically laid down and the economic inequalities that prevail. These statements apply internationally as well as nationally (cf. Robbins 1939, p. 6; Gilpin 1975).

It is surprising, then, that so much recent writing about interdependence reads as though it were written at the turn of the century. Economists and political scientists, like others, make free use of the clichés of our day: spaceship earth, the shrinking planet, our global village, international interdependence. These ubiquitous phrases assert that the world has to be taken whole. The world is treated as a unit and interpreted in market terms. For certain purposes that may be all right. The sensitivity of economic and other adjustments across national borders may never have been finer. In many parts of the world, although obviously not in all of the important ones, that is made true by more rapid communication and transport. Economic analysis must take account of that, but a different focus is required for some economic purposes and is indispensable for political understanding.

In defining interdependence as sensitivity of adjustment rather than as mutuality of dependence, Richard Cooper unwittingly reflects the lesser dependence of today's great powers as compared to those of earlier times. Data excerpted from Appendix Table I graphically show this.

Exports plus Imports as a Percentage of GNP

1909–13	U.K., France, Germany, Italy	33–52%
1975	U.S., Soviet Union	8–14%

To say that great powers then depended on one another and on the rest of the world much more than today's great powers do is not to deny that the adjustment of costs across borders is faster and finer now. Interdependence as sensitivity, however, entails little vulnerability. The more automatically, the more quickly, and the more smoothly factor costs adjust, the slighter the political consequences become. Before World War I, as Cooper says, large differences of cost meant that "trade was socially very profitable" but "less sensitive to small changes in costs, prices, and quality" (1968, p. 152). Minor variations of cost mattered little. Dependence on large quantities of imported goods and materials that could be produced at home only with difficulty, if they could be produced at all, mattered much. States that import and export 15 percent or more of their gross national products yearly, as most of the great powers did then and as most of the middle and smaller powers do now, depend heavily on having reliable access to markets outside their borders. Two or more parties involved in such relations are interdependent in the sense of being mutually vulnerable to the disruption of their exchanges. Sensitivity is a different matter.

As Cooper rightly claims, the value of a country's trade is more likely to vary with its magnitude than with its sensitivity. Sensitivity is higher if countries are able to move back and forth from reliance on foreign and on domestic production and investment "in response to relatively small margins of advantage." Under such conditions, the value of trade diminishes. If domestic substitutions for foreign imports cannot be made, or can be made only at high cost, trade becomes of higher value to a country and of first importance to those who conduct its foreign policy. The high value of Japan's trade, to use Cooper's example, "led Japan in 1941 to attack the Philippines and the United States fleet at Pearl Harbor to remove threats to its oil trade with the East Indies." His point is that high sensitivity reduces national vulnerability while creating a different set of problems. The more sensitive countries become, the more internal economic policies have to be brought into accord with external economic conditions. Sensitivity erodes the autonomy of states, but not of all states equally. Cooper's conclusion, and mine, is that even though problems posed by sensitivity are bothersome, they are easier for states to deal with than the interdependence of mutually vulnerable parties, and that the favored position of the United States enhances both its autonomy and the extent of its influence over others (1972, pp. 164, 176–80).

Defining interdependence as sensitivity leads to an economic interpretation of the world. To understand the foreign-policy implications of high or of low interdependence requires concentration on the politics of international economics, not on the economics of international politics. The common conception of interdependence omits inequalities, whether economic or political. And yet inequality is what much of politics is about. The study of politics, theories about politics, and the practice of politics have always turned upon inequalities, whether among interest groups, among religious and ethnic communities, among classes, or among nations. Internally, inequality is an important part of the political story, though far from being the whole of it. Internal politics is also the realm of authority and law, of established institutions, of socially settled and accepted ways of doing things. Internationally, inequality is more nearly the whole of the political story. Differences of national strength and power and of national capability and competence are what the study and practice of international politics are almost entirely about. This is so not only because international politics lacks the effective laws and the competent institutions found within nations but also because inequalities across nations are greater than inequalities within them (Kuznets 1951). A world of nations marked by great inequalities cannot usefully be taken as the unit of one's analysis.

Most of the confusion about interdependence follows from the failure to understand two points: first, how the difference of structure affects the meaning, the development, and the effects of the interactions of units nationally and internationally; and second, how the interdependence of nations varies with their capabilities. Nations are composed of differentiated parts that become integrated as they interact. The world is composed of like units that become dependent on one another in varying degrees. The parts of a polity are drawn together by their differences; each becomes dependent on goods and services that all specialize in providing. Nations pull apart as each of them tries to take care of itself and to avoid becoming dependent on others. How independent they remain, or how dependent they become, varies with their capabilities (recall Chapter 6, part I, section 2). To define interdependence as sensitivity, then, makes two errors. First, the definition treats the world as a whole, as reflected in the clichés cited earlier. Second, the definition compounds relations and interactions that represent varying degrees of independence for some, and of dependence for others, and lumps them all under the rubric of interdependence.

2. INTERDEPENDENCE AS MUTUAL VULNERABILITY

A politically more pertinent definition is found in everyday usage. Interdependence suggests reciprocity among parties. Two or more parties are interdependent if they depend on one another about equally for the supply of goods and services. They are interdependent if the costs of breaking their relations or of reducing their exchanges are about equal for each of them. Interdependence means that the parties are mutually dependent. The definition enables one to identify what is politically important about relations of interdependence that are looser or tighter. Quantitatively, interdependence tightens as parties depend on one another for larger supplies of goods and services; qualitatively, interdependence tightens as countries depend on one another for more important goods and services that would be harder to get elsewhere. The definition has two components: the aggregate gains and losses states experience through their interactions and the equality with which those gains and losses are distributed. States that are interdependent at high levels of exchange experience, or are subject to, the common vulnerability that high interdependence entails.

Because states are like units, interdependence among them is low as compared to the close integration of the parts of a domestic order. States do not interact with one another as the parts of a polity do. Instead, some few people and organizations in one state interact in some part of their affairs with people and organizations abroad. Because of their differences, the parts of a polity can do a lot for each other. Because of their similarity, states are more dangerous than useful to one another. Being functionally undifferentiated, they are distinguished primarily by their greater or lesser capabilities for performing similar tasks. This states formally what students of international politics have long noticed. The great powers of an era have always been marked off from others by both practitioners and theorists.

The structure of a system changes with changes in the distribution of capabilities across the system's units. As international structure changes, so does the extent of interdependence. As political systems go, the international-political one is loosely knit. With that proposition established, we want to know how interdependence varies in systems of different structure. Interdependence is a relation among equals. Interdependence is reduced by increases in the disparity of national capabilities. In the European-centered politics of the three centuries that ended with World War II, five or more great powers sought to coexist peacefully and at times contended for mastery. In the global politics of the three decades since that war, only two states have perched at the pinnacle of power. Economically as well as militarily, the United States and the Soviet Union act with an independence of the external world unknown to earlier great powers. When five or more great powers populated the world, most of them were geographically smaller than today's great powers are. They did a relatively high percentage of their business with one another and with the rest of the world. Interdependence decreased in the 1930s as countries strove for greater self-sufficiency. It decreased further and dramatically after World War II, for each of the superpowers that emerged from that war is vastly more self-sufficient than most of the previous great powers were. The United States and the Soviet Union are economically less dependent on each other and on other countries than great powers were in earlier days. If one is thinking of the international-political world, it is odd in the extreme that "interdependence" has become the word commonly used to describe it.

Why do I reach a conclusion so different from the accepted one? What one sees when looking at the world depends on one's theoretical perspective, which colors the meaning of concepts. When I say that interdependence is tighter or looser I am saying something about the international system, with systems-level characteristics defined, as ever, by the situation of the great powers. In any international-political system some of the major and minor states are closely interdependent; others are heavily dependent. The system, however, is tightly or loosely interdependent according to the relatively high or low dependence of the great powers. Interdependence is therefore looser now than it was before and between the two world wars of this century. Many who claim to measure economic interdependence find it closer in some or in all respects now than earlier in this century. The difference between us is conceptual, not empirical. They measure interdependence between certain countries or among all of them (see, e.g., Rosecrance and Stein, October 1973; Katzenstein, Autumn 1975; Rosecrance *et al.*, Summer 1977). They are concerned with interdependence as a unit-level phenomenon, as is to be expected since reduction dominates the field. Those who confine their analyses to the unit level infer from the growth of international business and the increased intensity of international activity that "international interdependence" has risen. They then dwell on the complex ways in which issues, actions, and policies have become intertwined and the difficulty everyone has in influencing or controlling them. They have discovered the complexity of processes and have lost sight of how processes are affected by structure. The growing complexity of public and private affairs is surely important, but so also is the effect of international-political structure on them. A systemic conception of interdependence is needed to answer such basic questions as these: What are the likely effects of complexity on the system? What is the likely response of the system's leading powers to it? How powers are placed in the system affects their abilities, their opportunities, and their inclinations to act. Their behaviors vary as the interdependence of the system changes, and the variations tell us something about the likely fate both of the system and of its parts—the great powers and the lesser ones as well.

Interdependence tends to decrease as the number of great powers diminishes; and two is the lowest possible number. The connection between change of system and extent of interdependence has to be carefully stated. The correlation is not perfect because economic interdependence varies with the size, and not necessarily with the number, of great powers. Though size tends to increase as numbers fall, one can imagine a world of four great powers, all of them at low levels of interdependence economically. The larger a country, the higher the proportion of its business it does at home. Bergsten and Cline point out that the West European Nine, if they began to play as a team, would import and export only about nine percent of GNP, which nicely shows both the political irrelevance of much writing about interdependence and how increased size would enhance the internal sector (1976, pp. 155–61). Western Europe with political unity achieved, and China with a modern economy, would be great powers and highly self-sufficient ones. To compete at the great-power level is now possible only for countries of continental size. Economically, although not militarily, among three or four powers of such size interdependence would remain low.

What do we see if we turn from theory to practice? How closely or how loosely interdependent does the international system appear to be?

1. ECONOMIC CONDITIONS

Even though the present great powers trade little of their product, do they not depend heavily on some essential imported raw materials? Consider the American rather than the Russian case, because we import more than they do. Three points should be made. First, in any international system the extent of interdependence varies. In the old multipolar world, economic interdependence peaked before and dropped after the First World War. In the new bipolar world, economic interdependence has increased from its low level at the end of the Second World War. Between those two systems the interdependence gap is considerable. Variations of interdependence within a system of low interdependence should not obscure the difference between systems.

Second, some raw materials will become scarcer, and we and others will become more dependent on their suppliers. The control of oil supplies and prices by the Organization of Petroleum Exporting Countries (OPEC) triggered worries about future raw-material scarcities, whether contrived or natural. As more studies are done, the more surely the conclusion emerges: By worrying a bit and taking appropriate actions, the United States can be reasonably sure of securing sufficient supplies. We make about a quarter of the world's goods, and we have at least that proportion of the world's resources. With more money, better technology, and larger research budgets, we can synthesize, stockpile, and substitute for critical materials more readily than other countries can. A study completed in 1976 by a group of seven economists for the Experimental Technologies Incentive Program of the National Bureau of Standards examined the advisability of governmental funding for projects aimed at achieving greater independence in seven critical commodities that we now import heavily—bauxite, chromium, manganese, cobalt, platinum-palladium, copper, and petroleum. They concluded that we should worry over the next ten years about cutoffs or price increases only in the case of chromium. They advised against funding new technologies and in favor of stockpiling supplies sufficient for specified periods. In all cases, save oil and copper, stockpiles already exceed the amounts recommended, and copper is not much of a problem anyway. The problem of stockpiling has not been to build up to targeted amounts, but to avoid exceeding them—and this despite the high targets that result from the Federal Preparedness Agency's planning on the basis of a three-year conventional war and the dislocations it would cause (Crittenden, December 31, 1976; Snyder 1966, p. 247; Finney, November 28, 1976; CIEP, December 1974, p. 16). Dependency, moreover, is a comparative matter. We have recently become more dependent, and so have many others. Our use of imported raw materials has increased, yet of 19 critical materials, the United States in 1973 imported 15 percent of the amount of its yearly use as compared to 75 percent for West European countries and 90 percent for Japan.* Of the American imports, two-thirds came from Canada, Australia, South Africa and other more developed countries, and over one-half from Canada alone (CIEP, December 1974, p. 4).

Third, although we trade a small percentage of our national product, this small percentage accounts for a large proportion of total world trade (see Appendix Table IV). The larger a country's trade, in absolute terms, the larger the number of its suppliers will be. As the world's largest trader, we draw on a multiplicity of sources of supply. Wayward political movements or revolutions or wars elsewhere in the world may shut off some of a country's supplies. Here, as in other matters, there is safety in numbers. As a big buyer, moreover, we enjoy the leverage that good customers have. We are also far and away the world's largest supplier of foodstuffs, of the technologically most advanced manufactures, and of capital. For the moment, consider the dependence of others on us for agricultural supplies alone. Throughout the 1960s and '70s, we accounted for 90 percent of world soybean exports, an important source of protein for people as well as for animals (Schneider 1976, p. 23). In 1975 we accounted for 48 percent of the world's wheat exports, 56 percent of feed grain exports, and 50 percent of oil seed exports (CIEP, March 1976, p. 16). The dependence of the Soviet Union on large, if sporadic, imports of American grain, of Europe on imports of American feed grains, of Japan and the less developed countries on imports of American food grains, has increased rapidly, and alarmingly, in the 1970s. Those who have what others want or badly need are in favored positions. States are the more independent if they have reliable access to important resources, if they have feasible alternatives, if they have the ability to do without, and if they have leverage to use against others. Dependency is a two-way street. Its extent varies both with how much we need them and with how much they need us.

Something should be said about American investments abroad. In 1974 we had about $265 billion in foreign assets of all sorts; in 1973 the sales of American firms operating abroad amounted to $292 billion, an amount exceeded only by the GNPs of the United States, the Soviet Union, Japan, and West Germany (CIEP, March 1976, p. 160, Table 42; *Survey of Current Business*, August 1975, p. 23). One may think that the vulnerability of American operations abroad is

---

*Oil, which is excluded, I shall discuss in a moment.

proportionate to the size of the stake. We do have plenty to lose, and other countries on occasion may want to take some of it from us. And yet, expropriations of American property have been of limited extent and are declining (UN Department of Economic Affairs, 1973, pp. 76–77; Barnet and Muller 1974, pp. 188–89). Again, three points should be made. First, we should separate the question of our vulnerability as a nation from the question of the vulnerability of American firms. How vulnerable are they? Measured by sales in 1971, eight of the top nine, and 52 of the top 90, multinational corporations (MNCs) are American. The percentage of profit earned abroad is shown for seven of the eight and for 22 of the 52. They earned, respectively, 34.4 and 33.5 percent of their profits abroad and made 29.2 percent of their total sales there (calculated from UN Department of Economic Affairs, 1973, pp. 130–32). Because foreign earnings account for large portions of their profits, firms use caution in deciding where to locate abroad. Though some risks are run, the larger firms gain safety through geographic diversification. The more important a firm is to the American economy, the less likely it is to suffer a fatal series of losses in various countries from their punitive regulations or expropriations. The diversity of American investment, in type of enterprise and in geographic location, provides ensurance against sudden and sharp reversals. Nations do not easily concert their policies, and that is a comfort for the nation whose operations are global. Some American firms may be vulnerable; America as a nation is not. Someone who has a lot to lose can afford to lose quite a bit of it. This maxim is a common proposition of oligopolistic economics. That a large and well-placed firm can afford to run at a loss for some years is taken not as a sign of weakness and vulnerability but as being a considerable strength. Where disparities are great, whether among firms or among states, the largest of them need worry least about the bothersome activities of others.

Second, the trend of American investments, away from extractive industries in less developed countries and toward manufacturing industries in more developed ones, makes investments safer. Data taken from Appendix Table V show

U.S. Foreign Direct Investment (FDI)

1950	In more developed countries (MDCs)	45%
	In less developed countries (LDCs)	55%
1975	In MDCs	68%
	In LDCs	32%
1950	U.S. FDI in extractive industries	38%
	of total U.S. FDI, of which	28% in LDCs
		10% in MDCs
1975	U.S. FDI in extractive industries	29%
	of total U.S. FDI, of which	10% in LDCs
		19% in MDCs

the trend. Investors in extractive industries have to put their money where the resources are. They are more vulnerable to pressures from host countries because they cannot easily move from less to more hospitable ones. In manufacturing sectors, "footloose corporations," to use Louis Turner's phrase, pick their countries with one eye to profitability and another to safety.

Third, in manufacturing sectors again the coin is biased in favor of American interests. On one side of the coin one sees that foreign countries are sensitive to the presence of American firms, many of which locate in fast-growing, high-technology, export-oriented sectors. Made wary by the depth of American penetration, foreign countries may try to reduce their dependence by barring American firms or by subsidizing their own to help them compete. At times during de Gaulle's rule France followed such policies, although at high cost and with little success. On the other side of the coin one sees the difficulties foreign countries have in resisting American firms. American firms have the technological lead, and it is hard for foreign firms to catch up. The size of the home market enables American firms to operate on a large scale and to generate resources that can be used abroad to compete with or to overwhelm native industries. In 1976, for example, IBM devoted about one billion dollars to research and development, an amount that exceeded the entire turnover of Britain's largest computer company and was four times greater than the money available to Britain's Science Research Council (*Economist*, August 13, 1977, pp. 64–65). The size of IBM's operations enables the company to spend money on a governmental scale.

The disadvantages of foreign firms relate directly to the smaller scale of their national economies. Although Britain, West Germany, and Japan now spend about as much on research and development, measured as a percentage of GNP, as we do, their absolute expenditures lag (see Appendix Table VI). Under these conditions, national governments are constrained to permit domestic firms to make arrangements with American companies. The smaller states' opportunities to maneuver are further limited by competition among them. If, say, France follows a policy of exclusion, American firms will locate in neighboring countries. Even one who believes that those countries become beholden to America cannot help but notice that they also become richer and better able to compete in foreign markets, including the markets of countries that exclude American firms. Lagging states only get weaker if American capital and technology are excluded. The American computer industry can get along without the assistance of French companies, but Machines Bull could not survive without American capital and technology. In 1962 the French government resisted the purchase by General Electric of 20 percent of Bull's shares. Unable to find another French or European partner, the French government was constrained in 1964 to accept a 50–50 arrangement with General Electric. By the middle 1960s GE's share in the company had grown to approximately two-thirds. GE's losses led it to quit challenging IBM in the European computer market. In 1970 GE sold out to

Honeywell. The story continues, but since it holds no surprises we can stop following it (see Tugendhat 1971, p. 36; *International Herald Tribune*, May 1977).

De Gaulle wanted to avoid American control and to maintain an independent French capability in the manufacturing of computers. Who wouldn't? The effective choice, however, was between a competitive American-controlled company and an uncompetitive French company technologically falling further and further behind. In France penetration of foreign capital is less than the West European average, but it is higher than average in fields using advanced technology. Notice what the averages for various fields are. A 1970 study by the EEC Commission showed American firms producing 95 percent of the EEC's integrated circuits, 80 percent of electronic computers, 40 percent of titanium, and 30 percent of cars and vehicles (Stephenson 1973, p. 27). The automotive industry does not operate at the technological frontier. American firms nevertheless command an impressive percentage of European markets. American firms have an edge not only in their technology and capital resources but also in their managerial skills and marketing networks.

General Electric, Honeywell, and other American firms may require foreign affiliations in order to compete with IBM. There may be genuine interdependence at the level of the firm. It is a mistake to identify interdependence at that level with the interdependence of states. Because of the technology they command, along with other advantages they offer, American firms are important to foreign firms. The attempts of foreign firms to band together are impeded by the greater attraction of establishing connections with American firms. Foreign countries as well feel the attraction because of the help American firms can give to their domestic economies and to their exports. In 1966 and 1970, seven countries were surveyed—Britain, France, West Germany, Belgium-Luxembourg, Canada, Mexico, and Brazil. In both years it was found that American-owned firms accounted on average for 13 percent of each country's gross fixed capital formation, and from 20 to 22 percent of capital formation in the vital machinery sector (see Appendix Table VII). Moreover, in those years American-owned firms generated 7 to 45 percent of the same countries' exports and accounted, respectively, for 21 and 24 percent of the world's total exports (see Appendix Table VIII; and for exports by manufacturing sector, Appendix Table IX).

The above figures and comments make clear why the urge to limit the intrusion of, or to exclude, American firms has given way to intense courting of them. In 1966 the Fairchild Corporation, when opening a new plant in de Gaulle's France, remarked that government officials had "moved heaven and earth to provide us with facilities" (Tugendhat 1971, p. 37). Competition for American firms has quickened. Britain won a Ford engine plant in 1977 after intense competition with other European states. The plant was worth competing for. It is expected to provide 2,500 jobs directly, another 5,000 indirectly, and a quarter of a billion dollars' worth of exports yearly (Collins, September 10, 1977). One may prefer domestic to foreign firms generally, but not lagging domestic firms to thriving foreign ones that will broadly stimulate the economy.

Multinational corporations are misnamed. They are nationally based firms that operate abroad, and more than one-half of the big ones are based in the United States. When the point is made that multinational corporations make their decisions on a global basis, one gets the impression that nations no longer matter. But that is grossly misleading. Decisions are made in terms of whole corporations and not just according to the condition and interest of certain subsidiaries. The picture usually drawn is one of a world in which economic activity has become transnational, with national borders highly permeable and businessmen making their decisions without even bearing them in mind. But most of the largest international corporations are based in America; most of their research and development is done there; most of their top personnel is American (Tugendhat 1971, pp. 17, 124). Under these conditions it is reasonable to suppose that in making corporate decisions the American perspective will be the prominent one. Similarly, although both American and foreign governments try to regulate the activities of these corporations, the fact that most of them are American based gives a big advantage to the latter government. We should not lightly conclude that decentralization of operations means that centers of control are lacking. From about the middle of the nineteenth century, the quicker transmission of ideas resulted, in the words of R. D. McKenzie, in "centralization of control and decentralization of operation." As he put it, "the modern world is integrated through information collected and distributed from fixed centers of dominance" (July 1927, pp. 34–35). Within the United States, when industry fanned out from the northeast, southern and western citizens complained that control remained in New York and Chicago where corporate decisions were made without regard for regional interests. Europeans and others now make similar complaints. One has to ask where most of the threads come together, and the answer is not in London, or Brussels, or Paris, but rather in New York City and Washington. The term "multinational corporation," like the term "interdependence," obscures America's special position—in this case, a position not shared by the Soviet Union.

2. POLITICAL EFFECTS

Interdependence has been low since the Second World War. Lately we have gained some sense of what dependence means by experiencing a bit more of it. We have gained no sense of how our, and the Soviet Union's, low interdependence compares with the high interdependence of previous powers and of the effects that has on behavior. Never in modern history have great powers been so sharply set off from lesser states and so little involved in each other's economic and social affairs. What political consequences follow from interdependence being closer or looser?

I have dwelt on the distinction between internal and external orders. That there is much of a distinction is denied by those who claim that interdependence has changed the character of international politics. Many believe that the mere mutualism of international exchange is becoming a true economic-social-political integration. One point can be made in support of this formulation. The common conception of interdependence is appropriate only if the inequalities of nations are fast lessening and losing their political significance. If the inequality of nations is still the dominant political fact of international life, then interdependence remains low. Economic examples in this section, and military examples in the next one, make clear that it is.

In placid times, statesmen and commentators employ the rich vocabulary of clichés that cluster around the notion of global interdependence. Like a flash of lightning, crises reveal the landscape's real features. What is revealed by the oil crisis following the Arab-Israeli War in October of 1973? Because that crisis is familiar to all of us and will long be remembered, we can concentrate on its lessons without rehearsing the details. Does it reveal states being squeezed by common constraints and limited to applying the remedies they can mutually contrive? Or does it show that the unequal capabilities of states continue to explain their fates and to shape international-political outcomes?

Recall how Kissinger traced the new profile of power. "Economic giants can be militarily weak," he said, "and military strength may not be able to obscure economic weakness. Countries can exert political influence even when they have neither military nor economic strength" (see above, p. 130). Economic, military, and political capabilities can be kept separate in gauging the ability of nations to act. Low politics, concerned with economic and such affairs, has replaced military concerns at the top of the international agenda. Within days the Arab-Israeli War proved that reasoning wrong. Such reasoning had supported references made in the early 1970s to the militarily weak and politically disunited countries of Western Europe as constituting "a great civilian power." Recall the political behavior of the great civilian power in the aftermath of the war. Not Western Europe as any kind of a power, but the separate states of Western Europe, responded to the crisis—in the metaphor of *The Economist*—by behaving at once like hens and ostriches. They ran around aimlessly, clucking loudly while keeping their heads buried deeply in the sand. How does one account for such behavior? Was it a failure of nerve? Is it that the giants of yesteryear—the Attlees and Bevins, the Adenauers and de Gaulles—have been replaced by men of lesser stature? Difference of persons explains some things; difference of situations explains more. In 1973 the countries of Western Europe depended on oil for 60 percent of their energy supply. Much of that oil came from the Middle East (see Appendix Table X). Countries that are highly dependent, countries that get much of what they badly need from a few possibly unreliable suppliers, must do all they can to increase the chances that they will keep getting it. The weak, lacking leverage, can plead their cause or panic. Most of the countries in question unsurprisingly did a little of each.

The behavior of nations in the energy crisis that followed the military one revealed the low political relevance of interdependence defined as sensitivity. Instead, the truth of the propositions I made earlier was clearly shown. Smooth and fine economic adjustments cause little difficulty. Political interventions that bring sharp and sudden changes in prices and supplies cause problems that are economically and politically hard to cope with. The crisis also revealed that, as usual, the political clout of nations correlates closely with their economic power and their military might. In the winter of 1973–74 the policies of West European countries had to accord with economic necessities. The more dependent a state is on others, and the less its leverage over them, the more it must focus on how its decisions affect its access to supplies and markets on which its welfare or survival may depend. This describes the condition of life for states that are no more than the equal of many others. In contrast, the United States was able to make its policy according to political and military calculations. Importing but two percent of its total energy supply from the Middle East, we did not have to appease Arab countries as we would have had to do if our economy had depended heavily on them and if we had lacked economic and other leverage. The United States could manipulate the crisis that others made in order to promote a balance of interests and forces holding some promise of peace. The unequal incidence of shortages led to the possibility of their manipulation. What does it mean then to say that the world is an increasingly interdependent one in which all nations are constrained, a world in which all nations lose control? Very little. To trace the effects that follow from inequalities, one has to unpack the word "interdependent" and identify the varying mixtures of relative dependence for some nations and of relative independence for others. As one should expect in a world of highly unequal nations, some are severely limited while others have wide ranges of choice; some have little ability to affect events outside of their borders while others have immense influence.

The energy crisis should have made this obvious, but it did not. Commentators on public affairs continue to emphasize the world's interdependence and to talk as though all nations are losing control and becoming more closely bound. Transmuting concepts into realities and endowing them with causal force is a habit easily slipped into. Public officials and students of international affairs once wrote of the balance of power causing war or preserving peace. They now attribute a comparable reality to the concept of interdependence and endow it with strong causal effect. Thus Secretary Kissinger, who can well represent both groups, wondered "whether interdependence would foster common progress or common disaster" (January 24, 1975, p. 1). He described American Middle-East policy as being to reduce Europe's and Japan's vulnerability, to engage in dialogue with the producers, and "to give effect to the principle of interdependence on a global basis" (January 16, 1975, p. 3). Interdependence has become a thing in itself: a "challenge" with its own requirements, "a physical and moral imperative" (January 24, 1975, p. 2; April 20, 1974, p. 3).

When he turned to real problems, however, Kissinger emphasized America's special position. The pattern of his many statements on such problems as energy, food, and nuclear proliferation was first to emphasize that our common plight denies all possibility of effective national action and then to place the United States in a separate category. Thus, two paragraphs after declaring our belief in interdependence, we find this query: "In what other country could a leader say, 'We are going to solve energy; we're going to solve food; we're going to solve the problem of nuclear war,' and be taken seriously?" (October 13, 1974, p. 2)

In coupling his many statements about interdependence with words about what we can do to help ourselves and others, was Kissinger not saying that we are much less dependent than most countries are? We are all constrained but, it appears, not equally. Gaining control of international forces that affect nations is a problem for all of them, but some solve the problem better than others. The costs of shortages fall on all of us, but in different proportion. Interdependence, one might think, is a euphemism used to obscure the dependence of most countries (cf. Goodwin 1976, p. 63). Not so, Kissinger says. Like others, we are caught in the web because failure to solve major resource problems would lead to recession in other countries and ruin the international economy. That would hurt all of us. Indeed it would, but again the uneven incidence of injuries inflicted on nations is ignored. Recession in some countries hurts others, but some more and some less so. An unnamed Arab oil minister's grip on economics appeared stronger than Kissinger's. If an oil shortage should drive the American economy into recession, he observed, all of the world would suffer. "Our economies, our regimes, our very survival, depend on a healthy U.S. economy" (*Newsweek*, March 25, 1974, p. 43). How much a country will suffer depends roughly on how much of its business is done abroad. As Chancellor Schmidt said in October of 1975, West Germany's economy depends much more than ours does on a strong international economic recovery because it exports 25 percent of its GNP yearly (October 7, 1975). The comparable figure for the United States was seven percent.

No matter how one turns it, the same answer comes up: We depend somewhat on the external world, and most other countries depend on the external world much more so. Countries that are dependent on others in important respects work to limit or lessen their dependence if they can reasonably hope to do so.* From late 1973 onward, in the period of oil embargo and increased prices, Presidents Nixon and Ford, Secretary Kissinger, and an endless number of American leaders proclaimed both a new era of interdependence and the goal of making the United States energy-independent by 1985. This is so much the natural behavior of major states that not only the speakers but seemingly also their audiences failed to notice the humor. Because states are in a self-help system, they try to avoid becoming dependent on others for vital goods and services. To achieve energy independence would be costly. Economists rightly point out that by their definition of interdependence the cost of achieving the goal is a measure of how much international conditions affect us. But that is to think of interdependence merely as sensitivity. Politically the important point is that only the few industrial countries of greatest capability are able to think seriously of becoming independent in energy supply. As Kissinger put it: "We have greater latitude than the others because we can do much on our own. The others can't" (January 13, 1975, p. 76).

And yet, though we may be able to "solve energy," we have not done so. Our dependence on foreign oil has increased in recent years, and because the price of oil multiplied by five between 1973 and 1977, we are inclined to believe that the cost of imported oil fueled inflation and impeded economic growth. We are more dependent than we used to be, but others continue to be more dependent still. In 1973 we imported 17 percent of our annual energy consumption; in 1976, about 20 percent. Meanwhile, Italy, France, Germany, and Japan continued to depend on imported resources for most of the energy they use. Data from Appendix Table X reveal the difference in dependency between the United States and others (see also Appendix Table XI).

Oil Imports as % of Energy Supply (col. 1) and Oil Imports from Middle East as % of Energy Supply (col. 2)

	W. Europe		Japan		U.S.	
	(1)	(2)	(1)	(2)	(1)	(2)
1967	50%	25%	62%	52%	9%	0.7%
1970	57	28	73	60	10	0.5
1973	60	41	80	61	17	2
1976	54	37	74	55	20	5

---

*Notice the implication of the following statement made by Leonid Brezhnev: "Those who think that we need ties and exchanges in the economic and scientific-technical fields more than elsewhere are mistaken. The entire volume of USSR imports from capitalist countries comes to less than 1.5% of our gross social product. It is clear that this does not have decisive importance for the Soviet economy's development" (October 5, 1976, p. 3).

Several points need to be made. Although we are in a better position than most countries, we have been slow to take steps to limit or reduce our dependency further, as Appendix Table XII suggests. Since we continue to use two to three times more energy per capita than the other industrial democracies do, and since we have more adequate energy resources than most of them have, we can lessen our dependency if we wish to. President Ford's goals, whether or not they were sensible, were not beyond our reach. As he described them they were to "end vulnerability to economic disruption by foreign suppliers by 1985" and to "develop our energy technology and resources so that the United States has the ability to supply a significant share of the energy needs of the free world by the end of this century" (January 16, 1975, p. 24). By turning coal into liquids and gases, by extracting oil from shale, and by building more nuclear power plants, we can place ourselves in the position of relying more on our own energy sources and of drawing less from others. But we need not rush into making such efforts. Having imposed quotas on foreign oil for decades to make sure, in the name of resource development, that we would use our own oil first, it makes sense now to rely more on imports. Given America's present situation, it may be wise to do the following: take steps to conserve energy; concentrate on research about, rather than on development of, our own energy sources; and build a petroleum stockpile sufficient for riding through, say, a six-month embargo.* A six-month stockpile would provide a comfortable margin of safety. Most OPEC countries, their oil riches aside, are weak economically as well as militarily and politically. All the more so because many of their interests diverge, one can safely bet on their inability to sustain punitive policies for more than a short time against the great and major powers of this world.

The conclusion is inescapable, or so one would think: The country that makes much of the world's goods finds many more ways of taking care of itself than most other countries can hope to. This is not to say that we depend on other countries not at all. This is not to say that some of the choices we may wish to make have not become costlier. This *is* to say that we, better than any other country, can afford to pay a higher price for choices we wish to make.

The tension between America's condition and the claim that the world is an interdependent one is obvious. How is the tension relaxed? Two ways stand out. First, those who find it pleasing to use words of current fashion turn "interdependence" into a protean term by endlessly varying the adjectives that precede it.

---

*The 1976 Strategic Petroleum Reserve Plan calls for 500 million barrels of oil to be stored by 1982, an amount that would carry us for four months at 1977 rates of consumption. The Carter administration in its first year decided to aim for one billion barrels to be stored by 1985. The International Energy Agency, moreover, requires its members to maintain emergency reserves equal to 70 days' imports, a requirement that will rise to 90 days' in 1980.

Psychological, sectoral, political, asymmetric: These words and others are used as modifiers of "interdependence." So used, they all convey this meaning: Parties that are not generally interdependent may in limited and particular ways be so. Asymmetric interdependence refers to parties that are not mutually dependent but in some ways affect each other. As compared to other nations, the United States is more independent than dependent. The term "asymmetric interdependence" suggests that one notices this but wishes to avoid blunt reference to the unequal condition of nations. "Sectoral" suggests that we know we are not locked into relations of mutual dependence, although in some few respects our dependence may be high. Varying the adjectives used to modify "interdependence" adapts the concept to different situations. The concept, then, does not illuminate the situations but instead is made to conform to them descriptively. The variety of adjectives used reflects the fashion of the word they modify. But conforming to fashion makes analytically useful distinctions all the more difficult to discern. Everything affects everything else. Interdependence usually suggests little more than that. The thought may be the beginning of wisdom, but not its end. One wants to know how, and how much, who is affected by and depends on whom.

Second, those who think of America as being entangled along with nearly everyone else shift the meaning of interdependence away from the condition of nations and toward the policies they follow. The game is ultimately given away by those who refer to psychological and political interdependence and thereby suggest that the United States is entangled, and thus constrained, because it cares about the well-being of many other nations and chooses to act to influence what happens to them.* To give that meaning to interdependence indicates that we are a great power and not simply one of the parts of an interdependent world. Nations that have the luxury of being able to care about, and the freedom to choose to act for, the presumed good of others are seen to be in a highly special position. The economics of interdependence gives way to the politics of our concern for others. Whatever we may say, we are not on the same economic footing as most countries. We cannot practice the economics of interdependence, as we are often advised to do, because unlike many other states we are not caught in the web. Nor can we adopt policies of interdependence since interdependence is a condition, not a policy. Dependent parties conform their behavior to the preferences of those they depend on. We, instead, make use of a favorable economic position to support national political ends. The economics of

---

*Cf. this statement, which appears in a Federal Energy Office Paper: The United States, by achieving independence in energy, would "benefit other importing nations by relieving strains on world oil supplies. In this sense, 'Project Independence' might better be called 'Project Interdependence' " (US Senate, Committee on Government Operations, 1974, p. 14).

*in*dependence makes possible the pursuit of American goals, just as one would expect (cf. Nau 1975).

IV

When the great powers of the world were small in geographic compass, they did a high proportion of their business abroad. The narrow concentration of power in the present and the fact that the United States and the Soviet Union are little dependent on the rest of the world produce a very different international situation. The difference between the plight of great powers in the new bipolar world and the old multipolar one can be seen by contrasting America's condition with that of earlier great powers. When Britain was the world's leading state economically, the portion of her wealth invested abroad far exceeded the portion that now represents America's stake in the world. In 1910 the value of total British investment abroad was one-and-one-half times larger than her national income. In 1973 the value of total American investments abroad was one-fifth as large as her national income. In 1910 Britain's return on investment abroad amounted to eight percent of national income; in 1973 the comparable figure for the United States was 1.6 percent (British figures computed from Imlah 1958, pp. 70–75, and Woytinsky and Woytinsky 1953, p. 791, Table 335; American figures computed from CIEP, March 1976, pp. 160–62, Tables 42, 47, and *US Bureau of the Census,* 1975, p. 384, and *Survey of Current Business,* October 1975, p. 48). Britain in its heyday had a huge stake in the world, and that stake loomed large in relation to her national product. From her immense and far-flung activities, she gained a considerable leverage. Because of the extent to which she depended on the rest of the world, wise and skillful use of that leverage was called for. Great powers in the old days depended on foodstuffs and raw materials imported from abroad much more heavily than the United States and the Soviet Union do now. Their dependence pressed them to make efforts to control the sources of their vital supplies.

Today the myth of interdependence both obscures the realities of international politics and asserts a false belief about the conditions that promote peace, as World War I conclusively showed. "The statistics of the economic interdependence of Germany and her neighbors," John Maynard Keynes remarked, "are overwhelming." Germany was the best customer of six European states, including Russia and Italy; the second best customer of three, including Britain; and the third best customer of France. She was the largest source of supply for ten European states, including Russia, Austria-Hungary, and Italy; and the second largest source of supply for three, including Britain and France (Keynes 1920, p. 17). And trade then was proportionately much higher than now. Then governments were more involved internationally than they were in their national economies. Now governments are more involved in their national economies than they are internationally. This is fortunate.

Economically, the low dependence of the United States means that the costs of, and the odds on, losing our trading partners are low. Other countries depend more on us than we do on them. If links are cut, they suffer more than we do. Given this condition, sustained economic sanctions against us would amount to little more than economic self-mutilation. The United States can get along without the rest of the world better than most of its parts can get along without us. But, someone will hasten to say, if Russia, or anyone, should be able to foreclose American trade and investment in successively more parts of the world, we could be quietly strangled to death. To believe that, one has to think not in terms of politics but in terms of the apocalypse. If some countries want to deal less with us, others will move economically closer to us. More so than any other country, the United States can grant or withhold a variety of favors, in matters of trade, aid, loans, the supply of atomic energy for peaceful purposes, and military security. If peaceful means for persuading other countries to comply with preferred American policies are wanted, the American government does not have to look far to find them. The Soviet Union is even less dependent economically on the outside world than we are, but has less economic and political leverage on it. We are more dependent economically on the outside world than the Soviet Union is, but have more economic and political leverage on it.

The size of the two great powers gives them some capacity for control and at the same time insulates them with some comfort from the effect of other states' behavior. The inequality of nations produces a condition of equilibrium at a low level of interdependence. This is a picture of the world quite different from the one that today's transnationalists and interdependers paint. They cling to an economic version of the domino theory: Anything that happens anywhere in the world may damage us directly or through its repercussions, and therefore we have to react to it. This assertion holds only if the politically important nations are closely coupled. We have seen that they are not. Seldom has the discrepancy been wider between the homogeneity suggested by "interdependence" and the heterogeneity of the world we live in. A world composed of greatly unequal units is scarcely an interdependent one. A world in which a few states can take care of themselves quite well and most states cannot hope to do so is scarcely an interdependent one. A world in which the Soviet Union and China pursue exclusionary policies is scarcely an interdependent one. A world of bristling nationalisms is scarcely an interdependent one. The confusion of concepts works against clarity of analysis and obscures both the possibilities and the necessities of action. Logically it is wrong, and politically it is obscurantist, to consider the world a unit and call it "interdependent." The intricacies of diplomacy are sometimes compared to those of chess. Neither game can be successfully played unless the chessboard is accurately described.

So far I have shown that smaller are better than larger numbers, at least for those states at the top. Defining the concept, and examining the economics, of interdependence did not establish just which small number is best of all. We could not answer that question because economic interdependence varies with the size of great powers and their size does not correlate perfectly with their number. In the next chapter, examination of military interdependence leads to an exact answer.

8

Structural Causes and Military Effects

Chapter 7 showed why smaller is better. To say that few are better than many is not to say that two is best of all. The stability of pairs—of corporations, of political parties, of marriage partners—has often been appreciated. Although most students of international politics probably believe that systems of many great powers would be unstable, they resist the widespread notion that two is the best of small numbers. Are they right to do so? For the sake of stability, peace, or whatever, should we prefer a world of two great powers or a world of several or more? Chapter 8 will show why two is the best of small numbers. We reached some conclusions, but not that one, by considering economic interdependence. Problems of national security in multi- and bipolar worlds do clearly show the advantages of having two great powers, and only two, in the system.

I

To establish the virtues of two-party systems requires comparing systems of different number. Because the previous chapter was concerned only with systems of small and of still smaller numbers, we did not have to consider differences made by having two, three, four, or more principal parties in a system. We must do so now. By what criteria do we determine that an international-political system changes, and conversely, by what criteria do we say that a system is stable? Political scientists often lump different effects under the heading of stability. I did this in 1964 and 1967 essays, using stability to include also peacefulness and the effective management of international affairs, which are the respective concerns of this chapter and the next one. It is important, I now believe, to keep different effects separate so that we can accurately locate their causes.

Anarchic systems are transformed only by changes in organizing principle and by consequential changes in the number of their principal parties. To say that an international-political system is stable means two things: first, that it remains anarchic; second, that no consequential variation takes place in the number of principal parties that constitute the system. "Consequential" variations in number are changes of number that lead to different expectations about the effect of structure on units. The stability of the system, so long as it remains anarchic, is then closely linked with the fate of its principal members. The close link is established by the relation of changes in number of great powers to transformation of the system. The link does not bind absolutely, however, because the number of great powers may remain the same or fail to vary consequentially even while some powers fall from the ranks of the great ones only to be replaced by others. International-political systems are remarkably stable, as Table 8.1 graphically shows. The multipolar system lasted three centuries because as some states fell from the top rank others rose to it through the relative increase of their capabilities. The system endured even as the identity of its members changed. The bipolar system has lasted three decades because no third state has been able to develop capabilities comparable to those of the United States and the Soviet Union. The system appears robust, although unlikely to last as long as its predecessor—a matter to be considered in the fourth part of this chapter.

Table 8.1 *GREAT POWERS, 1700–1979*

	1700	1800	1875	1910	1935	1945
Turkey	x					
Sweden	x					
Netherlands	x					
Spain	x					
Austria (Austria-Hungary)	x	x	x	x		
France	x	x	x	x	x	
England (Great Britain)	x	x	x	x	x	
Prussia (Germany)		x	x	x	x	
Russia (Soviet Union)		x	x	x	x	x
Italy			x	x	x	
Japan				x	x	
United States				x	x	x

Adapted from Wright, 1965, Appendix 20, Table 43.

The link between the survival of particular great powers and the stability of systems is also weakened by the fact that not all changes of number are changes of system. That bipolar and multipolar systems are distinct is widely accepted. Systems of two have qualities distinct from systems of three or more. What is the defining difference? The answer is found in the behavior required of parties in self-help systems: namely, balancing. Balancing is differently done in multi- and bipolar systems. Though many students of international politics believe that the balance-of-power game requires at least three or four players, we saw in Chapter 6 that two will do. Where two powers contend, imbalances can be righted only by their internal efforts. With more than two, shifts in alignment provide an additional means of adjustment, adding flexibility to the system. This is a crucial difference between multi- and bipolar systems. Beyond two, what variations of number are consequential? Three and four are threshold numbers. They mark the transition from one system to another because the opportunities offered for balancing through combining with others vary in ways that change expected outcomes. Systems of three have distinctive and unfortunate characteristics. Two of the powers can easily gang up on the third, divide the spoils, and drive the system back to bipolarity. In multipolar systems four is then the lowest acceptable number, for it permits external alignment and promises considerable stability. Five is thought of as another threshold number, being the lowest number that promises stability while providing a role for a balancer; and I shall examine that claim. Beyond five no threshold appears. We know that complications accelerate as numbers grow because of the difficulty everyone has in coping with the uncertain behavior of many others and because of the ever larger number and variety of coalitions that can be made, but we have no grounds for saying that complications pass a threshold as we move, say, from seven to eight. Luckily, as a practical matter, no increase in the number of great powers is in prospect.

Until 1945 the nation-state system was multipolar, and always with five or more powers. In all of modern history the structure of international politics has changed but once. We have only two systems to observe. By inference and analogy, however, some conclusions can be drawn about international systems with smaller or larger numbers of great powers. The next part of this chapter shows that five parties do not constitute a distinct system and considers the different implications of systems of two and of four or more.

II

With only two great powers, a balance-of-power system is unstable; four powers are required for its proper functioning. For ease and nicety of adjustment a fifth power, serving as balancer, adds a further refinement. This is the conventional wisdom. Should we accept it? Is five a nice compromise between the simplest possible system of two and numbers so large as to make anarchic systems hopelessly complex?

The notion of a balancer is more a historical generalization than a theoretical concept. The generalization is drawn from the position and behavior of Britain in the eighteenth and nineteenth centuries. British experience shows what conditions have to prevail if the role of balancer is to be effectively played. The first of these was that the margin of power on the side of the aggressor not be so large that British strength added to the weaker side would be insufficient to redress the balance. When the states of the continent were nearly in balance, Britain could act with effect. The second condition was that Britain's ends on the continent remain negative, for positive ends help to determine alignments. A state that wishes to secure a piece of territory ordinarily has to ally with states that do not already have it. The goals of the state then lessen the scope of its diplomatic maneuver. Finally, to be effective in the role of balancer, Britain required a status in power at least equal to that of the mightiest. British weakness vis-à-vis European countries has to the present day meant entanglement with them. Only when continental powers were nearly in balance or when Britain was impressively strong was she able to remain aloof until the moment arrived when her commitment could be diplomatically decisive. These are highly special conditions, made more so by the fact that political preferences must not lead the balancer to identify with any actual or potential grouping of states. Balance-of-power theory cannot incorporate the role of balancer because the playing of the role depends on such narrowly defined and historically unlikely conditions. The number five has no special charm, for there is no reason to believe that the odd party will be able and willing to serve as balancer.

Such considerations lead to more general doubts about the vaunted advantages of flexible alliances. To be helpful, flexibility has to mean that, where one or more states threaten others, some state will join one side or defect from the other in order to tilt the balance against the would-be aggressors. The old balance-of-power system here looks suspiciously like the new collective-security system of the League and the United Nations. Either system depends for its maintenance and functioning on neutrality of alignment at the moment of serious threat. To preserve the system, at least one powerful state must overcome the pressure of ideological preference, the pull of previous ties, and the conflict of present interests in order to add its weight to the side of the peaceful. It must do what the moment requires.

Since one of the interests of each state is to avoid domination by other states, why should it be difficult for one or a few states to swing to the side of the threatened? After all, they experience a common danger. But *A* may instead say to *B*: "Since the threat is to you as well as to me, I'll stand aside and let you deal with the matter." If *B* acts effectively, *A* gains free benefits. If *B*, having become resentful, does not, *A* and *B* both lose. Contemplation of a common fate may not lead to a fair division of labor—or to any labor at all. Whether or not it does depends on the size of the group and the inequalities within it, as well as on the character of its members (cf. Olson 1965, pp. 36, 45).

One sees the difficulties in any multipolar system where some states threaten others while alignments are uncertain. French Foreign Minister Flandin told British Prime Minister Baldwin that Hitler's military occupation of the Rhineland in 1936 provided the occasion for Britain to take the lead in opposing Germany. As the German threat grew, some British and French leaders could hope that if their countries remained aloof, Russia and Germany would balance each other off or fight each other to the finish (Nicolson 1966, pp. 247–49; Young 1976, pp. 128–30). Uncertainties about who threatens whom, about who will oppose whom, and about who will gain or lose from the actions of other states accelerate as the number of states increases. Even if one assumes that the goals of most states are worthy, the timing and content of the actions required to reach them become more and more difficult to calculate. Rather than making the matter simpler, pre-scribing general rules for states to follow simply illustrates the impossibility of believing that states can reconcile two conflicting imperatives—to act for their own sakes, as required by their situations, and to act for the system's stability or survival, as some scholars advise them to do. Political scientists who favor flexi-bility of national alignment have to accept that flexibility comes only as numbers increase and thus also as complexities and uncertainties multiply.

With more than two states, the politics of power turn on the diplomacy by which alliances are made, maintained, and disrupted. Flexibility of alignment means both that the country one is wooing may prefer another suitor and that one's present alliance partner may defect. Flexibility of alignment narrows one's choice of policies. A state's strategy must please a potential or satisfy a present partner. A comparable situation is found where political parties compete for votes by forming and re-forming electoral coalitions of different economic, ethnic, religious, and regional groups. The strategy, or policy, of a party is made for the sake of attracting and holding voters. If a party is to be an electoral success, its policy cannot simply be the one that its leaders believe to be best for the country. Policy must at least partly be made for the sake of winning elections. Similarly, with a number of approximately equal states, strategy is at least partly made for the sake of attracting and holding allies. If alliances may form, states will want to look like attractive partners. Suitors alter their appearance and adapt their behavior to increase their eligibility. Those who remain unattractive, find-ing that they compete poorly, are likely to try all the harder to change their appearance and behavior. One has to become attractive enough in personality and policy to be considered a possible choice. The alliance diplomacy of Europe in the years before World War I is rich in examples of this. Ever since the Napoleonic Wars, many had believed that the "Republican" and the "Cossack" could never become engaged, let alone contract a marriage. The wooing of France and Russia, with each adapting somewhat to the other, was nevertheless consummated in the alliance of 1894 and duly produced the Triple Entente as its progeny when first France and England and then Russia and England overcame their long-standing animosities in 1904 and 1907, respectively.

If pressures are strong enough, a state will deal with almost anyone. Litvinov remarked in the 1930s that to promote its security in a hostile world the Soviet Union would work with any state, even with Hitler's Germany (Moore 1950, pp. 350–55). It is important to notice that states will ally with the devil to avoid the hell of military defeat. It is still more important to remember that the question of who will ally with which devil may be the decisive one. In the end Hitler's acts determined that all of the great powers save Italy and Japan would unite against him.*

In the quest for security, alliances may have to be made. Once made, they have to be managed. European alliances beginning in the 1890s hardened as two blocs formed. The rigidity of blocs, it is thought, contributed strongly to the outbreak of the First World War. The view is a superficial one. Alliances are made by states that have some but not all of their interests in common. The common interest is ordinarily a negative one: fear of other states. Divergence comes when positive interests are at issue. Consider two examples. Russia would have preferred to plan and prepare for the occasion of war against Austria-Hungary. She could hope to defeat her, but not Germany, and Austria-Hungary stood in the way of Russia's gaining control of the Straits linking the Mediterranean and the Black Seas. France, however, could regain Alsace-Lorraine only by defeating Germany. Perception of a common threat brought Russia and France together. Alliance diplomacy, and a large flow of funds from France to Russia, helped to hold them together and to shape an alliance strategy more to the taste of France than of Russia. Alliance strategies are always the product of compromise since the interests of allies and their notions of how to secure them are never identical. In a multipolar system, moreover, despite the formation of blocs, one's allies may edge toward the opposing camp. If a member of one alliance tries to settle differences, or to cooperate in some ways, with a member of another alliance, its own allies become uneasy. Thus British-German cooperation in 1912 and 1913 to

---

*As Winston Churchill said to his private secretary the night before Germany's invasion of Russia, "If Hitler invaded Hell I would make at least a favourable reference to the Devil in the House of Commons" (Churchill 1950, p. 370).

dampen Balkan crises, and the settling of some colonial questions between them, may have been harmful. The reactions of their allies dissuaded Britain and Germany from playing similar roles in Southeastern Europe in 1914, yet gave each of them some hope that the other's alliance would not hold firm (Jervis 1976, p. 110). Greater cohesion of blocs would have permitted greater flexibility of policy. But then the cohesion of blocs, like the discipline of parties, is achieved through expert and careful management; and the management of blocs is exceedingly difficult among near-equals since it must be cooperatively contrived.

If competing blocs are seen to be closely balanced, and if competition turns on important matters, then to let one's side down risks one's own destruction. In a moment of crisis the weaker or the more adventurous party is likely to determine its side's policy. Its partners can afford neither to let the weaker member go to the wall nor to advertise their disunity by failing to back a venture even while deploring its risks. The prelude to World War I provides striking examples. The approximate equality of alliance partners made them closely interdependent. The interdependence of allies, plus the keenness of competition between the two camps, meant that while any country could commit its associates, no one country on either side could exercise control. If Austria-Hungary marched, Germany had to follow; the dissolution of the Austro-Hungarian Empire would have left Germany alone in the middle of Europe. If France marched, Russia had to follow; a German victory over France would be a defeat for Russia. And so it was all around the vicious circle. Because the defeat or the defection of a major ally would have shaken the balance, each state was constrained to adjust its strategy and the use of its forces to the aims and fears of its partners. In one sense the unstable politics of the Balkans carried the world into war. But that statement rather misses the point. Internationally, destabilizing events and conditions abound. The important questions to ask are whether they are likely to be managed better, and whether their effects are absorbed more readily, in one system than in another (see below, pp. 208–209).

The game of power politics, if really played hard, presses the players into two rival camps, though so complicated is the business of making and maintaining alliances that the game may be played hard enough to produce that result only under the pressure of war. Thus the six or seven great powers of the interwar period did not move into a two-bloc formation until more than two years after World War II began. The forming of two blocs, moreover, did not make the multipolar system into a bipolar one any more than the forming of opposing coalitions for the purpose of fighting an election turns a multiparty into a two-party system. Even with the greatest of external pressure, the unity of alliances is far from complete. States or parties in wartime or in electoral alliance, even as they adjust to one another, continue to jockey for advantage and to worry about the constellation of forces that will form once the contest is over.

In multipolar systems there are too many powers to permit any of them to draw clear and fixed lines between allies and adversaries and too few to keep the effects of defection low. With three or more powers flexibility of alliances keeps relations of friendship and enmity fluid and makes everyone's estimate of the present and future relation of forces uncertain. So long as the system is one of fairly small numbers, the actions of any of them may threaten the security of others. There are too many to enable anyone to see for sure what is happening, and too few to make what is happening a matter of indifference. Traditionally students of international politics have thought that the uncertainty that results from flexibility of alignment generates a healthy caution in everyone's foreign policy (cf. Kaplan 1957, pp. 22–36; Morgenthau 1961, part 4). Conversely they have believed that bipolar worlds are doubly unstable—that they easily erode or explode. This conclusion is based on false reasoning and scant evidence. Military interdependence varies with the extent to which, and the equality with which, great powers rely on others for their security. In a bipolar world, military interdependence declines even more sharply than economic interdependence. Russia and America depend militarily mainly on themselves. They balance each other by "internal" instead of "external" means, relying on their own capabilities rather than on the capabilities of allies. Internal balancing is more reliable and precise than external balancing. States are less likely to misjudge their relative strengths than they are to misjudge the strength and reliability of opposing coalitions. Rather than making states properly cautious and forwarding the chances of peace, uncertainty and miscalculation cause wars (cf. Blainey 1970, pp. 108–19). In a bipolar world uncertainty lessens and calculations are easier to make.

Much of the skepticism about the virtues of bipolarity arises from thinking of a system as being bipolar if two blocs form within a multipolar world. A bloc unskillfully managed may indeed fall apart. In a multipolar world the leaders of both blocs must be concerned at once with alliance management, since the defection of an ally may be fatal to its partners, and with the aims and capabilities of the opposing bloc. The prehistory of two world wars dramatically displays the dangers. The fair amount of effort that now goes into alliance management may obscure the profound difference between old-style and new-style alliances. In alliances among equals, the defection of one party threatens the security of the others. In alliances among unequals, the contributions of the lesser members are at once wanted and of relatively small importance. Where the contributions of a number of parties are highly important to all of them, each has strong incentive both to persuade others to its views about strategy and tactics and to make concessions when persuasion fails. The unity of major partners is likely to endure because they all understand how much they depend on it. Before World War I, Germany's acceptance of Italy's probable defection from the Triple Alliance signaled her relative unimportance. In alliances among unequals, alliance leaders need worry little about the faithfulness of their followers, who usually have little choice anyway. Contrast the situation in 1914 with that of the United States and Britain and France in 1956. The United States could dissociate itself from the Suez adventure of its two principal allies and subject them to heavy financial pressure. Like Austria-Hungary in 1914, they tried to commit or at least immobilize their alliance partner by presenting a *fait accompli*. Enjoying a position of predominance, the United States could continue to focus its attention on the major adversary while disciplining its allies. The ability of the United States, and the inability of Germany, to pay a price measured in intra-alliance terms is striking. It is important, then, to distinguish sharply between the formation of two blocs in a multipolar world and the structural bipolarity of the present system.

In bipolar as in multipolar worlds, alliance leaders may try to elicit maximum contributions from their associates. The contributions are useful even in a bipolar world, but they are not indispensable. Because they are not, the policies and strategies of alliance leaders are ultimately made according to their own calculations and interests. Disregarding the views of an ally makes sense only if military cooperation is fairly unimportant. This is the case both in the Warsaw Treaty Organization and in the North Atlantic Treaty Organization. In 1976, for example, the Soviet Union's military expenditures were well over 90 percent of the WTO total, and those of the United States were about 75 percent of the NATO total. In fact if not in form, NATO consists of guarantees given by the United States to its European allies and to Canada. The United States, with a preponderance of nuclear weapons and as many men in uniform as the West European states combined, may be able to protect them; they cannot protect her. Because of the vast differences in the capabilities of member states, the roughly equal sharing of burdens found in earlier alliance systems is no longer possible.

Militarily, interdependence is low in a bipolar world and high in a multipolar one. Great powers in a multipolar world depend on one another for political and military support in crises and war. To assure oneself of steadfast support is vital. This cannot be the case in a bipolar world, for third parties are not able to tilt the balance of power by withdrawing from one alliance or by joining the other. Thus two "losses" of China in the postwar world—first by the United States and then by the Soviet Union—were accommodated without disastrously distorting, or even much affecting, the balance between America and Russia. Nor did France, in withdrawing her forces from NATO, noticeably change the bipolar balance. That American policy need not be made for the sake of France helps to explain her partial defection. The gross inequality between the two superpowers and the members of their respective alliances makes any realignment of the latter fairly insignificant. The leader's strategy can therefore be flexible. In balance-of-power politics old style, flexibility of alignment made for rigidity of strategy or the limitation of freedom of decision. In balance-of-power politics new style, the obverse is true: Rigidity of alignment in a two-power world makes for flexibility of strategy and the enlargement of freedom of decision. Although concessions to allies are sometimes made, neither the United States nor the Soviet Union alters its strategy or changes its military dispositions simply to accommodate associated states. Both superpowers can make long-range plans and carry out their policies as best they see fit, for they need not accede to the demands of third parties.

In a multipolar world, states often pool their resources in order to serve their interests. Roughly equal parties engaged in cooperative endeavors must look for a common denominator of their policies. They risk finding the lowest one and easily end up in the worst of all possible worlds. In a bipolar world, alliance leaders make their strategies mainly according to their own calculations of interests. Strategies can be designed more to cope with the main adversary and less to satisfy one's allies. Alliance leaders are free to follow their own line, which may of course reflect their bad as well as their good judgment, their imaginary as well as their realistic fears, their ignoble as well as their worthy ends. Alliance leaders are not free of constraints. The major constraints, however, arise from the main adversary and not from one's own associates.

III

Neither the United States nor the Soviet Union has to make itself acceptable to other states; they do have to cope with each other. In the great-power politics of multipolar worlds, who is a danger to whom, and who can be expected to deal with threats and problems, are matters of uncertainty. In the great-power politics of bipolar worlds, who is a danger to whom is never in doubt. This is the first big difference between the politics of power in the two systems. The United States is the obsessing danger for the Soviet Union, and the Soviet Union for the United States, since each can damage the other to an extent no other state can match. Any event in the world that involves the fortunes of either automatically elicits the interest of the other. President Truman, at the time of the Korean invasion, could not very well echo Neville Chamberlain's words in the Czechoslovakian crisis by claiming that the Koreans were a people far away in the East of Asia of whom Americans knew nothing. We had to know about them or quickly find out. In the 1930s France lay between England and Germany. The British could believe, and we could too, that their frontier and ours lay on the Rhine. After World War II no third great power could lie between the United States and the Soviet Union, for none existed. The statement that peace is indivisible was controversial, indeed untrue, when it was made by Litvinov in the 1930s. Political slogans express wishes better than realities. In a bipolar world the wish becomes reality. A war or threat of war anywhere is a concern to both of the superpowers if it may lead to significant gains or losses for either of them. In a two-power competition a loss for one appears as a gain for the other. Because this is so, the powers in a bipolar world promptly respond to unsettling events. In a multipolar world dangers are diffused, responsibilities unclear, and definitions of vital interests easily obscured. Where a number of states are in balance, the skill-ful foreign policy of a forward power is designed to gain an advantage over one state without antagonizing others and frightening them into united action. At times in modern Europe, possible gains seemed greater than likely losses. Statesmen could hope to push an issue to the limit without causing all of the potential opponents to unite. When possible enemies are several in number, unity of action among them is difficult to arrange. National leaders could therefore think—or desperately hope as did Bethmann Hollweg and Adolf Hitler before two World Wars—that no united opposition would form. Interdependence of parties, diffusion of dangers, confusion of responses: These are the characteristics of great-power politics in multipolar worlds.

If interests and ambitions conflict, the absence of crises is more worrisome than their recurrence. Crises are produced by the determination of a state to resist a change that another state tries to make. The situation of the United States and of the Soviet Union disposes them to do the resisting, for in important matters they cannot hope that others will do it for them. Political action in the postwar world has reflected this condition. Communist guerrillas operating in Greece prompted the Truman Doctrine. The tightening of the Soviet Union's control over the states of Eastern Europe led to the Marshall Plan and the Atlantic Defense Treaty, and these in turn gave rise to the Cominform and the Warsaw Pact. The plan to form a West German government produced the Berlin Blockade. And so on through the 1950s, '60s, and '70s. Our responses are geared to the Soviet Union's actions, and theirs to ours, which has produced an increasingly solid bipolar balance.

In a bipolar world there are no peripheries. With only two powers capable of acting on a world scale, anything that happens anywhere is potentially of concern to both of them. Bipolarity extends the geographic scope of both powers' con-cern. It also broadens the range of factors included in the competition between them. Because allies add relatively little to the superpowers' capabilities, they concentrate their attention on their own dispositions. In a multipolar world, who is a danger to whom is often unclear; the incentive to regard all disequilibrating changes with concern and respond to them with whatever effort may be required is consequently weakened. In a bipolar world changes may affect each of the two powers differently, and this means all the more that few changes in the world at large or within each other's national realm are likely to be thought irrelevant. Competition becomes more comprehensive as well as more widely extended. Not just military preparation but also economic growth and technological develop-ment become matters of intense and constant concern. Self-dependence of parties, clarity of dangers, certainty about who has to face them: These are the characteristics of great-power politics in a bipolar world.

Miscalculation by some or all of the great powers is the source of danger in a multipolar world; overreaction by either or both of the great powers is the source of danger in a bipolar world. Bipolarity encourages the United States and the Soviet Union to turn unwanted events into crises, while rendering most of them relatively inconsequential. Each can lose heavily only in war with the other; in power and in wealth, both gain more by the peaceful development of internal resources than by wooing and winning—or by fighting and subduing—other states in the world. A five-percent growth rate sustained for three years increases the American gross national product by an amount exceeding one-half of West Germany's GNP, and all of Great Britain's (base year 1976). For the Soviet Union, with one-half of our GNP, imaginable gains double in weight. They would still be of minor importance. Only Japan, Western Europe, and the Middle East are prizes that if won by the Soviet Union would alter the balance of GNPs and the distribution of resources enough to be a danger.

Yet since World War II the United States has responded expensively in distant places to wayward events that could hardly affect anyone's fate outside of the region. Which is worse: miscalculation or overreaction? Miscalculation is more likely to permit the unfolding of a series of events that finally threatens a change in the balance and brings the powers to war. Overreaction is the lesser evil because it costs only money and the fighting of limited wars.

The dynamics of a bipolar system, moreover, provide a measure of correction. In a hot war or a cold war—as in any close competition—the external situation dominates. In the middle 1950s John Foster Dulles inveighed against the immoral neutralists. Russian leaders, in like spirit, described neutralists as either fools themselves or dupes of capitalist countries. But ideology did not long prevail over interest. Both Russia and America quickly came to accept neutralist states and even to lend them encouragement. The Soviet Union aided Egypt and Iraq, countries that kept their communists in jail. In the late 1950s and throughout the '60s, the United States, having already given economic and military assistance to communist Yugoslavia, made neutralist India the most favored recipient of economic aid.* According to the rhetoric of the Cold War, the root cleavage in the world was between capitalist democracy and godless communism. But by the size of the stakes and the force of the struggle, ideology was subordinated to interest in the policies of America and Russia, who behaved more like traditional great powers than like leaders of messianic movements. In a world in which two

---

*From 1960 to 1967 our economic aid to India exceeded our combined economic and military aid to any other country (US Agency for International Development, various years).

states united in their mutual antagonism far overshadow any other, the incentives to a calculated response stand out most clearly, and the sanctions against irresponsible behavior achieve their greatest force. Thus two states, isolationist by tradition, untutored in the ways of international politics, and famed for impulsive behavior, soon showed themselves—not always and everywhere, but always in crucial cases—to be wary, alert, cautious, flexible, and forbearing.

Some have believed that a new world began with the explosion of an atomic bomb over Hiroshima. In shaping the behavior of nations, the perennial forces of politics are more important than the new military technology. States remain the primary vehicles of ideology. The international brotherhood of autocrats after 1815, the cosmopolitan liberalism of the middle nineteenth century, international socialism before World War I, international communism in the decades following the Bolshevik revolution: In all of these cases international movements were captured by individual nations, adherents of the creed were harnessed to the nation's interest, international programs were manipulated by national governments, and ideology became a prop to national policy. So the Soviet Union in crisis became Russian, and American policy, liberal rhetoric aside, came to be realistically and cautiously constructed. By the force of events, they and we were impelled to behave in ways belied both by their words and by ours. Political scientists, drawing their inferences from the characteristics of states, were slow to appreciate the process. Inferences drawn from the characteristics of small-number systems are better borne out politically. Economists have long known that the passage of time makes peaceful coexistence among major competitors easier. They become accustomed to one another; they learn how to interpret one another's moves and how to accommodate or counter them. "Unambiguously," as Oliver Williamson puts it, "experience leads to a higher level of adherence" to agreements made and to commonly accepted practices (1965, p. 227). Life becomes more predictable.

Theories of perfect competition tell us about the market and not about the competitors. Theories of oligopolistic competition tell us quite a bit about both. In important ways, competitors become like one another as their competition continues. As we noticed in Chapter 6, this applies to states as to firms. Thus William Zimmerman found not only that the Soviet Union in the 1960s had abandoned its Bolshevik views of international relations but also that its views had become much like ours (1969, pp. 135, 282). The increasing similarity of competitors' attitudes, as well as their experience with one another, eases the adjustment of their relations.

These advantages are found in all small-number systems. What additional advantages do pairs enjoy in dealing with each other? As a group shrinks, its members face fewer choices when considering whom to deal with. Partly because they eliminate the difficult business of choosing, the smallest of groups manages its affairs most easily. With more than two parties, the solidarity of a group is always at risk because the parties can try to improve their lots by combining. Interdependence breeds hostility and fear. With more than two parties, hostility and fear may lead A and B to seek the support of C. If they both court C, their hostility and fear increase. When a group narrows to just two members, choice disappears. On matters of ultimate importance each can deal only with the other. No appeal can be made to third parties. A system of two has unique properties. Tension in the system is high because each can do so much for and to the other. But because no appeal can be made to third parties, pressure to moderate behavior is heavy (cf. Simmel 1902; Bales and Borgatta 1953). Bargaining among more than two parties is difficult. Bargainers worry about the points at issue. With more than two parties, each also worries about how the strength of his position will be affected by combinations he and others may make. If two of several parties strike an agreement, moreover, they must wonder if the agreement will be disrupted or negated by the actions of others.

Consider the problem of disarmament. To find even limited solutions, at least one of the following two conditions must be met. First, if the would-be winner of an arms race is willing to curtail its program, agreement is made possible. In the 1920s the United States—the country that could have won a naval arms race—took the lead in negotiating limitations. The self-interest of the would-be losers carried them along. Such was the necessary, though not the only, condition making the Washington Naval Arms Limitation Treaty possible. Second, if two powers can consider their mutual interests and fears without giving much thought to how the military capabilities of others affect them, agreement is made possible. The 1972 treaty limiting the deployment of antiballistic missiles is a dramatic example of this. Ballistic missile defenses, because they promise to be effective against missiles fired in small numbers, are useful against the nuclear forces of third parties. Because of their vast superiority, the United States and the Soviet Union were nevertheless able to limit their defensive weaponry. To the extent that the United States and the Soviet Union have to worry about the military strength of others, their ability to reach bilateral agreements lessens. So far those worries have been small.*

The simplicity of relations in a bipolar world and the strong pressures that are generated make the two great powers conservative. Structure, however, does not by any means explain everything. I say this again because the charge of structural determinism is easy to make. To explain outcomes one must look at the capabilities, the actions, and the interactions of states, as well as at the structure of their systems. States armed with nuclear weapons may have stronger incen-

---

*Richard Burt has carefully considered some of the ways in which the worries are growing (1976).

tives to avoid war than states armed conventionally. The United States and the Soviet Union may have found it harder to learn to live with each other in the 1940s and '50s than more experienced and less ideological nations would have. Causes at both the national and the international level make the world more or less peaceful and stable. I concentrate attention at the international level because the effects of structure are usually overlooked or misunderstood and because I am writing a theory of international politics, not of foreign policy.

In saying that the United States and the Soviet Union, like duopolists in other fields, are learning gradually how to cope with each other, I do not imply that they will interact without crises or find cooperation easy. The quality of their relations did, however, perceptibly change in the 1960s and '70s. Worries in the 1940s and '50s that tensions would rise to intolerable levels were balanced in the 1960s and '70s by fears that America and Russia would make agreements for their mutual benefit at others' expense. West Europeans—especially in Germany and France—have fretted. Chinese leaders have sometimes accused the Soviet Union of seeking world domination through collaboration with the United States. Worries and fears on any such grounds are exaggerated. The Soviet Union and the United States influence each other more than any of the states living in their penumbra can hope to do. In the world of the present, as of the recent past, a condition of mutual opposition may require rather than preclude the adjustment of differences. Yet first steps toward agreement do not lead to second and third steps. Instead they mingle with other acts and events that keep the level of tension quite high. This is the pattern set by the first major success enjoyed by the Soviet Union and the United States in jointly regulating their military affairs—the Test Ban Treaty of 1963. The test ban was described in the United States as possibly a first big step toward wider agreements that would increase the chances of maintaining peace. In the same breath it was said that we cannot lower our guard, for the Soviet Union's aims have not changed (cf. Rusk, August 13, 1963). Because they must rely for their security on their own devices, both countries are wary of joint ventures. Since they cannot know that benefits will be equal, since they cannot be certain that arrangements made will reliably bind both of them, each shies away from running a future risk for the sake of a present benefit. Between parties in a self-help system, rules of reciprocity and caution prevail. Their concern for peace and stability draws them together; their fears drive them apart. They are rightly called *frère ennemi* and adversary partners.

But may not the enmity obliterate the brotherhood and the sense of opposition obscure mutual interests? A small-number system can always be disrupted by the actions of a Hitler and the reactions of a Chamberlain. Since this is true, it may seem that we are in the uncomfortable position of relying on the moderation, courage, and good sense of those holding positions of power. Given human vagaries and the unpredictability of the individual's reaction to events, one may feel that the only recourse is to lapse into prayer. We can nonetheless take comfort from the thought that, like others, those who direct the activities of great states are by no means free agents. Beyond the residuum of necessary hope that leaders will respond sensibly, lies the possibility of estimating the pressures that encourage them to do so. In a world in which two states united in their mutual antagonism far overshadow any other, the incentives to a calculated response stand out most clearly, and the sanctions against irresponsible behavior achieve their greatest force. The identity as well as the behavior of leaders is affected by the presence of pressures and the clarity of challenges. One may lament Churchill's failure to gain control of the British government in the 1930s, for he knew what actions were required to maintain a balance of power. Churchill was not brought to power by the diffused threat of war in the '30s but only by the stark danger of defeat after war began. If a people representing one pole of the world now tolerates inept rulers, it runs clearly discernible risks. Leaders of the United States and the Soviet Union are presumably chosen with an eye to the tasks they will have to perform. Other countries, if they wish to, can enjoy the luxury of selecting leaders who will most please their peoples by the way in which internal affairs are managed. The United States and the Soviet Union cannot.

It is not that one entertains the utopian hope that all future American and Russian rulers will combine in their persons a complicated set of nearly perfect virtues, but rather that the pressures of a bipolar world strongly encourage them to act internationally in ways better than their characters may lead one to expect. I made this proposition in 1964; Nixon as president confirmed it. It is not that one is serenely confident about the peacefulness, or even about the survival, of the world, but rather that cautious optimism is justified so long as the dangers to which each must respond are so clearly present. Either country may go berserk or succumb to inanition and debility. That necessities are clear increases the chances that they will be met, but gives no guarantees. Dangers from abroad may unify a state and spur its people to heroic action. Or, as with France facing Hitler's Germany, external pressures may divide the leaders, confuse the public, and increase their willingness to give way. It may also happen that the difficulties of adjustment and the necessity for calculated action simply become too great. The clarity with which the necessities of action can now be seen may be blotted out by the blinding flash of nuclear explosions. The fear that this may happen strengthens the forces and processes I have described.

IV

A system of two has many virtues. Before explaining any more of them, the question of the durability of today's bipolar world should be examined. The system is dynamically stable, as I have shown. I have not, however, examined the many assertions that America and Russia are losing, or have lost, their effective edge over other states, as has happened to previous great powers and surely may happen again. Let us first ask whether the margin of American and Russian superiority *is* seriously eroding, and then examine the relation between military power and political control.

Surveying the rise and fall of nations over the centuries, one can only conclude that national rankings change slowly. War aside, the economic and other bases of power change little more rapidly in one major nation than they do in another. Differences in economic growth rates are neither large enough nor steady enough to alter standings except in the long run. France and her major opponents in the Napoleonic Wars were also the major initial participants in World War I, with Prussia having become Germany and with the later addition of the United States. Even such thorough defeats as those suffered by Napoleonic France and Wilhelmine Germany did not remove those countries from the ranks of the great powers. World War II did change the cast of great-power characters; no longer could others compete with the United States and the Soviet Union, for only they combine great scale in geography and population with economic and technological development. Entering the club was easier when great powers were larger in number and smaller in size. With fewer and bigger ones, barriers to entry have risen. Over time, however, even they can be surmounted. How long a running start is needed before some third or fourth state will be able to jump over the barriers? Just how high are they?

Although not as high as they once were, they are higher than many would have us believe. One of the themes of recent American discourse is that we are a "declining industrial power." C.L. Sulzberger, for example, announced in November of 1972 that "the U.S. finds itself no longer the global giant of twenty years ago." Our share of global production, he claimed, "has slipped from 50 to 30 percent" (November 15, 1972, p. 47). Such a misuse of numbers would be startling had we not become accustomed to hearing about America's steady decline. In the summer of 1971 President Nixon remarked that 25 years ago "we were number one in the world militarily" and "number one economically" as well. The United States, he added, "was producing more than 50 percent of all the world's goods." But no longer. By 1971, "instead of just America being number one in the world from an economic standpoint, the preeminent world power, and instead of there being just two superpowers, when we think in economic terms and economic potentialities, there are five great power centers in the world today" (July 6, 1971).

The trick that Sulzberger and Nixon played on us, and no doubt on themselves, should be apparent. In 1946, Nixon's year of comparison, most of the industrial world outside of the United States lay in ruins. By 1952, Sulzberger's year of comparison, Britain, France, and Russia had regained their prewar levels of production but the German and Japanese economic miracles had not been performed. In the years just after the war, the United States naturally produced an unusually large percentage of the world's goods.* Now again, as before the war, we produce about one quarter of the world's goods, which is two and three times as much as the two next-largest economies—namely, the Soviet Union's and Japan's. And that somehow means that rather than being number one, we have become merely one of five?

A recovery growth rate is faster than a growth rate from a normal base. The recovery rates of other economies reduced the huge gap between America and other industrial countries to one still huge, but less so. No evidence suggests further significant erosion of America's present position. Much evidence suggests that we became sufficiently accustomed to our abnormal postwar dominance to lead us now to an unbecoming sensitivity to others' advances, whether or not they equal our own. In the economic/technological game, the United States holds the high cards. Economic growth and competitiveness depend heavily on technological excellence. The United States has the lead, which it maintains by spending more than other countries on research and development. Here again recent statements mislead. The *International Economic Report of the President*, submitted in March of 1976, warned the Congress that "the United States has not been keeping pace with the growth and relative importance of R&D efforts of some of its major foreign competitors, especially Germany and Japan" (CIEP, p. 119). This should be translated to read as follows: Germany's and Japan's increases in R&D expenditures brought them roughly to the American level of spending by 1973 (see Appendix Table II). Much of America's decline in expenditure over the decade reflects reduced spending on space and defense-related research and development, which have little to do with economic standing anyway. Since expenditure is measured as a percentage of GNP, moreover, America's national expenditure is still disproportionately large. The expenditure is reflected in results, as several examples suggest. In 29 years following the 1943 resumption of Nobel Prize awards in science Americans won 86 of the 178 given (Smith and Karlesky 1977, p. 4). In 1976 we became the first country ever to sweep the Nobel Prizes. (This of course led to articles in the press warning of an approaching decline in America's scientific and cultural eminence, partly because other countries are catching up in research expenditures in ways that I have just summarized. One suspects the warning is merited; we can scarcely do better.)

---

*Nixon and Sulzberger do, however, overestimate American postwar economic dominance. W. S. and E. S. Woytinsky credit the United States with 40.7 percent of world income in 1948, compared to 26 percent in 1938. Theirs seems to be the better estimate (1953, pp. 389, 393–95).

Between 1953 and 1973 the United States produced 65 percent of 492 major technological innovations. Britain was second with 17 percent (*ibid.*). In 1971, of every ten thousand employees in the American labor force, 61.9 were scientists and engineers. The comparable figures for the next ranking noncommunist countries were 38.4 for Japan, 32.0 for West Germany, and 26.2 for France. Finally, our advantage in the export of manufactured goods has depended heavily on the export of high technology products. In the three years from 1973 through 1975 those exports grew at an annual average rate of 28.3 percent (IERP, 1976, p. 120).

However one measures, the United States is the leading country. One may wonder whether the position of leader is not a costly one to maintain. Developing countries, Russia and Japan for example, have gained by adopting technology expensively created in countries with more advanced economies. For four reasons this is no longer easily possible. First, the complexity of today's technology means that competence in some matters can seldom be separated from competence in others. How can a country be in the forefront of any complicated technology without full access to the most sophisticated computers? Countries as advanced as the Soviet Union and France have felt the difficulties that the question suggests. Second, the pace of technological change means that lags lengthen and multiply. "The countries only a little behind," as Victor Basiuk has said, "frequently find themselves manufacturing products already on the threshold of obsolescence" (n.d., p. 489). Third, even though the United States does not have an internal market big enough to permit the full and efficient exploitation of some possible technologies, it nevertheless approaches the required scale more closely than anyone else does. The advantage is a big one since most projects will continue to be national rather than international ones. Fourth, economic and technological leads are likely to become more important in international politics. This is partly because of the military stalemate. It is also because in today's world, and more so in tomorrow's, adequate supplies of basic materials are not easily and cheaply available. To mine the seabeds, to develop substitutes for scarce resources, to replace them with synthetics made from readily available materials: These are the abilities that will become increasingly important in determining the prosperity, if not the viability, of national economies.

I have mentioned a number of items that have to be entered on the credit side of the American ledger. Have I not overlooked items that should appear as debit entries? Have I not drawn a lopsided picture? Yes, I have; but then, it's a lopsided world. It is hard to think of disadvantages we suffer that are not more severe disadvantages for other major countries. The Soviet Union enjoys many of the advantages that the United States has and some that we lack, especially in natural resource endowments. With half of our GNP, she nevertheless has to run hard to stay in the race. One may think that the question to ask is not whether a third or fourth country will enter the circle of great powers in the foreseeable future but rather whether the Soviet Union can keep up.

The Soviet Union, since the war, has been able to challenge the United States in some parts of the world by spending a disproportionately large share of her smaller income on military means. Already disadvantaged by having to sustain a larger population than America's on one-half the product, she also spends from that product proportionately more than the United States does on defense—perhaps 11 to 13 percent as compared to roughly 6 percent of GNP that the United States spent in the years 1973 through 1975.* The burden of such high military spending is heavy. Only Iran and the confrontation states of the Middle East spend proportionately more. Some have worried that the People's Republic of China may follow such a path, that it may mobilize the nation in order to increase production rapidly while simultaneously acquiring a large and modern military capability. It is doubtful that she can do either, and surely not both, and surely not the second without the first. As a future superpower, the People's Republic of China is dimly discernible on a horizon too distant to make speculation worthwhile.

Western Europe is the only candidate for the short run—say, by the end of the millennium. Its prospects may not be bright, but at least the potential is present and needs only to be politically unfolded. Summed, the nine states of Western Europe have a population slightly larger than the Soviet Union's and a GNP that exceeds hers by 25 percent. Unity will not come tomorrow, and if it did, Europe would not instantly achieve stardom. A united Europe that developed political competence and military power over the years would one day emerge as the third superpower, ranking probably between the United States and the Soviet Union.

Unless Europe unites, the United States and the Soviet Union will remain economically well ahead of other states. But does that in itself set them apart? In international affairs, force remains the final arbiter. Thus some have thought that by acquiring nuclear weapons third countries reduce their distance from the great powers. "For, like gunpowder in another age," so one argument goes, "nuclear weapons must have the ultimate result of making the small the equal of the great" (Stillman and Pfaff 1961, p. 135). Gunpowder did not blur the distinction between the great powers and the others, however, nor have nuclear weapons done so. Nuclear weapons are not the great equalizers they were sometimes thought to be. The world was bipolar in the late 1940s, when the United States had few atomic bombs and the Soviet Union had none. Nuclear weapons did not cause the condition of bipolarity; other states by acquiring them cannot change the condition. Nuclear weapons do not equalize the power of nations because they do not

---

*Some estimates of the Soviet Union's spending are higher. Cf. Brennan 1977.

change the economic bases of a nation's power. Nuclear capabilities reinforce a condition that would exist in their absence: Even without nuclear technology the United States and the Soviet Union would have developed weapons of immense destructive power. They are set apart from the others not by particular weapons systems but by their ability to exploit military technology on a large scale and at the scientific frontiers. Had the atom never been split, each would far surpass others in military strength, and each would remain the greatest threat and source of potential damage to the other.

Because it is so research-intensive, modern weaponry has raised the barriers that states must jump over if they are to become members of the superpower club. Unable to spend on anywhere near the American or Russian level for research, development, and production, middle powers who try to compete find themselves constantly falling behind.* They are in the second-ranking powers' customary position of imitating the more advanced weaponry of their wealthier competitors, but their problems are now much bigger. The pace of the competition has quickened. If weaponry changes little and slowly, smaller countries can hope over time to accumulate weapons that will not become obsolete. In building a nuclear force, Britain became more dependent on the United States. Contemplating the example, de Gaulle nevertheless decided to go ahead with France's nuclear program. He may have done so believing that missile-firing submarines were the world's first permanently invulnerable force, that for them military obsolescence had ended. The French are fond of invulnerability. Given the small number of submarines France has planned, however, only one or two will be at sea at any given time. Continuous trailing makes their detection and destruction increasingly easy. And France's 18 land-based missiles can be blanketed by Russia's intermediate-range ballistic missiles, which she has in abundant supply. French officials continue to proclaim the invulnerability of their forces, as I would do if I were they. But I would not find my words credible. With the United States and the Soviet Union, each worries that the other may achieve a first-strike capability, and each works to prevent that. The worries of lesser nuclear powers are incomparably greater, and they cannot do much to allay them.

In the old days weaker powers could improve their positions through alliance, by adding the strength of foreign armies to their own. Cannot some of the middle states do together what they are unable to do alone? For two decisive reasons, the answer is no. Nuclear forces do not add up. The technology of warheads, of delivery vehicles, of detection and surveillance devices, of command

---

*Between 1955 and 1965, Britain, France, and Germany spent 10 percent of the American total on military R&D; between 1970 and 1974, 27 percent. As Richard Burt concludes, unless European countries collaborate on producing and procuring military systems and the United States buys European, exploitation of new technology will widen the gap in the capabilities of allies (1976, pp. 20–21; and see Appendix Table VI).

and control systems, counts more than the size of forces. Combining separate national forces is not much help. To reach top technological levels would require complete collaboration by, say, several European states. To achieve this has proved politically impossible. As de Gaulle often said, nuclear weapons make alliances obsolete. At the strategic level he was right. That is another reason for calling NATO a treaty of guarantee rather than an old-fashioned alliance. To concert their power in order to raise their capabilities to the level of the super-powers, states would have to achieve the oligopolists' unachievable "collusive handling of all relevant variables." Recalling Fellner, we know that this they cannot do. States fear dividing their strategic labors fully—from research and development through production, planning and deployment. This is less because one of them might in the future be at war with another, and more because anyone's decision to use the weapons against third parties might be fatal to all of them. Decisions to use nuclear weapons may be decisions to commit suicide. Only a national authority can be entrusted with the decision, again as de Gaulle always claimed. The reasons Europeans fear American unwillingness to retaliate on their behalf are the reasons middle states cannot enhance their power to act at the global and strategic levels through alliances compounded among themselves.* I leave aside the many other impediments to nuclear cooperation. These are impediments enough. Only by merging and losing their political identities can middle states become superpowers. The nonadditivity of nuclear forces shows again that in our bipolar world efforts of lesser states cannot tilt the strategic balance.

Saying that the spread of nuclear weapons leaves bipolarity intact does not imply indifference to proliferation. It will not make the world multipolar; it may have other good or bad effects. The bad ones are easier to imagine. Bipolarity has been proof against war between the great powers, but enough wars of lesser scale have been fought. The prospect of a number of states having nuclear weapons that may be ill-controlled and vulnerable is a scary one, not because proliferation would change the system, but because of what lesser powers might do to one another. In an influential 1958 article, Albert Wohlstetter warned of the dangers of a "delicate balance of terror." Those dangers may plague countries having small nuclear forces, with one country tempted to fire its weapons preemptively against an adversary thought to be momentarily vulnerable. One must add that these dangers have not in fact appeared. Reconsideration of nuclear proliferation is called for, but not here since I want only to make the point that an increase in the number of nuclear states does not threaten the world's bipolar structure.

---

*For the same reasons, a lagging superpower cannot combine with lesser states to compensate for strategic weakness.

Limitations of technology and scale work decisively against middle states competing with the great powers at the nuclear level. The same limitations put them ever further behind in conventional weaponry. Increasingly, conventional weaponry has become unconventional. Weapons systems of high technology may come to dominate the battlefield. One American officer describes an escort plane, under development for tactical strike missions, that "will throw an electronic blanket over their air defenses that will allow our aircraft to attack without danger from anything more than lucky shots." Another describes electronic-warfare capability as "an absolute requirement for survival in any future conflicts" (Middleton, September 13, 1976, p. 7). Though the requirement may be an absolute one, it is a requirement that only the United States and, belatedly, the Soviet Union will be able to meet. From rifles to tanks, from aircraft to missiles, weapons have multiplied in cost. To buy them in numbers and variety sufficient for military effectiveness exceeds the economic capability of most states. From about 1900 onward, only great powers, enjoying economies of scale, could deploy modern fleets. Other states limited their ships to older and cheaper models, while their armies continued to be miniatures of the armies of great powers. Now armies, air forces, and navies alike can be mounted at advanced levels of technology only by great powers. Countries of German or British size enjoy economies of scale in manufacturing steel and refrigerators, in providing schools, health services, and transportation systems. They no longer do so militarily. Short of the electronic extreme, the cost and complication of conventional warfare exclude middle states from developing the full range of weapons for land, air, and sea warfare.*

Great powers are strong not simply because they have nuclear weapons but also because their immense resources enable them to generate and maintain power of all types, military and other, at strategic and tactical levels. The barriers to entering the superpower club have never been higher and more numerous. The club will long remain the world's most exclusive one.

V

No one doubts that capabilities are now more narrowly concentrated than ever before in modern history. But many argue that the concentration of capabilities does not generate effective power. Military power no longer brings political control. Despite its vast capability, is the United States "a tied Gulliver, not a master

---

*Vital has made these points nicely for small states. They apply to middle states as well (1967, pp. 63–77).

with free hands" (Hoffmann, January 11, 1976, sec. iv, p. 1)? And does the Soviet Union also fit the description? The two superpowers, each stalemated by the other's nuclear force, are for important political purposes effectively reduced to the power of lesser states. That is a common belief. The effective equality of states emerges from the very condition of their gross inequality. We read, for example, that the "change in the nature of the mobilizable potential has made its actual use in emergencies by its unhappy owners quite difficult and self-defeating. As a result, nations endowed with infinitely less can behave in a whole range of issues as if the difference in power did not matter." The conclusion is driven home by adding that the United States thinks in "cataclysmic terms," lives in dread of all-out war, and bases its military calculations on the forces needed for the ulti-mate but unlikely crisis rather than on what might be needed in the less spectacu-lar cases that are in fact more likely to occur (Hoffmann, Fall 1964, pp. 1279, 1287–88; cf. Knorr 1966).

In the widely echoed words of John Herz, absolute power equals absolute impotence, at least at the highest levels of force represented by the American and Russian nuclear armories (1959, pp. 22, 169). At lesser levels of violence many states can compete as though they were substantially equal. The best weapons of the United States and the Soviet Union are useless, and the distinct advantage of those two states is thus negated. But what about American or Russian nuclear weapons used against minor nuclear states or against states having no nuclear weapons? Here again the "best" weapon of the most powerful states turns out to be the least usable. The nation that is equipped to "retaliate massively" is not likely to find the occasion to use its capability. If amputation of an arm were the only remedy available for an infected finger, one would be tempted to hope for the best and leave the ailment untreated. The state that can move effectively only by commiting the full power of its military arsenal is likely to forget the threats it has made and acquiesce in a situation formerly described as intolerable. Instru-ments that cannot be used to deal with small cases—those that are moderately dangerous and damaging—remain idle until the big case arises. But then the use of major force to defend a vital interest would run the grave risk of retaliation. Under such circumstances the powerful are frustrated by their strength; and although the weak do not thereby become strong, they are, it is said, able to behave as though they were.

Such arguments are repeatedly made and have to be taken seriously. In an obvious sense, part of the contention is valid. When great powers are in a stale-mate, lesser states acquire an increased freedom of movement. That this phe-nomenon is now noticeable tells us nothing new about the strength of the weak or the weakness of the strong. Weak states have often found opportunities for maneuver in the interstices of a balance of power. In a bipolar world, leaders are free to set policy without acceding to the wishes of lesser alliance members. By the same logic, the latter are free not to follow the policy that has been set. As we once did, they enjoy the freedom of the irresponsible since their security is mainly provided by the efforts that others make. To maintain both the balance and its by-product requires the continuing efforts of America and Russia. Their instincts for self-preservation call forth such efforts. The objective of both states must be to perpetuate an international stalemate as a minimum basis for the security of each of them—even if this should mean that the two big states do the work while the small ones have the fun.

Strategic nuclear weapons deter strategic nuclear weapons (though they may also do more than that). Where each state must tend to its own security as best it can, the means adopted by one state must be geared to the efforts of others. The cost of the American nuclear establishment, maintained in peaceful readiness, is functionally comparable to the cost incurred by a government in order to maintain domestic order and provide internal security. Such expenditure is not productive in the sense that spending to build roads is, but it is not unproductive either. Its utility is obvious, and should anyone successfully argue otherwise, the consequences of accepting the argument would quickly demonstrate its falsity. Force is least visible where power is most fully and most adequately present (cf. Carr 1946, pp. 103, 129-32). Power maintains an order; the use of force signals a possible breakdown. The better ordered a society and the more competent and respected its government, the less force its policemen are required to employ. Less shooting occurs in present-day Sandusky than did on the western frontier. Similarly, in international politics states supreme in their power have to use force less often. "Non-recourse to force"—as both Eisenhower and Khrushchev seem to have realized—is the doctrine of powerful states. Powerful states need to use force less often than their weaker neighbors because the strong can more often protect their interests or work their wills in other ways—by persuasion and cajolery, by economic bargaining and bribery, by the extension of aid, and finally by posing deterrent threats. Since states with large nuclear armories do not actually "use" them, force is said to be discounted. Such reasoning is fallacious. Possession of power should not be identified with the use of force, and the usefulness of force should not be confused with its usability. To introduce such confusions into the analysis of power is comparable to saying that the police force that seldom if ever employs violence is weak or that a police force is strong only when policemen are shooting their guns. To vary the image, it is comparable to saying that a man with large assets is not rich if he spends little money or that a man is rich only if he spends a lot of it.

But the argument, which we should not lose sight of, is that just as the miser's money may depreciate grossly in value over the years, so the great powers' military strength has lost much of its usability. If military force is like currency that cannot be spent or money that has lost much of its worth, then is not forbearance in its use merely a way of disguising its depreciated value? Conrad von Hötzendorf, Austrian Chief of Staff prior to the First World War, looked at military power as though it were a capital sum, useless unless invested. In his view, to invest military force is to commit it to battle.* In the reasoning of Conrad, military force is most useful at the moment of its employment in war. Depending on a country's situation, it may make much better sense to say that military force is most useful when it dissuades other states from attacking, that is, when it need not be used in battle at all. When the strongest state militarily is also a status-quo power, nonuse of force is a sign of its strength. Force is most useful, or best serves the interests of such a state, when it need not be used in the actual conduct of warfare. Throughout a century that ended in 1914, the British navy was powerful enough to scare off all comers, while Britain carried out occasional imperial ventures in odd parts of the world. Only as Britain's power weakened were her military forces used to fight a full-scale war. In being used, her military power surely became less useful.

Force is cheap, especially for a status-quo power, if its very existence works against its use. What does it mean, then, to say that the cost of using force has increased while its utility has lessened? It is highly important, indeed useful, to think in "cataclysmic terms," to live in dread of all-out war, and to base military calculations on the forces needed for the ultimate but unlikely crisis. That the United States does so, and that the Soviet Union apparently does too, makes the cataclysm less likely to occur. The web of social and political life is spun out of inclinations and incentives, deterrent threats and punishments. Eliminate the latter two, and the ordering of society depends entirely on the former—a utopian thought impractical this side of Eden. Depend entirely on threat and punishment, and the ordering of society is based on pure coercion. International politics tends toward the latter condition. The daily presence of force and recurrent reliance on it mark the affairs of nations. Since Thucydides in Greece and Kautilya in India, the use of force and the possibility of controlling it have been the preoccupations of international-political studies (Art and Waltz 1971, p. 4).

John Herz coined the term "security dilemma" to describe the condition in which states, unsure of one anothers' intentions, arm for the sake of security and in doing so set a vicious circle in motion. Having armed for the sake of security, states feel less secure and buy more arms because the means to anyone's security is a threat to someone else who in turn responds by arming (1950, p. 157). What-

---

*"The sums spent for the war power is money wasted," he maintained, "if the war power remains unused for obtaining political advantages. In some cases the mere threat will suffice and the war power thus becomes useful, but others can be obtained only through the warlike use of the war power itself, that is, by war undertaken in time; if this moment is missed, the capital is lost. In this sense, war becomes a great financial enterprise of the State" (quoted in Vagts 1956, p. 361).

ever the weaponry and however many states in the system, states have to live with their security dilemma, which is produced not by their wills but by their situations. A dilemma cannot be solved; it can more or less readily be dealt with. Force cannot be eliminated. How is peace possible when force takes its awesome nuclear form? We have seen in this chapter that two can deal with the dilemma better than three or more. Second-strike nuclear forces are the principal means used. Those means look almost entirely unusable. Is that a matter of regret? Why is "usable" force preferred—so that the United States and the Soviet Union would be able to fight a war such as great powers used to do on occasion? The whole line of reasoning implied in assertions that the United States and the Soviet Union are hobbled by the unusability of their forces omits the central point. Great powers are best off when the weapons they use to cope with the security dilemma are ones that make the waging of war among them unlikely. Nuclear forces are useful, and their usefulness is reinforced by the extent to which their use is forestalled. The military forces of great powers are most useful and least costly if they are priced only in money and not also in blood.

Odd notions about the usability and usefulness of force result from confused theory and a failure of historical recall. Great powers are never "masters with free hands." They are always "Gullivers," more or less tightly tied. They usually lead troubled lives. After all, they have to contend with one another, and because great powers have great power, that is difficult to do. In some ways their lot may be enviable; in many ways it is not. To give a sufficient example, they fight more wars than lesser states do (Wright 1965, pp. 221–23 and Table 22; Woods and Baltzly 1915, Table 46). Their involvement in wars arises from their position in the international system, not from their national characters. When they are at or near the top, they fight; as they decline, they become peaceful. Think of Spain, Holland, Sweden, and Austria. And those who have declined more recently enjoy a comparable benefit.* Some people seem to associate great power with great good fortune, and when fortune does not smile, they conclude that power has evaporated. One wonders why.

As before, great powers find ways to use force, although now not against each other. Where power is seen to be balanced, whether or not the balance is nuclear, it may seem that the resultant of opposing forces is zero. But this is misleading. The vectors of national force do not meet at a point, if only because the

---

*Notice how one is misled by failing to understand how a state's behavior is affected by its placement. With Thucydides (see above, p. 127), contrast this statement of A.J.P. Taylor's: "For years after the second world war I continued to believe that there would be another German bid for European supremacy and that we must take precautions against it. Events have proved me totally wrong. I tried to learn lessons from history, which is always a mistake. The Germans have changed their national character" (June 4, 1976, p. 742).

power of a state does not resolve into a single vector. Military force is divisible, especially for states that can afford a lot of it. In a nuclear world, contrary to some assertions, the dialectic of inequality does not produce the effective equality of strong and weak states. Nuclear weapons deter nuclear weapons; they also serve to limit escalation. The temptation of one country to employ increasingly larger amounts of force is lessened if its opponent has the ability to raise the ante. Force can be used with less hesitation by those states able to parry, to thrust, and to threaten at varied levels of military endeavor. For more than three decades, power has been narrowly concentrated; and force has been used, not orgiastically as in the world wars of this century, but in a controlled way and for conscious political purposes, albeit not always the right ones. Power may be present when force is not used, but force is also used openly. A catalogue of examples would be both complex and lengthy. On the American side of the ledger it would contain such items as the garrisoning of Berlin, its supply by airlift during the blockade, the stationing of troops in Europe, the establishment of bases in Japan and elsewhere, the waging of war in Korea and Vietnam, and the "quarantine" of Cuba. Seldom if ever has force been more variously, more persistently, and more widely applied; and seldom has it been more consciously used as an instrument of national policy. Since World War II we have seen the political organization and pervasion of power, not the cancellation of force by nuclear stalemate.

Plenty of power has been used, although at times with unhappy results. Just as the state that refrains from applying force is said to betray its weakness, so the state that has trouble in exercising control is said to display the defectiveness of its power. In such a conclusion the elementary error of identifying power with control is evident. If power is identical with control, then those who are free are strong; and their freedom has to be taken as an indication of the weakness of those who have great material strength. But the weak and disorganized are often less amenable to control than those who are wealthy and well disciplined. Here again old truths need to be brought into focus. One old truth, formulated by Georg Simmel, is this: When one "opposes a diffused crowd of enemies, one may oftener gain isolated victories, but it is very hard to arrive at decisive results which definitely fix the relationships of the contestants" (1904, p. 675).

A still older truth, formulated by David Hume, is that "force is always on the side of the governed." "The soldan of Egypt or the emperor of Rome," he went on to say, "might drive his harmless subjects like brute beasts against their sentiments and inclination. But he must, at least, have led his *mamalukes* or *praetorian bands*, like men, by their opinion" (1741, p. 307). The governors, being few in number, depend for the exercise of their rule on the more or less willing assent of their subjects. If sullen disregard is the response to every command, no government can rule. And if a country, because of internal disorder and lack of coherence, is unable to rule itself, no body of foreigners, whatever the military force at its command, can reasonably hope to do so. If insurrection is the problem, then it can hardly be hoped that an alien army will be able to pacify a country that is unable to govern itself. Foreign troops, though not irrelevant to such problems, can only be of indirect help. Military force, used internationally, is a means of establishing control over a territory, not of exercising control within it. The threat of a nation to use military force, whether nuclear or conventional, is preeminently a means of affecting another state's external behavior, of dissuading a state from launching a career of aggression and of meeting the aggression if dissuasion should fail.

Dissuasion, whether by defense or by deterrence, is easier to accomplish than "compellence," to use an apt term invented by Thomas C. Schelling (1966, pp. 70–71). Compellence is more difficult to achieve, and its contrivance is a more intricate affair. In Vietnam, the United States faced not merely the task of compelling a particular action but of promoting an effective political order. Those who argue from such a case that force has depreciated in value fail in their analyses to apply their own historical and political knowledge. The master builders of imperial rule, such men as Bugeaud, Galliéni, and Lyautey, played both political and military roles. In like fashion, successful counterrevolutionary efforts have been directed by such men as Templer and Magsaysay, who combined military resources with political instruments (cf. Huntington 1962, p. 28). Military forces, whether domestic or foreign, are insufficient for the task of pacification, the more so if a country is rent by faction and if its people are politically engaged and active. Some events represent change; others are mere repetition. The difficulty experienced by the United States in trying to pacify Vietnam and establish a preferred regime is mere repetition. France fought in Algeria between 1830 and 1847 in a similar cause. Britain found Boers terribly troublesome in the war waged against them from 1898 to 1903. France, when she did the fighting, was thought to have the world's best army, and Britain, an all powerful navy (Blainey 1970, p. 205). To say that militarily strong states are feeble because they cannot easily bring order to minor states is like saying that a pneumatic hammer is weak because it is not suitable for drilling decayed teeth. It is to confuse the purpose of instruments and to confound the means of external power with the agencies of internal governance. Inability to exercise *political* control over others does not indicate *military* weakness. Strong states cannot do everything with their military forces, as Napoleon acutely realized; but they are able to do things that militarily weak states cannot do. The People's Republic of China can no more solve the problems of governance in some Latin American country than the United States can in Southeast Asia. But the United States can intervene with great military force in far quarters of the world while wielding an effective deterrent against escalation. Such action exceeds the capabilities of all but the strongest of states.

Differences in strength do matter, although not for every conceivable purpose. To deduce the weakness of the powerful from this qualifying clause is a misleading use of words. One sees in such a case as Vietnam not the *weakness* of great military power in a nuclear world but instead a clear illustration of the *limits* of military force in the world of the present as always.

Within the repeated events, an unmentioned difference lurks. Success or failure in peripheral places now means less in material terms than it did to previous great powers. That difference derives from the change in the system. Students of international politics tend to think that wars formerly brought economic and other benefits to the victors and that in contrast the United States cannot now use its military might for positive accomplishment (e.g., Morgenthau 1970, p. 325; Organski 1968, pp. 328–29). Such views are wrong on several counts. First, American successes are overlooked. Buttressing the security of Western Europe is a positive accomplishment; so was defending South Korea, and one can easily lengthen the list. Second, the profits of past military ventures are overestimated. Before 1789, war may have been "good business"; it has seldom paid thereafter (Schumpeter 1919, p. 18; cf. Sorel, pp. 1–70, and Osgood and Tucker 1967, p. 40). Third, why the United States should be interested in extending military control over others when we have so many means of nonforceful leverage is left unspecified. America's internal efforts, moreover, add more to her wealth than any imaginable gains scored abroad. The United States, and the Soviet Union as well, have more reason to be satisfied with the status quo than most earlier great powers had. Why should we think of using force for positive accomplishment when we are in the happy position of needing to worry about using force only for the negative purposes of defense and deterrence? To fight is hard, as ever; to refrain from fighting is easier because so little is at stake. Léon Gambetta, French premier after France's defeat by Prussia, remarked that because the old continent is stifling, such outlets as Tunis are needed. This looks like an anticipation of Hobson. The statement was merely expediential, for as Gambetta also said, Alsace-Lorraine must always be in Frenchmen's hearts, although for a long time it could not be on their lips (June 26, 1871). Gains that France might score abroad were valued less for their own sake and more because they might strengthen France for another round in the French-German contest. Jules Ferry, a later premier, argued that France needed colonies lest she slip to the third or fourth rank in Europe (Power 1944, p. 192). Such a descent would end all hope of retaking Alsace-Lorraine. And Ferry, known as *Le Tonkinoise*, fell from power in 1885 when his southeast Asian ventures seemed to be weakening France rather than adding to the strength she could show in Europe. For the United States in the same part of the world, the big stake, as official statements described it, was internally generated—our honor and credibility, although the definition of those terms was puzzling. As some saw early in that struggle, and as most saw later on, in terms of global politics little was at stake in Vietnam (Stoessinger 1976, Chapter 8, shows that this was Kissinger's view). The international-political insignificance of Vietnam can be understood only in terms of the world's structure.

America's failure in Vietnam was tolerable because neither success nor failure mattered much internationally. Victory would not make the world one of American hegemony. Defeat would not make the world one of Russian hegemony. No matter what the outcome, the American-Russian duopoly would endure.

Military power no longer brings political control, but then it never did. Conquering and governing are different processes. Yet public officials and students alike conclude from the age-old difficulty of using force effectively that force is now obsolescent and that international structures can no longer be defined by the distribution of capabilitites across states.

How can one account for the confusion? In two ways. The first, variously argued earlier, is that the usefulness of force is mistakenly identified with its use. Because of their favored positions, the United States and the Soviet Union need to use force less than most earlier great powers did. Force is more useful than ever for upholding the status quo, though not for changing it, and maintaining the status quo is the minimum goal of any great power. Moreover, because the United States has much economic and political leverage over many other states, and because both the United States and the Soviet Union are more nearly self-sufficient than most earlier great powers were, they need hardly use force to secure ends other than their own security. Nearly all unfavorable economic and political outcomes have too little impact to call for their using force to prevent them, and strongly preferred economic and political outcomes can be sufficiently secured without recourse to force. For achieving economic gains, force has seldom been an efficient means anyway. Because the United States and the Soviet Union are secure in the world, except in terms of each other, they find few international-political reasons for resorting to force. Those who believe that force is less useful reach their conclusion without asking whether there is much reason for today's great powers to use force to coerce other states.

The second source of confusion about power is found in its odd definition. We are misled by the pragmatically formed and technologically influenced American definition of power—a definition that equates power with control. Power is then measured by the ability to get people to do what one wants them to do when otherwise they would not do it (cf. Dahl 1957). That definition may serve for some purposes, but it ill fits the requirements of politics. To define "power" as "cause" confuses process with outcome. To identify power with control is to assert that only power is needed in order to get one's way. That is obviously false, else what would there be for political and military strategists to do? To use power is to apply one's capabilities in an attempt to change someone else's behavior in certain ways. Whether *A*, in applying its capabilities, gains the wanted compliance of *B* depends on *A*'s capabilities and strategy, on *B*'s capabilities and counterstrategy, and on all of these factors as they are affected by the situation at hand. Power is one cause among others, from which it cannot be isolated. The common relational definition of power omits consideration of how acts and relations are affected by the structure of action. To measure power by compliance rules unintended effects out of consideration, and that takes much of the politics out of politics.

According to the common American definition of power, a failure to get one's way is proof of weakness. In politics, however, powerful agents fail to impress their wills on others in just the ways they intend to. The intention of an act and its result will seldom be identical because the result will be affected by the person or object acted on and conditioned by the environment within which it occurs. What, then, can be substituted for the practically and logically untenable definition? I offer the old and simple notion that an agent is powerful to the extent that he affects others more than they affect him. The weak understand this; the strong may not. Prime Minister Trudeau once said that, for Canada, being America's neighbor "is in some ways like sleeping with an elephant. No matter how friendly or even tempered is the beast . . . one is affected by every twitch and grunt" (quoted in Turner 1971, p. 166). As the leader of a weak state, Trudeau understands the meaning of our power in ways that we overlook. Because of the weight of our capabilities, American actions have tremendous impact whether or not we fashion effective policies and consciously put our capabilities behind them in order to achieve certain ends.

How is power distributed? What are the effects of a given distribution of power? These two questions are distinct, and the answer to each of them is extremely important politically. In the definition of power just rejected, the two questions merge and become hopelessly confused. Identifying power with control leads one to see weakness wherever one's will is thwarted. Power is a means, and the outcome of its use is necessarily uncertain. To be politically pertinent, power has to be defined in terms of the distribution of capabilities; the extent of one's power cannot be inferred from the results one may or may not get. The paradox that some have found in the so-called impotence of American power disappears if power is given a politically sensible definition. Defining power sensibly, and comparing the plight of present and of previous great powers, shows that the usefulness of power has increased.

VI

International politics is necessarily a small-number system. The advantages of having a few more great powers is at best slight. We have found instead that the advantages of subtracting a few and arriving at two are decisive. The three-body problem has yet to be solved by physicists. Can political scientists or policymakers hope to do better in charting the courses of three or more interacting states? Cases that lie between the simple interaction of two entities and the statistically predictable interactions of very many are the most difficult to unravel. We have seen the complications in the military affairs of multipolar worlds. The fates of great powers are closely linked. The great powers of a multipolar world, in taking steps to make their likely fates happier, at times need help from others. Friedrich Meinecke described the condition of Europe at the time of Frederick the Great this way: "A set of isolated power-States, alone yet linked together by their mutually grasping ambitions—that was the state of affairs to which the development of the European State-organism had brought things since the close of the Middle Ages" (1924, p. 321). Militarily and economically, interdependence developed as the self-sufficient localities of feudal Europe were drawn together by modern states. The great powers of a bipolar world are more self-sufficient, and interdependence loosens between them. This condition distinguishes the present system from the previous one. Economically, America and Russia are markedly less interdependent and noticeably less dependent on others than earlier great powers were. Militarily, the decrease of interdependence is more striking still, for neither great power can be linked to any other great power in "their mutually grasping ambitions."

Two great powers can deal with each other better than more can. Are they also able to deal with some of the world's common problems better than more numerous great powers can? I have so far emphasized the negative side of power. Power does not bring control. What does it bring? The question is considered in the next chapter, where the possibilities of, and the need for, international management and control are considered.

9

The Management of International Affairs

If power does not reliably bring control, what *does* it do for you? Four things, primarily. First, power provides the means of maintaining one's autonomy in the face of force that others wield. Second, greater power permits wider ranges of action, while leaving the outcomes of action uncertain. These two advantages we have discussed. The next two require elaboration.

Third, the more powerful enjoy wider margins of safety in dealing with the less powerful and have more to say about which games will be played and how. Duncan and Schnore have defined power in ecological terms as "the ability of one cluster of activities or niches to set the conditions under which others must function" (1959, p. 139). Dependent parties have some effect on independent ones, but the latter have more effect on the former. The weak lead perilous lives. As Chrysler's chairman, John Riccardo, remarked: "We've got to be right. The smaller you are, the more right you've got to be" (Salpukas, March 7, 1976, III, p. 1). General Motors can lose money on this model or that one, or on all of them, for quite a long time. Chrysler, if it does so, goes bankrupt. Be they corporations or states, those who are weak and hard pressed have to be careful. Thus with the following words Nguyen Van Thieu rejected the agreement for ending the war in Vietnam that Kissinger, the ally, and Le Duc Tho, the enemy, had made in October of 1972:

> You are a giant, Dr. Kissinger. So you can probably afford the luxury of being easy in this agreement. I cannot. A bad agreement means nothing to you. What is the loss of South Vietnam if you look at the world's map? Just a speck. The loss of South Vietnam may even be good for you. It may be good to contain China, good for your world strategy. But a little Vietnamese doesn't play with a strategic map of the world. For us, it isn't a question of choosing between Moscow and Peking. It is a question of choosing between life and death (quoted in Stoessinger 1976, p. 68).

Weak states operate on narrow margins. Inopportune acts, flawed policies, and mistimed moves may have fatal results. In contrast, strong states can be inattentive; they can afford not to learn; they can do the same dumb things over again. More sensibly, they can react slowly and wait to see whether the apparently threatening acts of others are truly so. They can be indifferent to most threats because only a few threats, if carried through, can damage them gravely. They can hold back until the ambiguity of events is resolved without fearing that the moment for effective action will be lost.

Fourth, great power gives its possessors a big stake in their system and the ability to act for its sake. For them management becomes both worthwhile and possible. To show how and why managerial tasks are performed internationally is the subject of this chapter. In self-help systems, as we know, competing parties consider relative gains more important than absolute ones. Absolute gains become more important as competition lessens. Two conditions make it possible for the United States and the Soviet Union to be concerned less with scoring relative gains and more with making absolute ones. The first is the stability of two-party balances, a stability reinforced by second-strike nuclear weapons. Where a first-strike capability is almost as difficult to imagine as to achieve, gains and losses need not be so carefully counted. The second condition is the distance between the two at the top and the next most powerful states, a distance that removes the danger of third states catching up. The United States gained relatively when OPEC multiplied oil prices by five between 1973 and 1977 (cf. above, pp. 153–55). The other noncommunist industrial countries suffered more than we did. At times it was hinted that, for this reason, the United States more readily acquiesced in OPEC's actions. In the past, with many competing powers, one might have credited the aspersion, but not now. In a self-help system, when the great-power balance is stable and when the distribution of national capabilities is severely skewed, concern for absolute gains may replace worries about relative ones. Those who are unduly favored can lead in, or lend themselves to, collective efforts even though others gain disproportionately from them.

In this chapter, I first show how managing is done internationally despite the difficulties, and then consider three tasks that the managers may perform. We shall, as usual, notice how tasks are differently performed as the number of their performers varies.

I

In the relations of states, with competition unregulated, war occasionally occurs. Although in one of its aspects war is a means of adjustment within the international system, the occurrence of war is often mistakenly taken to indicate that the system itself has broken down. At times, as during much of the eighteenth and nineteenth centuries, war was tolerable, since it was circumscribed and of limited destructive effect. The costs of war now appear to be frighteningly high. Since the most impressive of large and complicated self-regulatory systems operate only within contrived orders, the effective management of the affairs of nations appears to be a crying need. With power internationally uncontrolled, is it reasonable to expect states to adjust their relations through their independent policies without war serving as a means of regulation? This would be to ask for more from international-political systems than is expected in domestic economics or politics. But in describing expectations this way, it is at once implicitly assumed that war and the risk of war are more painful to bear than the costs of constructing and sustaining systems of management and that managerial functions are now badly performed. We have already examined the costs of managerial systems. Does their absence mean that managerial functions are not performed? Are governmental tasks performed in anarchic realms, and if so, what are the conditions that promote their performance? Since there are important managerial tasks to be accomplished internationally and no present or likely future agency exists to perform them, we have to search for a surrogate of government. We can best begin the search by asking why collective action for the common good is hard to achieve in anarchic realms.

Two difficulties stand out. The first is illustrated by considering a number of industries polluting a river with their wastes. For some to quit dumping their wastes in the river while others continue to do so will not do much good. The proper disposal of wastes is costly. If some plants unload their costs on the community, all of them will follow the practice. The industries enjoy free waste disposal; the community, say of would-be swimmers and fishermen, bears the costs. Under the circumstances nothing will be done unless all the industries can be forced to bear the full costs of their operations by paying for the proper disposal of wastes. That is the Alfred Kahn side of the coin (cf. above, Chapter 6, part I, section 3).

The second difficulty is seen by looking at the coin's other side. Certain goods and services, if made available, benefit all of the members of a group whether or not they help pay for them. Public parks, fire departments, police forces, and military establishments serve the citizens at large. Those who pay for such services, and those who do not, benefit equally. Such services are collective goods—goods that once supplied by any members of a group can be consumed by all of them. Thus all have reason to hang back, hoping that others will bear the costs—something that nobody may have an incentive to do. Such services will not be provided, or will be undersupplied, unless all are required to pay.

To get work done for the common good is difficult. How do the difficulties vary in societies of different structure? Regulation of collective affairs is the more needed as parties affect each other more severely through their interactions. The further the division of labor proceeds, the more complicated the regulation of joint activities becomes until finally either the system breaks down from lack of regulation or some of the parties emerge as specialists in managing system-wide affairs. Given an effective manager of collective affairs, specialization proceeds apace. To get more work done, the further differentiation of parties is required. As interdependence becomes integration, the division of labor becomes political as well as economic. Units previously alike become functionally distinct as some of them take on system-wide tasks (cf. Durkheim 1893; Park 1941). This is the governmental solution. Governments coerce those whose cooperation is required for the success of common projects and force payment for the services provided by suppliers of collective goods. Nationally, the tyranny of small decisions is broken and collective goods can be adequately supplied. The costs of organizing to get these results may, however, exceed the benefits expected. Internationally, common projects may not be undertaken because the cooperation of recalcitrant states is difficult to secure. Internationally, collective goods may not be provided because the providers would be serving some who evade paying their share of the costs. To organize for the coercion of the uncooperative and for collecting payments from free riders is forbiddingly difficult. Internationally, the tyranny of small decisions is not broken, and collective goods are not adequately supplied.* Does this mean that no international work gets done? Surely less gets done abroad than at home, but less does not mean nothing. What gets done, and how, varies with the number of great powers in the system. "The more the merrier" is the conclusion that most students have reached; that is, the chances of peace supposedly increase as the number of states playing the power-political game grows, at least up to some such number as five. Little heed is paid to another good old saying: "Everybody's business is nobody's business." Existence of a number of states is said to ease adjustments in the distribution of power among them, and even though we know that is not true, international politics is not supposed to be anyone's business anyway. Here again, attention focuses on relations to the exclusion of structure, thus emphasizing adjustment rather than control.

What do we see if we focus on the management and control of states rather than on relations among them? An example used by Baumol is suggestive, although he omits the size factor (1952, pp. 90–91). Suppose a few drought-stricken farmers are able to make rain by hiring someone to seed clouds. They will alleviate drought for themselves and also for neighboring farmers, who may refuse to pay their share of the costs since they will benefit anyway. Rainmaking

---

*From the extensive and excellent literature on collective goods, I find Baumol 1952, and Olson 1965, especially suggestive. Ruggie 1972 deftly describes the organizational difficulties I refer to.

is a collective good. The few farmers having the largest spreads may decide to provide it. Because the number of parties is small, they can hope to reach agreement, and they are spurred on by the size of their stakes and the urgency of their need. As Mancur Olson, Jr., has shown, "the larger the group, the less it will further its common interests" (1965, pp. 36, 45). Conversely, the smaller the group, and the less equal the interests of its members, the likelier it becomes that some members—the larger ones—will act for the group's interest, as they define it, and not just for their own. The greater the relative size of a unit the more it identifies its own interest with the interest of the system. This is made clear by considering the extreme case. If units grow in size as they compete, finally one of them will supplant the others. If one unit swallows the system, the distinction between the unit's and the system's interest disappears. Short of this extreme, in any realm populated by units that are functionally similar but of different capability, those of greatest capability take on special responsibilities. This is true whether the units are kinship groups, business firms, or nations. United States Steel, a firm organized to make steel and profits, in its heyday took on regulatory tasks as well—the maintenance of price stability at levels high enough to maintain profits and low enough to discourage new entrants (Berglund 1907; Burns 1936). System-wide tasks are difficult to perform. Why do larger units shoulder them? Like others, they want their system to be orderly and peaceful, and they want common interests to be cared for. Unlike others, they can act to affect the conditions of their lives. Organizations seek to reduce uncertainties in their environment. Units having a large enough stake in the system will act for its sake, even though they pay unduly in doing so. The large corporations lobby for laws to serve their industries' interests. The large corporations set wage levels for their industries when they reach agreements with trade unions. The large corporations police their industries and act to exclude new competitors. The large corporations translate the power that is the product of their superior capabilities into a degree of control unless governments prevent them from doing so.

Internationally, how can the problems of securing payment for, and participation in, collective tasks be solved? The smaller the number of great powers, and the wider the disparities between the few most powerful states and the many others, the more likely the former are to act for the sake of the system and to participate in the management of, or interfere in the affairs of, lesser states. The likelihood that great powers will try to manage the system is greatest when their number reduces to two. With many great powers, the concerns of some of them are regional, not global. With only two, their worries about each other cause their concerns to encompass the globe. For all but the United States and the Soviet Union, problems are local or regional. They are certainly less than global. For the United States, and increasingly so for the Soviet Union, regional problems are part of their global concerns. Each of them takes a system-wide view. The

United States and the Soviet Union account for about 38 percent of the world's gross product and for about 80 percent of the world's military expenditure. The other 150 or so states account for the rest. Neither the United States nor the Soviet Union can behave as "ordinary" states because that is not what they are. Their extraordinary positions in the system lead them to undertake tasks that other states have neither the incentive nor the ability to perform.

What are these tasks? In descending order of importance, they are the transforming or maintaining of the system, the preservation of peace, and the management of common economic and other problems.

II

Systems are either maintained or transformed. Let us consider possibilities of systems transformation before problems of maintenance. In economic systems, any one of several dominating firms has more to say about all of the matters that affect it than has one firm among hundreds of small ones. Oligopolists may prefer duopoly while disagreeing as to which two of several firms should survive. Duopolists may prefer monopoly or conceivably wish that worries about the management of markets were shared by a wider circle of firms. In international politics the possibilities are not fewer but more numerous than in a constricted sector of an economy, precisely because no agency is able to limit the efforts that states may make to transform their system. The principal entities that constitute the system are also its managers. They try to cope with the affairs of each day; they may also seek to affect the nature and direction of change. The system cannot be transcended; no authorized manager of the affairs of nations will emerge in the foreseeable future. Can international systems be changed by the actions of their major constituents? In a multipolar world one great power, or two or three in combination, can eliminate other states as great powers by defeating them in war. Reducing a multi- to a tri- or a bipolar world would change the system's structure. Wars that eliminate enough rival great powers are system-transforming wars. In modern history only World War II has done this. In a bipolar world, one of the leading powers may drive for hegemony or may seek to enlarge the circle of great powers by promoting the amalgamation of some of the middle states. Since the Second World War, the United States has pursued both of these uneasily reconciled ends much of the time. The United States has been the more active power in this period, so let us consider her policy.

The United States can justify her actions abroad in either or both of two ways. First, we can exaggerate the Russian or the communist threat and overreact to slight dangers. The domino theory is a necessary one if a traditional rationale in terms of security is to be offered for peripheral military actions. Second, we can act for the good of other people. Like some earlier great powers, we can identify the presumed duty of the rich and powerful to help others with our own beliefs about what a better world would look like. England claimed to bear the white man's burden; France spoke of her *mission civilisatrice*. In like spirit, we say that we act to make and maintain world order. The conviction that we must be concerned with every remote danger is analytically distinguishable from the world-order theme that developed out of old American ideas about national self-determination. In practice, however, they are closely connected. The interest of the country in security came to be identified with the maintenance of a certain order. For countries at the top, this is predictable behavior. They blend necessary or exaggerated worries about security with concern for the state of the system. Once a state's interests reach a certain extent, they become self-reinforcing. In attempting to contrive an international-security order, the United States also promoted its economic interests and gave expression to its political aspirations for the world.

A few examples, grouped so as to bring out different aspects of the world-order theme, will make its importance clear. Early postwar expressions of the theme, and some even today, incorporate the anticommunist concern in quite simple ways. As early as September of 1946, Clark Clifford argued in a memorandum written for President Truman that "our best chances of influencing Soviet leaders consist in making it unmistakably clear that action contrary to our conception of a decent world order will redound to the disadvantage of the Soviet regime whereas friendly and cooperative action will pay dividends. If this position can be maintained firmly enough and long enough the logic of it must permeate eventually into the Soviet system" (p. 480). Anticommunism is not merely an end in itself; it is also a means of making a decent world. More recently, Adam Ulam remarked that postwar history can suggest "which changes in Russian behavior favor a rapprochement with the United States, which developments in America threaten her influence in the world and hence the future of democratic institutions" (Ulam 1971, p. vi). Both Clifford and Ulam link opposition to the Soviet Union and the extension of American influence with the maintenance and development of a proper world order.

A second set of examples transcends the anticommunist theme, without eliminating it, by concentrating directly on the importance of building a world order. Our responsibility for reordering the world became America's theme song during the presidencies of Kennedy and Johnson. President Kennedy, speaking on the Fourth of July, 1962, made this declaration: "Acting on our own by ourselves, we cannot establish justice throughout the world. We cannot insure its domestic tranquility, or provide for its common defense, or promote its general welfare, or secure the blessings of liberty to ourselves and our posterity. But joined with other free nations, we can do all this and more. . . . We can mount a deterrent powerful enough to deter any aggression, and ultimately we can help achieve a world of law and free choice, banishing the world of war and coercion" (July 23, 1962). Such would be the benefits of an American-European union. A few years later, Senator Fulbright, ever an effective spokesman for the developing trends of the day, conveyed a full sense of our world aspirations. In *The Arrogance of Power*, an aptly titled book, he urged that because the world is able to destroy itself, it is "essential that the competitive instinct of nations be brought under control." And he added that America, "as the most powerful nation in the world, is the only nation equipped to lead the world in an effort to change the nature of its politics" (1966, p. 256). More simply, President Johnson described the purpose of American military strength as being "to put an end to conflict" (June 4, 1964). Never have the leaders of a nation expressed more overweening ambitions, but then never in modern history has a great power enjoyed so wide an economic and technological lead over the only other great power in the race.

An Atlantic imperium is hard to construct. For non-Americans, it goes against the international imperative, which reads "take care of yourself." Any seeming American success is a further spur to Russian efforts. The weak, moreover, fearing the loss of their identity, limit their cooperation with the stronger. They want to see not the aggrandizing but the balancing of power. De Gaulle voiced fears that others have felt—in the American scheme, European states would occupy subordinate places. To construct an Atlantic imperium with Western Europe disunited, we would have to bring European states separately, successively, and reliably under our influence. Efforts to do so might themselves provoke European states to seek political union more diligently, as in other ways we have often encouraged them to do.

To promote a change of system, whether by building a world hegemony or by promoting an area to great power status by helping it find political unity, is one of history's grandiose projects. We should be neither surprised nor sad that it failed. The humane rhetoric that expressed our aspirations, and the obvious good intentions it embodied, should not disguise the dangers. Consider hegemony first. One cannot assume that the leaders of a nation superior in power will always define policies with wisdom, devise tactics with fine calculation, and apply force with forbearance. The possession of great power has often tempted nations to the unnecessary and foolish employment of force, vices to which we are not immune. For one state or combination of states to foreclose others' use of force in a world where grievances and disputes abound, to end conflict in a contentious world, would require as much wisdom as power. Since justice cannot be objectively defined, the temptation of a powerful nation is to claim that the solution it seeks to impose is a just one. The perils of weakness are matched by the temptations of power.

And what about the American hope that its global burdens could be shared within a wider circle once a West European state became a third great power? Although many Americans have hoped for a united Europe, few have considered its unfavorable implications. The United States need worry little about wayward movements and unwanted events in weak states. We do have to be concerned with the implications of great power wherever it may exist. The principal pains of a great power, if they are not self-inflicted, arise from the effects of policies pursued by other great powers, whether or not the effects are intended. That thought suggests that a united Europe would be troublesome. Henry Kissinger noticed this. Ambivalence runs through his *Troubled Partnership*, a book about NATO. United, Europe would be a bastion against the Soviet Union, but a Europe of separate states is easier for an alliance leader to deal with. His ambivalence may explain why as Secretary of State he called for a new "Charter" for Europe without himself chartering anything. He did, however, make this remark: "We knew that a united Europe would be a more independent partner. But we assumed, perhaps too uncritically, that our common interests would be assured by our long history of cooperation" (April 24, 1973). The assumption is unwarranted. The emergence of a united Europe would shift the structure of international politics from bi- to tripolarity. For reasons of tradition, of political compatibility, and of ideological preference, a new Europe might well pull westward; but we know that the internal characteristics and the preferences of nations do not provide sufficient grounds for predicting behavior. A newly united Europe and the Soviet Union would be the weaker of the three great powers. In self-help systems, external forces propel the weaker parties toward one another. Weaker parties, our theory predicts, incline to combine to offset the strength of the stronger. The Soviet Union would work for that result, and Europe would benefit because weaker parties pay more for support that is given. Not in one grand confrontation, but on many issues of importance, the Soviet Union and the new Europe would cooperate in ways that we would find unpleasant.

Kissinger might have added, as few do when discussing the prospects for European unity, that students of international politics, who do not agree on much else, have always suspected that a world of three great powers would be the least stable of all. People who believe this, and would nevertheless welcome a united Europe, must rely on the second-strike forces that the old superpowers have, and the new one would develop, to overcome systemic instability. The question posed is whether a unit-level cause may negate a systems-level effect. That is surely possible. The argument would not be that the effects of tripolarity become different but that weaponry of certain characteristics overcomes them. Although second-strike forces may perpetuate a stalemate among more than two powers, one has to accept more doubts about who will help whom, and more uncertainty about who has second- and who has first-strike capabilities, and *then* bet that the system would remain peaceful and stable despite the greater difficulties. We should prefer bipolarity. In the event we probably would, despite statements, dwindling in frequency and fervor, to the contrary. Even such a good European as George Ball might balk at the prospect of a tripolar world if it threatened to become reality. As we would expect of sensible duopolists, the United States and the Soviet Union would like to maintain their positions. At times they cooperate to do so, as in the nonproliferation treaty. One of its aims was expressed by William C. Foster when he was director of the Arms Control and Disarmament Agency: "When we consider the cost to us of trying to stop the spread of nuclear weapons, we should not lose sight of the fact that widespread nuclear proliferation would mean a substantial erosion in the margin of power which our great wealth and industrial base have long given us relative to much of the rest of the world" (July 1965, p. 591). The United States would like to maintain its favored position, and so apparently would the Soviet Union (see Waltz 1974, p. 24). Putative gains in a tripolar world are less attractive than keeping the club exclusive.

Despite some outdated rhetoric from the doughtiest of cold warriors, American aims have shifted from changing the system to maintaining the system and working within it. The Nixon doctrine announced the shift. Other states would have to do more, although we would continue to buttress their security. Clearly our help would be designed not to change the balance of world power but merely to preserve it. Kissinger, as Secretary of State, defined our task from the early 1970s onward as being to disengage from the war in Vietnam "in a way that preserved our ability to design and to influence the development of a new international order" (January 10, 1977, p. 2). This sounds like the aspiration America has entertained intermittently from the presidency of Woodrow Wilson onward, the aspiration to reorder the world; but it is not. Kissinger was not thinking of world order in precisely defined structural terms, but rather of the task of shaping orderly and peaceful relations over the years among the world's principal parts. This is the task of maintaining and working the system, rather than of trying to transform it.

This profound change in the definition of the American mission marks the maturation of the bipolar world. "Maturation" is meant in two senses. First, America's earlier, extraordinary dominance in a world heavily damaged by war has diminished through a less drastically skewed distribution of national capabilities. As Kissinger put it, the Soviet Union has recently emerged "into true superpower status" by removing the overwhelming "disparity in strategic power between the United States and the Soviet Union" (December 23, 1975, p. 2). Second, the United States and the Soviet Union have increasingly shown that they have learned to behave as sensible duopolists should—moderating the intensity of their competition and cooperating at times to mutual advantage while continuing to eye each other warily. This condition, if properly seen and exploited, permits some reversal of America's global expansion, an expansion undertaken ironically in the name of opposing communism.

The maturation of the bipolar world is easily confused with its passing. In the middle 1970s, the waning of hegemonic competition in an era of détente and the increased prominence of north-south relations led many to believe that the world could no longer be defined in bipolar terms. But the waning of American-Russian competition and the increased importance of third-world problems do not imply the end of bipolarity. American and Russian behavior has changed somewhat over time, but it has changed in the direction one may expect it to take so long as the world remains bipolar (cf. Chapter 8, part III).

III

With only two great powers, both can be expected to act to maintain the system. Are they likely to provide such other services as promoting the general peace and helping others solve their security problems? Nationally, management is institutionally provided. Internationally, it is not. Managerial tasks are performed in both realms, but in markedly different ways. This difference, structurally derived, causes the possibility of managing international affairs to be played down unduly. The domestic realm is seen as the realm of ordered expectations in which governments control the acts of citizens by offering rewards and imposing deprivations, by passing laws and making regulations. Domestic problems lie within the arena of the state's control; foreign-policy problems do not. The proposition appears to be a truism, but its truistic quality disappears if one emphasizes control rather than arena. Which has been more difficult—to moderate and control Russian behavior in Berlin and Cuba or, within the United States, to get persons of different color to accept each other as equals, to cope with juvenile delinquency, to secure adhesion to wage guidelines by fragmented trade unions, and to manage mobs and prevent riots in cities? Problems of management in the two realms are different, but not uniformly more difficult in one than in the other. Because even the most powerful nations neither control everything nor influence everyone to their own satisfaction, it is easy, but wrong, to conclude that control over international affairs is inordinately difficult to contrive. Whether or not it is depends on the type of control envisaged and varies from one international system to another.

States strive to maintain their autonomy. To this end, the great powers of a multipolar world maneuver, combine, and occasionally fight. Some states fight wars to prevent others from achieving an imbalance of power in their favor. Out of their own interest, great powers fight power-balancing wars. Fighting in their own interest, they produce a collective good as a by-product, which should be appreciated by states that do not want to be conquered.* The war aims that

---

*In an unpublished paper, Stephen Van Evera nicely makes this point.

Germany developed in the course of fighting World War I called for annexing all or parts of small nearby countries. They could not prevent Germany from realizing her ambitions; only other great powers could do so. A benign result is not guaranteed. Maintaining a balance was earlier achieved by dividing and sharing Poland among Prussia, Russia, and Austria, which again shows great powers actively managing their system, although not to Poland's taste. That suggests a point always to be kept in mind. Internationally, quite a bit of managing is done, although the managers may not like the bother and the danger of doing it, and the managed may dislike the managers and the results they produce. Nothing about that is unusual. Managers and their works are often unpopular, a statement that holds alike for corporate executives, trade-union bosses, public officials, and great powers. Old-style imperialist countries were not warmly appreciated by most of their subjects, nor were the Japanese when they were assembling their "Greater East Asian Co-Prosperity Sphere," nor the Germans when they were building Hitler's new order. All of these are examples of great powers managing, influencing, controlling, and directing world or regional affairs.

For the most part, we should expect, and have experienced, more managerial effort in a bipolar world than is usually seen in a multipolar one. The attention of the managers is divided only between the two of them and, as we know, they have sufficient incentive to keep global affairs under their scrutiny. Both the United States and the Soviet Union have taken the fate of many others as being their concern. Edward W. Brooke caught the spirit well in his maiden speech in the Senate. We were not, he declared, fighting in Vietnam "as a necessary sacrifice to the global balance of power." We were instead fighting a "just" war to secure what is "best for South Vietnam, and most honorable and decent for ourselves" (March 23, 1967, p. 8). He was right. We surely did not fight for profit or out of necessity. States, and especially the major ones, do not act only for their own sakes. They also act for the world's common good. But the common good is defined by each of them for all of us, and the definitions conflict. One may fear the arrogance of the global burden-bearers more than the selfishness of those who tend to their own narrowly defined interests. Agents with great capabilities may use them to help others or to harm them. The urge to act for the good of other people as we define it became especially dangerous in the early 1960s when we converted superior economic resources into military capability at a pace that the Soviet Union did not match. Close competition subordinates ideology to interest; states that enjoy a margin of power over their closest competitors are led to pay undue attention to minor dangers and to pursue fancies abroad that reach beyond the fulfillment of interests narrowly defined in terms of security. In the years of American war in Vietnam, we enjoyed such a margin of military superiority over the Soviet Union that we could commit half a million men to war without increasing the percentage of gross national product that went into defense and without weakening our strategic position vis-à-vis the Soviet Union. With such vast capability the United States could act, not against the Soviet Union, but aside from the threat that her power entails. How can we hope that the wielders of great power will not savage a region in the name of making and maintaining world order? At the level of the international system, one may hope that power, which has recently come into closer balance, remains there. A military competition, if it is a close one, calls for caution on the part of the competitors. At the level of the nation, we may hope that internal forces restrain national leaders from dangerous and unnecessary adventures. The pressures of public opposition to adventurous policies may do this in the United States; the weaknesses of a lagging economy and a backward technology may do it in the Soviet Union.

We cannot hope that powerful agents will follow policies that are just right; we can hope that they will not get it all wrong. American failures in Southeast Asia should not obscure the useful role the United States has played and continues to play in Northeast Asia, in Europe, in the Middle East, and in other places. As American officials have said often enough, we are not the world's policeman. But, alas, in the words of President Johnson "there is no one else who can do the job" (May 5, 1965, p. 18). The statement "that the United States cannot be the world's policeman," as Kissinger later remarked, "is one of those generalities that needs some refinement. The fact of the matter is that security and progress in most parts of the world depend on some American commitment" (December 23, 1975, p. 3). The United States, with a million men stationed abroad even before fighting in Vietnam, garrisoned the noncommunist world from the 38th parallel in Korea eastward all the way to Berlin. We did serve as the world's policeman, and still do, and policing is a governmental task. We discharge the task, pretty much to the satisfaction of many others, at much more expense to ourselves than to them. Basic satisfaction is shown by the dwindling popularity of the slogan once found chalked on walls in many foreign cities: "Americans go home." We now find that we are asked more often to come than to go, more often to intervene than to stay out. Obvious examples abound. Arabs want us to bring pressures on Israelis. Israelis want us to supply and support them. Southern African leaders want us to solve residual colonial problems in their favor. South Koreans are reluctantly saying a slow goodbye to American troops and will continue to receive American military supplies along with naval and air support. Chinese leaders want American troops withdrawn from Asia but, they make clear, not too many of them and not too fast. Many countries have become accustomed to their dependence and continue to rely on us to help care for them. Western Europe is the most striking case of protracted dependence. West Europeans, despite an imbalance of economic assets favoring them over Russia, continue to expect us to provide the major part of their defense. "Please stay" has replaced "go home" as a popular slogan. Indeed, Georg Leber and Helmut Schmidt have made "you must stay" the imperious message of their repeated statements on European security. Leber, German Defense Minister from

1972 to 1978, has warned us that for our military commitment to Europe "there is neither a political nor a military nor a psychological substitute nor one provided by a single European state nor by various European states together" (February 27, 1973, p. 50). Schmidt, Defense Minister and Finance Minister before becoming Chancellor in 1974, has over the years insistently ruled out a greater German effort because "lack of money, manpower, and popular support would preclude such a solution—quite apart from the grave political effects it would have in the East as well as in the West" (quoted in Newhouse 1971, p. 83). In arguing that politically and economically West Germany could not increase its efforts, he might have added that the defense cost she was struggling to bear amounted to 3.3 percent of GNP. At the same time we were spending almost eight percent of GNP on defense with about two percent of GNP going for military personnel and equipment that we keep either in or for Europe. From 1973 through 1976, among West European states only Britain spent more than four percent of GNP on defense, and we were spending about six percent. Some European states could afford to do more. The additional contribution that any of them might make, however, would have little impact. They have less incentive to increase their contributions than they have to make arguments and take measures designed to maintain the effectiveness of the American commitment, which Germany, France, and Britain all do, each in its separate way (cf. Waltz 1974).

In a world of nation-states, some regulation of military, political, and economic affairs is at times badly needed. Who will provide it? In the most important cases—those of far-reaching economic importance and those that threaten to explode in military violence—the United States is often the only country that has a reasonable chance of intervening effectively. In these matters, a reasonable chance may not be a high one. In giving some help, we do gain some control. We influence the political-military strategies that others follow and occasionally decide whether or not they should initiate war. Thus Kissinger warned the Israeli Ambassador, Dinitz, in the fall of 1973 "not to pre-empt." And our Ambassador, Keating, underscored the warnings by telling the Israelis that if they struck first without irrefutable proof of Arab aggression, they would fight alone (Stoessinger 1976, p. 179). The United States has not been able to prevent fighting between Israelis and Arabs. It has curbed wars and pushed the parties toward a settlement. It may expect no more than a comparable mixture of failure and success in southern Africa. Yet if the United States does not lend a hand in trying to solve the most important and difficult problems, who will? "We can move forward from a Pax Americana or even a Pax Russo-Americana," a Canadian scholar has said, "but we are doomed if we revert to the graceless state in which only the weak care about international order" (Holmes 1969, p. 244).

Despite the difficulties of international management, the United States has probably overmanaged the affairs of the world since World War II. The clarity with which dangers and duties are defined in a bipolar world easily leads the country that identifies its own security with the maintenance of world order to overreact. Minding much of the world's business for one-third of a century has made it easy for us to believe that the world will be worse off if we quit showing such solicitude for it. Some have worried that after the war in Vietnam America would shed global responsibilities too quickly. For three reasons the worry is unfounded. First, the interest of preeminent powers in the consumption of collective goods is strong enough to cause them to undertake the provision of those goods without being properly paid. They have incentives to act in the interest of the general peace and the wider security of nations even though they will be working for the benefit of others as much as for themselves and even though others pay disproportionately small amounts of the costs. Thus Mancur Olson, Jr., deduces a *"tendency for the 'exploitation' of the great by the small"* (1965, p. 35). Leading states play leading roles in managing world affairs, and they do this the more so as their number shrinks to two. Second, others may have to worry about the credibility of our commitments, but we don't. Our credibility is their problem, not ours, although in the middle 1970s many American leaders put the problem the wrong way around. We sometimes have reasons to bear others' burdens; we hardly need assume their worries about our reliability when those worries may prompt them to do more to help themselves and leave us with less to do for them. Third, the managerial habits of three decades are so deeply ingrained that the danger continues to be that we will do too much rather than too little.

Managing is hard to do; regulation of the affairs of states is difficult to contrive. Those statements are certainly true, which makes the extent, and even the success, of American—and yes, also of Russian—management impressive. I have said little about the Soviet Union because the United States has borne the major burden of global management militarily and even more so economically. The Soviet Union has, of course, devotedly ordered her sphere insofar as she could maintain it. By doing so she has contributed to international peace and stability, although not to the liberties of East Europeans (see Licklider 1976–77). Great powers have an interest in areas whose instability may lead to their involvement and, through involvement, to war. Balkan instabilities triggered World War I. Could our bipolar world tolerate crises and wars among East European states any more readily than the old multipolar world did? Believing the answer to be "no," some have argued that the previous and the present worlds are comparably unstable and war prone. That obscures a vital difference between the two systems. Now the control of East European affairs by one great power is tolerated by the other precisely because their competing interventions would pose undue dangers. Thus John Foster Dulles, apostle of liberation, assured the Soviet Union when Hungarians rebelled in October of 1956 that we would not interfere with efforts to suppress them. Although we would prefer that East Europeans freely choose their governors, we may nevertheless understand that the Soviet Union's managing a traditionally volatile part of the world has its good points. Through tests and probes, in Eastern Europe and elsewhere, a division of managerial labor is more readily arranged in bipolar than in multipolar worlds.

In asking what the possibilities of managing world affairs are, we should also ask how great the need for management may be. The need for management increases as states become more closely interdependent. If interdependence is really close, each state is constrained to treat other states' acts as though they were events within its own borders. Mutuality of dependence leads each state to watch others with wariness and suspicion. A decrease in interdependence lessens the need for control. We have learned, one may hope, that the domino theory holds neither economically nor militarily. A measure of self-sufficiency and the possession of great capabilities insulate a nation from the world by muting the effects of adverse movements that originate outside of one's national arena. At the same time, the narrow concentration of power, which is implied in lessened interdependence, gives to the small number of states at the top of the pyramid of power both a larger interest in exercising control and a greater ability to do so. The size of the two great powers gives them some capacity for control and at the same time insulates them to a considerable extent from the effects of other states' behavior. The inequality of nations produces a condition of equilibrium at a low level of interdependence. In the absence of authoritative regulation, loose coupling and a certain amount of control exercised by large states help to promote peace and stability. If the members of an anarchic realm are in a condition of low interdependence, the concerting of effort for the achievement of common aims is less often required. Control rather than precise regulation, and prevention rather than coordination for positive accomplishment, are the operations of key importance. To interdict the use of force by the threat of force, to oppose force with force, to influence the policies of states by the threat or use of force: These have been and continue to be the most important means of control in security matters. With a highly unequal distribution of world power, some states, by manipulating the threat of force, are able to moderate others' use of force internationally. These same states, by virtue of their superior power, are able to absorb possibly destabilizing changes that emanate from uses of violence that they do not or cannot control.

IV

And what about all those other problems that require the concerted efforts of a number of nations? The problems that I have referred to as the four "p's"—poverty, population, pollution, and proliferation—sometimes creep to the top of the international agenda. Military stalemate between the United States and the Soviet Union may permit them to stay there for long periods. Who will deal with them? Many in the 1970s began to believe that the United States cannot, because ours is no longer the world's dominant economy (cf. Ullman, October 1976, pp. 3–4). True, we cannot in the sense that international problems of any consequence can never be solved by one nation unaided. True, we cannot now get our own way in dealing with international problems of trade, money, and finance as much as we did at Bretton Woods in 1944. True, we cannot stop the spread of nuclear weapons, although we can do more than anyone else to keep them from proliferating (cf. Kissinger, September 30, 1976, pp. 8–9; Nye, June 30, 1977, pp. 5–6).

No one will deny that collective efforts are needed if common problems are to be solved or somehow managed. Carrying out common projects requires some concerting, more so now than earlier in the postwar world. Global problems can be solved by no nation singly, only by a number of nations working together. But who can provide the means and who will pay the major share of the costs? Unless we do, the cooperative ventures of nations will be of limited extent and effect. I have already said enough about our role in economic and other such matters, about the leverage we gain from our relatively independent position, and about the inability of the Soviet Union, whatever its inclinations, to contribute much to the management of the nonmilitary affairs of the world. Economically the United States is far and away the leading power. If the leading power does not lead, the others cannot follow. All nations may be in the same leaky world boat, but one of them wields the biggest dipper. In economic and social affairs, as in military matters, other countries are inclined to leave much of the bailing to us. The increase of interdependence, according to the accepted view, has shrunk the globe and established possibilities for the central management of world affairs. Increased interdependence certainly leads to increased need for the management of collective affairs, but it does not produce a manager capable of doing it. From the global, or macro, perspective, the United States and the Soviet Union most of all need to be managed. Our theory changes the perspective to a micro one. The problem seen in the light of the theory is not to say how to manage the world, including its great powers, but to say how the possibility that great powers will constructively manage international affairs varies as systems change.

Appendix

The following tables were prepared by Stephen Peterson.

Table I *Exports plus imports as percentage of national product[a]*

Periods	Countries												
	United Kingdom		France		Germany		Italy		Japan		Soviet Union		United States	
	Years	%	Years	%	Years	%	Years	%	Years	%	Years	%	Years	%
Late 19th Century	1877–85	49	1875–84	52	1880–89	34	1889–90	26	1878–87	13			1879–88	14
	1887–95	45	1885–94	50	1890–99	30	1891–00	25	1888–97	26			1889–98	14
Pre-World War I	1897–05	41	1895–04	49	1901–09	34	1901–10	31	1898–07	34			1899–08	11
	1909–13	52	1905–13	54	1910–13	38	1911–13	34	1908–13	33			1904–13	12
Inter-War	1924–28	38	1920–24	51	1925–29	31	1925–29	30	1918–27	41			1919–28	12
	1929–33	28	1925–34	42	1930–34	22	1930–34	20	1928–37	41		b	1929–38	8
	1934–38	24	1935–38	33	1935–38	12	1935–38	15	1938–42	31			1939–48	10
Post-World War II	1949–53	37	1950–54	38	1950–54	26	1950–52	26	1950–56	21	1955	4	1944–53	10
	1960	32	1960	23	1960	30	1960	26	1960	20	1960	5	1960	7
	1965	30	1965	22	1965	32	1965	26	1965	19	1965	5	1965	7
	1970	33	1970	25	1970	34	1970	30	1970	20	1970	5	1970	9
	1975	41	1975	32	1975	39	1975	41	1976	23	1975	7	1975	14

Notes:

[a]Exports as a percentage of GNP plus imports as a percentage of GNP.
[b]Interwar data for the Soviet Union are not given. They are misleading because of the rapid depreciation of the domestic ruble and the discrepancy between the domestic and the international ruble as a unit of account. For the latter reason, and because of the difference in measurement of international and intrabloc trade, postwar data should be interpreted cautiously.

Sources: All data through the mid-1950s, except for the Soviet Union, are from Kuznets, January 1967, Table I, pp. 96–120. All data from 1960 onward, except for the Soviet Union, are from CIEP, January 1977, Tables 1, 18, 19. GNP data for the Soviet Union are from CIEP, January 1977, Table 2, p. 138. Trade data for 1955 are from Mitchell 1975, p. 499; for 1960 and 1965, from International Monetary Fund; for 1970 and 1975, from UN Statistical Office, 1977, pp. 424–27.

Table II *Net capital flow from selected countries as percentage of gross capital formation and gross national product*

Country and amounts	1880–89	1890–99	1900–09	1910–13	1922–25
United Kingdom					
NCF/GCF[a]	80.0	48.0	49.0	139.0	27.0
NCF/GNP[b]	4.8	3.3	3.9	7.7	2.0
France					
NCF/GCF	46.0	13.0	19.0	17.0	7.3
NCF/GNP	0.9	2.6	4.0	3.5	2.0
Germany					
NCF/GCF	30.0	11.0	10.0	17.0	n.a.
NCF/GNP	3.1	1.4	1.5	2.6	n.a.
Japan					
NCF/GCF	n.a.	n.a.	n.a.	n.a.	n.a.
NCF/GNP	n.a.	n.a.	n.a.	n.a.	n.a.
United States					
NCF/GCF	+3.2	0.2	+0.5	+2.7	2.0
NCF/GNP	+0.7	0.1	+0.1	+0.5	0.4

1926–30	1931–35	1951–55	1956–59	1961–65	1966–70	1971–75
15.0	+6.0[c]	9.0	9.0	5.0	1.0	+9.0
1.3	+0.5	1.0	1.0	0.9	0.2	+2.0
17.0	+3.4	4.0	0.1	0.2	1.4	+1.0
3.2	+0.7	1.0	0.02	0.1	0.4	0.2
33.0	104.0	2.0	3.0	+1.0	5.3	+5.4
3.1	3.1	0.5	1.0	+0.2	1.3	+1.3
n.a.	n.a.	0.7	0.2	1.4	1.4	3.0
n.a.	n.a.	0.2	0.04	0.4	0.5	1.0
3.0	+3.0	4.6	7.1	4.7	2.0	2.5
0.5	+0.4	1.0	1.2	1.0	0.4	0.4

Notes:
[a]Net capital flow divided by gross capital formation.
[b]Net capital flow divided by gross national product.
[c]Plus sign stands for net inflow.

Table II   *Continued*

Sources: Pre-World War I data are from three sources. Net capital flow averages are computed from Bloomfield 1968, Appendix I, pp. 42–43. European GNPs and GCFs are computed from Mitchell 1975, pp. 781–82, 785, 790, 797. US GNPs and GCFs are from US Bureau of the Census, 1976, Part I, pp. 224–31. Interwar data are from three sources. Net capital flow averages for all countries, except Germany, are computed from Royal Institute of International Affairs, 1937, pp. 139–40, 175, 200–201. German capital flows are from UN Department of Economic Affairs, 1949, Table 1, pp. 10–11. European GNPs and GCFs are from Mitchell, pp. cited. US GNPs and GCFs are from US Bureau of the Census, 1976. Data for 1951 to 1959 are from four sources. Capital flows are from UN Department of Economic Affairs, 1961, Table 3, pp. 6–7. European GNPs and GCFs are from Mitchell, pp. 792–95. US GNPs are from US Bureau of the Census, 1976. US GCFs are from UN Statistical Office, 1957 and 1961. Data for 1961 to 1975 are from three sources. Capital flows are from OECD, various years, as are GNPs for 1961 to 1970. GNPs for 1971 to 1975 are from CIEP, March 1976, p. 137. GCFs for Europe 1961 to 1975 are from OECD, various years, and US GCFs are from UN Statistical Office, 1961, 1970, and 1974.

Table III   *European emigration as a percentage of total European population*[a]

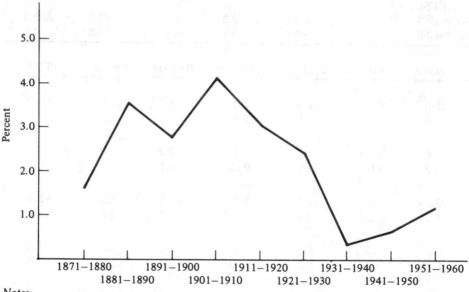

Notes:

[a]Each point represents a decade's total emigration as a percentage of a decade's average population. The graph excludes European Russia. For perspective, note that from 1846 to 1932 about 95 percent of intercontinental emigration was from Europe and from 1821 to 1932 about 58 percent of emigrants went to the US (Kuznets 1966).

Sources: Emigration data are from Mitchell 1975, p. 135. Population data for 1871 to 1930 are computed from Kucyzynski 1969, Table I, pp. 230–31. Population data for 1931 to 1960 are from UN Statistical Office, 1966, p. 103.

Table IV *Exports plus imports as percentage of world trade for selected countries*

Years	United Kingdom[a]	France	Germany	Italy	Japan	Soviet Union	United States[b]
1870–80	24.0	10.8	9.7	3.0	n.a.	4.5	8.0
1880–89	22.4	10.2	10.3	2.9	n.a.	3.9	9.8
1913	15.5	7.3	12.1	2.9	n.a.	12.8	12.9
1928	13.7	6.1	9.3	2.8	n.a.	8.3	17.3
1937	14.1	4.8	8.3	2.3	5.1	7.4	16.0
1955	9.7	5.3	6.6	2.4	2.3	3.3	14.6
1960	8.7	4.9	8.1	3.1	3.3	4.2	13.4
1965	8.0	5.7	9.4	4.0	4.2	4.8	14.4
1970	6.9	6.3	11.0	4.9	6.2	3.9	15.0
1975	5.8	6.4	10.0	4.5	6.6	4.0	13.0

Notes:
[a]United Kingdom and Ireland through 1937.
[b]North America for years 1913–1937.

Sources: Data for 1870 to 1937 are from Kuznets 1966, pp. 306–308. Data for 1955, except for the Soviet Union, are from CIEP, March 1976, Tables 17–18, pp. 146–47. Data for 1955 for the Soviet Union are from Mitchell 1975, p. 499. Data for 1960 and 1965 are from International Monetary Fund; for 1970 and 1975, from UN Statistical Office, 1977, pp. 424–27.

Table V *US direct investment by area and selected sectors*

Year and type of area	Book value[a]	Percent of USDI[b]	Percent in extractive	Percent in manufacturing
1945				
Developed[c]	$ 4,809	57%	14%	24%
Developing[d]	3,560	43	16	7
Total USDI	8,369		30	31
1950				
Developed	5,356	45	10	24
Developing	6,447	55	28	8
Total USDI	11,804		38	32
1955				
Developed	10,070	53	16	25
Developing	9,115	47	26	8
Total USDI	19,185		42	33
1960				
Developed	19,319	61	21	29
Developing	12,546	39	23	5
Total USDI	31,865		44	34
1965				
Developed	32,312	65	20	32
Developing	17,162	35	19	7
Total USDI	49,474		39	39
1970				
Developed	51,819	69	19	34
Developing	19,168	31	12	7
Total USDI	75,456		31	41
1975				
Developed	91,139	68	19	34
Developing	34,874	32	10	8
Total USDI	133,168		29	42

Notes:
[a]Millions of current US $
[b]US Direct Investment
[c]Includes Western Europe, Canada, Australia, New Zealand, South Africa
[d]All other countries

Sources: All data, except for 1970, are from the following issues of *Survey of Current Business:* data for 1945, from January 1951, Table 4, p. 22; for 1950, from December 1952, Table 1, p. 8; for 1955, from August 1956, Table 3, p. 19; for 1960 and 1965, from October 1970, Table 9, p. 31; for 1975, from August 1976, Table 14, p. 49. Data for 1970 are from US Department of Commerce, Bureau of Economic Analysis, 1975, Table 5, p. 5.

Table VI *National expenditures for research and development*

Nation	Annual average growth of R&D spending, 1963–1973	Gross expenditure and percentage of GNP spent on R&D					
		1963		1967		1973	
		Amount[a]	Percent	Amount	Percent	Amount	Percent
United Kingdom	4.3%	$ 2,160	2.3%	$ 2,649	2.3%	$ 3,340	1.9%
France	10.2	1,300	1.6	2,562	2.3	3,982	1.6
West Germany	14.1	1,463	1.4	2,084	1.7	8,329	2.4
Canada	8.7	430	1.3	828	1.5	1,092	0.9
Japan	15.5	1,023	1.4	1,952	1.5	8,159	2.0
Soviet Union[b]	9.4	7,665[c]	3.6	9,100	3.6	21,323	4.7
United States	4.4	19,215	3.4	25,330	3.0	30,120	2.3

Notes:
[a]Millions of current US dollars.
[b]Data are for "basic science" expenditures.
[c]1965 data.

Sources: OECD data for 1963 and 1967 are from Ruggie 1974, Tables III–1 and III–2, pp. 181–83. OECD gross expenditures and percentages of GNP for 1973 are from CIEP, March 1976, p. 119, and OECD, 1976, pp. 10, 48, 88, 260, 290, 532. R&D data for the Soviet Union are from Nolting 1976, Table I, p. 8. GNP data for the Soviet Union are from UN Statistical Office, 1976, p. 185.

Table VII Shares of plant and equipment spending by US-owned MNCs in gross fixed capital formation in the manufacturing industries of seven key countries, 1966 and 1970

Industry	Plant and equipment spending by MNCs as percentage of gross fixed capital formation							Aggregate for all 7 countries		
	United Kingdom	France	West Germany	Belgium-Luxembourg	Canada	Mexico	Brazil[a]	P&E spending by MNCs (million dollars)	GFCF[b] (million dollars)	P&E as percent of GFCF[c]
1966										
All manufacturing	16.3%	4.3%	9.2%	17.0%	42.7%	6.7%	12.4%	$3,014	$22,407	13%
Food	4.6	1.9	1.4	n.a.[d]	22.5	2.7	n.a.[d]	109[e]	2,670[e]	4
Chemicals	15.8	1.9	5.1	23.3	86.6	20.8	16.8	561	4,348	12
Primary and fabricated metals	11.3	1.7	1.8			4.0	n.a.[d]	195[f]		
Machinery	21.5	15.4	19.4	19.3	64.0	5.3	50.8	748	8,579[f]	20
Transportation equipment	47.6	8.8	37.8			3.1	28.2	831		
All other manufacturing	11.6	1.0	1.1	10.6	23.6	8.2	6.7	570	6,810	8
1970										
All manufacturing	20.9	5.8	12.3	14.1	32.2	9.3	18.3	4,152	29,739	13
Food	4.4	0.9	2.0	n.a.[d]	23.5	3.1	11.1	163[g]	4,030[g]	4
Chemicals	17.9	2.1	10.4	24.9	68.1	10.7	27.4	691	5,155	13
Primary and fabricated metals	21.1	1.0	8.4			8.3	11.9	457		
Machinery	29.0	23.3	27.8	12.0	57.8	13.9	57.1	1,292	11,482	22
Transportation equipment	45.5	9.8	27.8			17.9	25.6	870		
All other manufacturing	18.2	2.8	2.7	10.8	20.5	13.0	5.9	679	9,072	7

a Figures for 1970 are based on 1969 data for GFCF.

b Gross fixed capital formation.

c Plant and equipment expenditures as percent of gross fixed capital formation.

d Included in "all other manufacturing."

e Excludes food processing in Belgium-Luxembourg and Brazil. Figures for these countries are included in "all other manufacturing."

f Excludes primary metals and fabricated metals in Brazil. These figures are included in "all other manufacturing."

g Excludes food processing in Belgium-Luxembourg, for which the relevant data are included in "all other manufacturing."

Source: US Senate, Committee on Finance, February 1973, Table 9, p. 411.

Table VIII *All merchandise: Exports of the world and of selected countries compared to exports generated by US MNCs and their majority-owned foreign affiliates, 1966 and 1970*

| Area or country | Amount[a] | | | | Increase or decrease (—) 1966 to 1970 | | | | MNC Exports as percentage of total exports | |
| | 1966 | | 1970 | | Amount[a] | | Percent | | | |
	Total	MNC	Total	MNC	Total	MNC	Total	MNC	1966	1970
World total	$201,800	$43,046	$309,200	$72,755	$107,400	$29,713	53.2%	69.0%	21%	24%
United States	29,998	19,241	42,593	29,420	12,595	10,173	41.2	52.9	64	69
Canada	9,551	3,327	16,187	6,852	6,636	3,525	69.5	105.9	35	42
Latin America and other Western Hemisphere	10,871	4,333	13,260	4,746	2,389	413	22.0	9.5	40	36
—Mexico[b]	1,199	126	1,402	217	203	91	16.9	72.2	11	16
—Brazil[b]	1,741	152	2,738	222	997	70	57.3	46.1	9	8
United Kingdom	14,132	2,664	19,351	3,374	5,219	710	36.9	26.7	19	17
European Economic Community (EEC)	52,650	4,532	88,520	8,607	35,870	4,075	68.1	89.9	9	10
—Belgium/Luxembourg[b]	6,832	875	11,609	1,558	4,777	683	69.9	78.1	13	13
—France[b]	10,889	779	17,742	1,552	6,853	773	62.9	99.2	7	9
—W. Germany[b]	20,134	1,424	34,189	2,666	14,055	1,242	69.8	87.2	7	8
Japan	9,777	84	19,318	350	9,541	266	97.6	316.7	1	2
Other Western Europe	19,538	2,494	29,639	4,409	10,101	1,915	51.7	76.8	13	15
Eastern Europe and USSR	21,200	n.a.	31,000	n.a.	9,800	-	46.2	-	-	-
Australia/New Zealand/ South Africa	5,844	340	7,993	758	2,149	418	36.8	122.9	6	9
Other Asia and Africa	25,210	4,655	37,100	10,029	11,890	5,374	47.2	115.4	18	27
International, unallocated	89	1,369	99	3,747	10	-	11.2	-	-	-

Notes:

[a]In millions of US current dollars.

[b]Partially estimated by Tariff Commission in lieu of entry or entries suppressed by the source agency.

Source: US Senate, Committee on Finance, February 1973, Table A-1, p. 354.

Table IX *Manufactured products: Exports of US MNCs and of their majority-owned foreign affiliates as a percentage of selected country exports, 1966 and 1970*

Countries

Industry	Total all countries listed 1966	1970	United States 1966	1970	Canada 1966	1970	United Kingdom 1966	1970	France 1966	1970	West Germany 1966	1970	Belgium-Luxembourg 1966	1970	Mexico 1966	1970	Brazil 1966	1970
All manufacturing	28%	30%	65%	68%	39%	44%	16%	16%	6%	10%	7%	8%	10%	14%	16%	30%	15%	29%
Food products	38	38	132	176	42	25	12	13	3	7	13	15	6	10	11	22	5	6
Paper and allied products	36	68	61	54	31	30	3	7	3	7	1	5	9	14	0	0	66	83
Chemicals and allied products	31	28	73	61	57	29	16	22	7	8	2	5	28	41	23	24	19	213
Rubber	33	30	72	79	21	42	16	18	13	8	0	3	15	41	100	200	0	60
Primary and fabricated materials	13	16	64	75	4	6	9	6	1	0.6	1	3	0.4	5	3	15	0	3
Machinery, except electrical	27	26	47	45	23	34	21	19	23	21	7	7	37	33	0	37	22	716
Electrical machinery	34	30	76	69	38	26	20	17	8	7	4	7	15	26	56	71	20	28
Transportation equipment	53	56	102	104	104	85	30	32	2	17	21	22	20	6	275	110	120	40
Textiles and apparel	3	7	15	26	11	34	0.4	0.4	0.3	0.3	0.1	0.6	1	14	2	7	6	3
Printing and publishing	18	18	36	44	7	29	14	8	3	4	0	2	17	8	13	11	n.a.	n.a.
Instruments	34	44	57	75	431	442	28	45	17	20	7	9	8	4	300	50	200	n.a.
Other manufacturing	11	15	26	36	22	35	3	2	0.7	10	2	7	1	1	17	11	14	n.a.

Source: Data are computed from US Senate, Committee on Finance, February 1973, Tables A–24 to 27, pp. 377–80.

Table X *Oil import dependence: United States, Japan, and Western Europe for selected years*

Countries and years	Oil imports: millions of metric tons	Oil imports: percentage of energy supply	Oil imports from Middle East: millions of metric tons	Oil imports from Middle East: percentage of energy supply
Western Europe				
1967	451	50%	230	25%
1970	644	57	309	28
1973	756	60	513	41
1976	682	54	467	37
Japan				
1967	121	62	102	52
1970	211	73	173	60
1973	284	80	216	61
1976	262	74	196	55
United States				
1967	130	9	10	0.7
1970	170	10	9	0.5
1973	313	17	41	2
1976	365	20	95	5

Sources: Total oil imports and oil imports from the Middle East are from British Petroleum Company, 1967, 1970, 1973, 1976; total energy consumption for all years, from 1976, p. 25.

Table XI *United States, Western European, and Japanese energy projections, 1973–90*

Countries and years	Oil imports as percentage of energy consumption	Net energy imports as percentage of energy consumption[a]
Western Europe		
1973[b]	59%	62%
1980[c]	36	42
1985	28	35
1990	24	33
Japan		
1973[b]	77	89
1980	67	85
1985	61	80
1990	56	75
United States[d]		
1973[b]	18	17
1980	20	19
1985	20	19
1990	18	17

Notes:
[a]Energy imports include coal, petroleum, and natural gas.
[b]Actual data.
[c]Projected US figures are based on these main assumptions: GNP growing 4.3 percent yearly to 1980 and 4.0% thereafter; population growing 1 percent yearly; only evolutionary changes in energy technology except for coal gasification and liquefaction and control of sulfur oxide emissions before 1985 and commercial introduction of breeder reactors thereafter (Dupree and West, US Department of the Interior, 1972, pp. 14–15).
[d]Energy import figures are lower than oil imports in all years due to the export of coal.
Source: US Department of the Interior, June 1976, pp. 43, 45, 47.

Table XII *Percentage change in daily oil consumption in selected countries, 1973–77 and 1976–77*

Country	1973–77	1976–77
United Kingdom	−19.5%	−1.5%
France	−8.6	−1.4
West Germany	−10.8	−0.5
Italy	−5.0	−2.6
Japan	−0.7	+7.0
United States	+7.5	+8.8

Source: Stabler and Tanner, October 31, 1977, p. 1.

Bibliography

ALLISON, GRAHAM T. (1971). *Essence of Decision*. Boston: Little, Brown.

_____ and MORTON HALPERIN (Spring 1972). "Bureaucratic politics: a paradigm and some policy implications." *World Politics*, vol. 24.

ANDRADE, E. N. de C. (1957). *An Approach to Modern Physics*. New York: Doubleday.

ANGELL, NORMAN (1913). *The Great Illusion*, 4th rev. and enlarged ed. New York: Putnam's.

ANGYAL, ANDRAS (January 1939). "The structure of wholes." *Philosophy of Science*, vol. 6.

ARON, RAYMOND (1962). *Peace and War: A Theory of International Relations*. Translated by Richard Howard and Annette Baker Fox. Garden City: Doubleday, 1966.

_____ (1967). "What is a theory of international relations?" *Journal of International Affairs*, vol. 21.

_____ (1970). "Theory and theories in international relations: a conceptual analysis." In Norman D. Palmer (ed.), *A Design for International Relations Research*, monograph 10. Philadelphia: American Academy of Political and Social Science.

ART, ROBERT J. (1973). "The influence of foreign policy on seapower: new weapons and Weltpolitik in Wilhelminian Germany." *Sage Professional Paper in International Studies*, vol. 2. Beverly Hills: Sage Publications.

_____ and KENNETH N. WALTZ (1971). "Technology, strategy, and the uses of force." In Art and Waltz (eds.), *The Use of Force*. Boston: Little, Brown.

ASHBY, W. ROSS (1956). *An Introduction to Cybernetics*. London: Chapman and Hall, 1964.

BAIN, JOE S. (1956). *Barriers to New Competition*. Cambridge, Mass.: Harvard University Press.

BALES, ROBERT F., and EDGAR F. BORGATTA (1953). "Size of group as a factor in the interaction profile." In A. Paul Hare, Edgar F. Borgatta, and Robert F. Bales (eds.), *Small Groups: Studies in Social Interaction*. New York: Knopf, 1965.

BARAN, PAUL A., and PAUL M. SWEEZY (1966). *Monopoly Capital: An Essay on the American Economic and Social Order.* New York: Monthly Review Press.

BARNARD, CHESTER I. (1944). "On planning for world government." In Barnard (ed.), *Organization and Management.* Cambridge: Harvard University Press, 1948.

BARNET, RICHARD J., and R. E. MULLER (1974). *Global Reach.* New York: Simon and Schuster.

BASIUK, VICTOR (n.d.). "Technology, Western Europe's alternative futures, and American policy." New York: Institute of War and Peace Studies, Columbia University.

BAUMOL, WILLIAM J. (1952). *Welfare Economics and the Theory of the State.* London: Longmans, Green.

BEAUFRE, ANDRÉ (1965). "Nuclear deterrence and world strategy." In Karl H. Cerny and Henry W. Briefs (eds.), *NATO in Quest of Cohesion.* New York: Praeger.

BERGLUND, ABRAHAM (1907). *The United States Steel Corporation.* New York: Columbia University Press.

BERGSTEN, C. FRED, and WILLIAM R. CLINE (May 1976). "Increasing international economic interdependence: the implications for research." *American Economic Review*, vol. 66.

BERTALANFFY, LUDWIG VON (1968). *General Systems Theory.* New York: Braziller.

BLAINEY, GEOFFREY (1970). *The Causes of War.* London: Macmillan.

BLOOMFIELD, ARTHUR I. (1968). "Patterns of fluctuation in international investment before 1914." Princeton Studies in International Finance, no. 21: Department of Economics.

BOLTZMAN, LUDWIG (1905). "Theories as representations." Excerpt translated by Rudolf Weingartner. In Arthur Danto and Sidney Morgenbesser (eds.), *Philosophy of Science.* Cleveland: World, Meridian Books, 1960.

BOULDING, KENNETH E., and TAPAN MUKERJEE (1971). "Unprofitable empire; Britain in India, 1800–1967: a critique of the Hobson-Lenin thesis on imperialism." *Peace Research Society Papers*, vol. 16.

BRENNAN, DONALD G. (Spring 1977). "The Soviet military build-up and its implications for the negotiations on strategic arms limitations." *Orbis*, vol. 21.

BREZHNEV, L. I. (October 5, 1976). "Brezhnev gives interview on French TV." In *The Current Digest of the Soviet Press*, vol. 28. Columbus: Ohio State University, November 3, 1976.

BRIGGS, ASA (1968). "The world economy: interdependence and planning." In C. L. Mowat (ed.), *The New Cambridge Modern History*, vol. 12. Cambridge: Cambridge University Press.

British Petroleum Company Ltd. (various years). *B.P. Statistical Review of the World Oil Industry.* London: Britannic House.

BROOKE, EDWARD (March 23, 1967). "Report on Vietnam and Asia." *Congressional Record.* Washington, D.C.: GPO.

BROWN, MICHAEL BARRATT (1970). *After Imperialism,* rev. ed. New York: Humanities Press.

BUCHANAN, JAMES M., and GORDON TULLOCK (1962). *The Calculus of Consent.* Ann Arbor: University of Michigan Press.

BUCKLEY, WALTER (ed.) (1968). *Modern Systems Research for the Behavioral Scientist, A Sourcebook.* Chicago: Aldine.

BUKHARIN, NIKOLAI (1917). *Imperialism and World Economy.* Translator unnamed, 1929. New York: Monthly Review Press, 1973.

BURNS, ARTHUR ROBERT (1936). *The Decline of Competition.* New York: McGraw-Hill.

BURT, RICHARD (1976). *New Weapons Technologies: Debate and Directions.* London: Adelphi Papers, no. 126.

CARR, EDWARD HALLET (1946). *The Twenty Years' Crisis: 1919–1939,* 2nd. ed. New York: Harper and Row, 1964.

CHAMBERLIN, E. H. (1936). *The Theory of Monopolistic Competition, a Re-orientation of the Theory of Value.* Cambridge: Harvard University Press.

CHOU EN-LAI (September 1, 1973). " Excerpts from Chou's report to the 10th Congress of the Chinese Communist Party." *New York Times.*

CHURCHILL, WINSTON S. (1950). *The Grand Alliance.* Boston: Houghton Mifflin.

CIEP: Council on International Economic Policy (December 1974). *Special Report. Critical Imported Materials.* Washington, D.C.: GPO.

_____(March 1976). *International Economic Report of the President.* Washington, D.C.: GPO.

_____(January 1977). *International Economic Report of the President.* Washington, D.C.: GPO.

CLIFFORD, CLARK (September 1946). "American relations with the Soviet Union." In Arthur Krock, *Memoirs.* New York: Funk and Wagnalls, 1968.

COLLINS, JOSEPH (September 10, 1977). "Britain is awarded Ford engine plant in stiff competition." *New York Times.*

CONANT, JAMES B. (1947). *On Understanding Science.* New Haven: Yale University Press.

_____(1952). *Modern Science and Modern Man.* New York: Columbia University Press.

COOPER, RICHARD N. (1968). *The Economics of Interdependence.* New York: McGraw-Hill.

_____ (January 1972). "Economic interdependence and foreign policy in the seventies." *World Politics,* vol. 24.

CRITTENDEN, ANN (December 31, 1976). "U.S. seen safe from supply cuts of major minerals." *International Herald Tribune.*

CROSSMAN, RICHARD (1977). *The Diaries of a Cabinet Minister,* vol. 3: *Secretary of State for Social Services, 1968–70.* London: Hamish Hamilton and Jonathan Cape.

DAHL, ROBERT A. (July 1957). "The concept of power." *Behavioral Science*, vol. 2.

DE GAULLE, CHARLES (January 14, 1963). "Seventh press conference held by General de Gaulle as President of the French Republic in Paris at the Elysee Palace." *Major Addresses, Statements and Press Conferences: May 19, 1958—January 31, 1964.* New York: Service de Presse et d'information, Ambassade de France.

DE TOCQUEVILLE, ALEXIS (1840). *Democracy in America.* Edited by J. P. Mayer and Max Lerner and translated by George Lawrence. New York: Harper and Row, 1966.

DEUTSCH, KARL W. (1966). "Recent trends in research methods in political science." In James C. Charlesworth (ed.), *A Design for Political Science: Scope, Objectives, and Methods*, monograph 10. Philadelphia: American Academy of Political and Social Science.

_____ and J. DAVID SINGER (April 1964). "Multipolar power systems and international stability." *World Politics*, vol. 16.

DIESING, PAUL (1962). *Reason in Society.* Urbana: University of Illinois Press.

DISRAELI, Earl of Beaconsfield (1880). *Endymion.* London: Longmans, Green.

DJILAS, MILOVAN (1962). *Conversations with Stalin.* Translated by Michael B. Petrovich. New York: Harcourt, Brace and World.

DOWNS, ANTHONY (1967). *Inside Bureaucracy.* Boston: Little, Brown.

DOWTY, ALAN (1969). "Conflict in war potential politics: an approach to historical macroanalysis." *Peace Research Society Papers*, vol. 13.

DUNCAN, OTIS D., and LEO F. SCHNORE (September 1959). "Cultural, behavioral, and ecological perspectives in the study of social organization." *Journal of American Sociology*, vol. 65.

DUPREE, WALTER G., and JAMES A. WEST (1972). *United States Energy Through the Year 2000.* US Department of the Interior, Washington, D.C.: GPO.

DURKHEIM, EMILE (1893). *The Division of Labor in Society.* Translated by George Simpson, 1933. New York: Free Press, 1964.

The Economist (August 13, 1977). "Business brief: imitating IBM."

EMMANUEL, ARGHIRI (1972). *Unequal Exchange: A Study of the Imperialism of Trade.* Translated by Brian Pearce. New York: Monthly Review Press.

FEIS, HERBERT (1930). *Europe, the World's Banker, 1870-1914.* New York: August M. Kelly, 1964.

FELLNER, WILLIAM (1949). *Competition among the Few.* New York: Knopf.

FINNEY, JOHN W. (January 18, 1976). "Dreadnought or dinosaur." *New York Times Magazine.*

_____(November 28, 1976). "Strategic stockpile: for whose security." *New York Times.*

FOLLETT, MARY PARKER (1941). *Dynamic Administration; the Collected Papers of Mary Parker Follett.* Edited by H. C. Metcalf and L. Urwick. Bath, England: Management Publications Trust.

FORD, GERALD R. (January 16, 1975). "State of the union message to Congress." *New York Times.*

FORTES, MEYER (1949). "Time and social structure: an Ashanti case study." In Fortes (ed.), *Social Structure: Studies Presented to A. R. Radcliffe-Brown.* Oxford: Clarendon Press.

FOSTER, WILLIAM C. (July 1965). "Arms control and disarmament." *Foreign Affairs,* vol. 43.

FOX, WILLIAM T. R. (1959). "The uses of international relations theory." In Fox (ed.), *Theoretical Aspects of International Relations.* Notre Dame: University of Notre Dame Press.

FRANKE, WINFRIED (1968). "The Italian city-state system as an international system." In Morton A. Kaplan (ed.), *New Approaches to International Relations.* New York: St. Martin's.

FULBRIGHT, J. WILLIAM (1966). *The Arrogance of Power.* New York: Random House.

GAITSKELL, HUGH (March 1, 1960). House of Commons, *Parliamentary Debates,* vol. 618. London: HMSO.

GALLAGHER, JOHN, and RONALD ROBINSON (August 1953). "The imperialism of free trade." *Economic History Review,* 2nd series, vol. 6.

GALTUNG, JOHAN (1971). "A structural theory of imperialism." *Journal of Peace Research,* vol. 8.

GAMBETTA, LÉON (June 26, 1871). "France after the German conquest," from the speech at Bordeaux. In *The World's Best Orations,* vol. 6. Edited by David J. Brewer. St. Louis: Fred P. Kaiser, 1899.

GILPIN, ROBERT (1975). *U.S. Power and the Multinational Corporation.* New York: Basic Books.

GISCARD D'ESTAING, VALERY (June 1, 1976). "France's defense policy." New York: Service de Presse et d'information, Ambassade de France.

GOODWIN, GEOFFREY L. (1976). "International institutions and the limits of interdependence." In Avi Shlaim (ed.), *International Organisations in World Politics: Yearbook, 1975.* London: Croom Helm.

GREENE, MURRAY (1952). "Schumpeter's imperialism—a critical note." In Harrison M. Wright (ed.), *The "New Imperialism."* Boston: Heath, 1961.

GREGOR, JAMES (June 1968). "Political science and the uses of functional analysis." *American Political Science Review,* vol. 62.

GRUNDY, KENNETH W. (April 1963). "Nkrumah's theory of underdevelopment, an analysis of recurrent themes." *World Politics,* vol. 15.

HAAS, ERNST B. (July 1953). "The balance of power: prescription, concept, or propaganda?" *World Politics,* vol. 5.

HALLE, LOUIS J. (1955). *Civilization and Foreign Policy.* New York: Harper.

HALPERIN, MORTON (1974). *Bureaucratic Politics and Foreign Policy.* Washington: Brookings..

HAMILTON, ALEXANDER; JOHN JAY; and JAMES MADISON (1787–1788). *The Federalist.* New York: Modern Library, Random House, n.d.

HARRIS, ERROL E. (1970). *Hypothesis and Perception.* London: Allen and Unwin.

HEISENBERG, WERNER (1971). *Physics and Beyond.* Translated by Arnold J. Pomerans. New York: Harper and Row.

HERTZ, HEINRICH (1894). *The Principles of Mechanics.* Translated by D. E. Jones and J. T. Walley, 1899. Introduction reprinted in Arthur Danto and Sidney Morgenbesser (eds.), *Philosophy of Science.* Cleveland: World Meridian Books, 1970.

HERZ, JOHN H. (January 1950). "Idealist internationalism and the security dilemma." *World Politics,* vol. 2.

_____(1959). *International Politics in the Atomic Age.* New York: Columbia University.

HESSLER, ELLYN (forthcoming). Ph.D. dissertation. Waltham, Mass.: Brandeis University.

HOBBES, THOMAS (1651). *Leviathan.* Edited by Michael Oakeshott. Oxford: Basil Blackwell, n.d.

HOBSON, J. A. (1902). *Imperialism: A Study.* London: Allen and Unwin, 1938.

HOFFMANN, STANLEY (April 1959). "International relations: the long road to theory." *World Politics,* vol. 11.

_____(1961). "International systems and international law." In Hoffmann, *The State of War: Essays on the Theory and Practice of International Politics.* New York: Praeger, 1965.

_____(1963a). "Minerve et Janus." In Hoffmann, *The State of War.* New York: Praeger.

_____(1963b). "Rousseau on war and peace." In Hoffmann, *The State of War.*

_____(January 30, 1964). "Cursing de Gaulle is not a policy." *The Reporter,* vol. 30.

_____(Fall 1964). "Europe's identity crisis: between the past and America." *Daedalus,* vol. 93.

_____(1968). *Gulliver's Troubles.* New York: McGraw-Hill.

_____(March 6 and 7, 1972). "Over there, part I and part II." *New York Times.*

_____(January 11, 1976). "Groping toward a new world order." *New York Times.*

HOLMES, JOHN W. (Spring 1969). "The American problem." *International Journal,* vol. 24.

HOSOYA, CHIHIRO (April 1974). "Characteristics of the foreign policy decision-making system in Japan." *World Politics,* vol. 26.

HUME, DAVID (1741). "Of the first principles of government." In Henry D. Aiken (ed.), *Hume's Moral and Political Philosophy.* New York: Hafner, 1948.

_____(1742). "Of the balance of power." In Charles W. Hendel (ed.), *David Hume's Political Essays.* Indianapolis: Bobbs-Merrill, 1953.

HUNTINGTON, SAMUEL P. (1962). "Patterns of violence in world politics." In Huntington (ed.), *Changing Patterns of Military Politics.* New York: Free Press.

HYMER, STEPHEN (May 1970). "The efficiency (contradictions) of multinational corporations." *American Economic Review,* vol. 60.

IMLAH, A. H. (1958). *Economic Elements in the Pax Britannica.* Cambridge: Harvard University Press.

International Herald Tribune (May 1977). "The outlook for France."

International Monetary Fund, Bureau of Statistics (various years). *Direction of Trade.* New York.

ISAAK, ALAN C. (1969). *Scope and Methods of Political Science.* Homewood, Ill.: Dorsey.

JAEGER, WERNER (1939). *Paideia: The Ideals of Greek Culture,* vol. 1. Translated from the second German edition by Gilbert Highet. New York: Oxford University Press.

JERVIS, ROBERT (1976). *Perception and Misperception in International Politics.* Princeton: Princeton University Press.

_____(January 1978). "Cooperation under the security dilemma." *World Politics,* vol. 30.

JOHNSON, CHALMERS A. (1966). *Revolutionary Change.* Boston: Little, Brown.

JOHNSON, LYNDON BAINES (June 4, 1964). "Excerpts from speech to Coast Guard." *New York Times.*

_____(May 5, 1965). "Text of President's message on funds for Vietnam." *New York Times.*

KAHN, ALFRED E. (1966). "The tyranny of small decisions: market failures, imperfections, and the limits of econometrics." In Bruce M. Russett (ed.), *Economic Theories of International Relations.* Chicago: Markham, 1968.

KAPLAN, MORTON A. (1957). *System and Process in International Politics.* New York: Wiley, 1964.

_____(October 1966). "The new great debate: traditionalism vs. science in international relations." *World Politics,* vol. 19.

_____(1969). *Macropolitics: Selected Essays on the Philosophy and Science of Politics.* Chicago: Aldine.

KATONA, GEORGE (September 1953). "Rational behavior and economic behavior." *Psychological Review,* vol. 60.

KATZENSTEIN, PETER J. (Autumn 1975). "International interdependence: some long-term trends and recent changes." *International Organization,* vol. 29.

KEEFE, EUGENE K. et al. (1971). *Area Handbook for the Soviet Union.* Washington, D.C.: GPO.

KENNEDY, JOHN F. (July 23, 1962). "The goal of an Atlantic partnership: address by President Kennedy." *Department of State Bulletin,* vol. 42.

KEYNES, JOHN MAYNARD (1920). *The Economic Consequences of the Peace.* New York: Harcourt, Brace and Howe.

————(September 1, 1926). "The end of laissez-faire—II." *New Republic,* vol. 48.

————(n.d.). *The General Theory of Employment, Interest, and Money.* New York: Harcourt, Brace.

KINDLEBERGER, CHARLES P. (1969). *American Business Abroad.* New Haven: Yale University Press.

KISSINGER, HENRY A. (1957). *Nuclear Weapons and Foreign Policy.* New York: Harper.

————(1964). *A World Restored.* New York: Grosset and Dunlap.

————(1965). *The Troubled Partnership.* New York: McGraw-Hill.

————(Summer 1968). "The white revolutionary: reflections on Bismarck." *Daedalus,* vol. 97.

————(April 24, 1973). "Text of Kissinger's talk at A.P. meeting here on U.S. relations with Europe." *New York Times.*

————(October 10, 1973). "At Pacem in Terris conference." *News Release.* Bureau of Public Affairs: Department of State.

————(April 20, 1974). "Good partner policy for Americas described by Secretary Kissinger." *News Release.* Bureau of Public Affairs: Department of State.

————(October 13, 1974). "Interview by James Reston of the *New York Times.*" *The Secretary of State.* Bureau of Public Affairs: Department of State.

————(January 13, 1975). "Kissinger on oil, food, and trade." *Business Week.*

————(January 16, 1975). "Interview: for Bill Moyers' Journal." *The Secretary of State.* Bureau of Public Affairs: Department of State.

————(January 24, 1975). "A new national partnership." *The Secretary of State.* Bureau of Public Affairs: Department of State.

————(September 13, 1975). "Secretary Henry A. Kissinger interviewed by William F. Buckley, Jr." *The Secretary of State.* Bureau of Public Affairs: Department of State.

————(December 23, 1975). "Major topics: Angola and detente." *The Secretary of State.* Bureau of Public Affairs: Department of State.

————(September 30, 1976). "Toward a new understanding of community." *The Secretary of State.* Bureau of Public Affairs: Department of State.

————(January 10, 1977). "Laying the foundations of a long-term policy." *The Secretary of State.* Bureau of Public Affairs: Department of State.

KNIGHT, FRANK HYNEMAN (1936). *The Ethics of Competition and Other Essays.* London: Allen and Unwin.

KNORR, KLAUS (1966). *On the Uses of Military Power in the Nuclear Age.* Princeton: Princeton University Press.

KOESTLER, ARTHUR (1971). "Beyond atomism and holism—the concept of the holon." In Koestler and J. R. Smythies (eds.), *Beyond Reductionism*. Boston: Beacon.

KUCYZNSKI, ROBERT R. (1969). *The Measurement of Population Growth: Methods and Results*. New York: Gordon Breach.

KUHN, THOMAS (1970). "Reflections on my critics." In Imre Lakatos and Alan Musgrave (eds.), *Criticism and the Growth of Knowledge*. Cambridge: Cambridge University Press.

KUZNETS, SIMON (Winter 1951). "The state as a unit in study of economic growth." *Journal of Economic History*, vol. 11.

_____(1966). *Modern Economic Growth*. New Haven: Yale University Press.

_____(January 1967). "Quantitative aspects of the economic growth of nations: paper X." *Economic Development and Cultural Change*, vol. 15.

LAKATOS, IMRE (1970). "Falsification and the methodology of scientific research programs." In Imre Lakatos and Alan Musgrave (eds.), *Criticism and the Growth of Knowledge*. Cambridge: Cambridge University Press.

LANDAU, MARTIN (1972). *Political Theory and Political Science*. New York: Macmillan.

LANGER, WILLIAM L. (1950). *European Alliances and Alignments, 1871–1890*, 2nd ed. New York: Random House.

LASKI, HAROLD J. (1933). "The economic foundations of peace." In Leonard Woolf (ed.), *The Intelligent Man's Way to Prevent War*. London: Victor Gollancz.

LEBER, GEORG (February 27, 1973). "Retain balance of power although at lower profile." *The Bulletin*, vol. 23. Bonn: Press and Information Office, Government of the Federal Republic of Germany.

LE BON, GUSTAVE (1896). *The Crowd*. Translator unnamed. London: T. Fisher Unwin.

LENIN, V. I. (1916). *Imperialism, the Highest Stage of Capitalism*. Translator unnamed. New York: International Publishers, 1939.

LÉVI-STRAUSS, CLAUDE (1963). *Structural Anthropology*. Translated by Claire Jacobson and Brooke Grundfest Schoepf. New York: Basic Books.

LEVY, MARION J. (1966). *Modernization and the Structure of Societies*, vol. 2. Princeton: Princeton University Press.

LICKLIDER, ROY E. (Winter 1976–77). "Soviet control of eastern Europe: morality versus American national interests." *Political Science Quarterly*, vol. 91.

LIEBER, ROBERT J. (1972). *Theory and World Politics*. Cambridge, Mass.: Winthrop.

LIPPMANN, WALTER (April 1950). "Break-up of the two power world." *Atlantic Monthly*, vol. 85.

_____(December 5, 1963). "NATO crisis—and solution: don't blame De Gaulle." *Boston Globe*.

LIST, FRIEDRICH (1844). *The National System of Political Economy.* Translated by Sampson S. Lloyd. London: Longmans, Green, 1916.

LIVERNASH, E. R. (1963). "The relation of power to the structure and process of collective bargaining." In Bruce M. Russett (ed.), *Economic Theories of International Politics.* Chicago: Markham, 1968.

MAGDOFF, HARRY (1969). *The Age of Imperialism.* New York: Monthly Review Press.

_____(September/October 1970) "The logic of imperialism." *Social Policy,* vol. 1.

MANNING, C. A. W. (1962). *The Nature of International Society.* New York: Wiley.

MAO TSE-TUNG (January 1930). "A single spark can start a prairie fire." In *Mao Tse Tung: Selected Works,* vol. 1. Translator unnamed. New York: International Publishers, 1954.

_____(1936). "Strategic problems of China's revolutionary war." In *Selected Works,* vol. 1. New York: International Publishers, 1954.

_____(1939). "The Chinese Revolution and the Chinese Communist Party." In *Selected Works,* vol. 3. New York: International Publishers, 1954.

MARCH, J. G., and H. A. SIMON (1958). *Organizations.* New York: Wiley.

MARTINEAU, HARRIET (1853). *The Positive Philosophy of Auguste Comte: Freely Translated and Condensed,* 3rd ed., vol. 2. London: Kegan Paul, Trench, Trubner, 1893.

MARX, KARL, and FREDERICK ENGELS (1848). *Communist Manifesto.* Translator unnamed. Chicago: Charles H. Kerr, 1946.

McCLELLAND, CHARLES A. (1970). "Conceptualization, not theory." In Norman D. Palmer (ed.), *A Design for International Relations Research,* monograph 10. Philadelphia: American Academy of Political and Social Science.

McKENZIE, R. D. (July 1927). "The concept of dominance and world-organization." *American Journal of Sociology,* vol. 33.

MEINECKE, FRIEDRICH (1924). *Machiavellism.* Translated by Douglas Scott. London: Routledge and Kegan Paul, 1957.

MIDDLETON, DREW (September 13, 1976). "Growing use of electronic warfare is becoming a source of major concern for world's military powers." *New York Times.*

MITCHELL, B. R. (1975). *European Historical Statistics, 1750–1970.* New York: Columbia University Press.

MOORE, BARRINGTON, JR. (1950). *Soviet Politics: The Dilemma of Power.* Cambridge: Harvard University Press.

MORGENTHAU, HANS J. (1961). *Purpose of American Politics.* New York: Knopf.

_____(1970a). "International relations: quantitative and qualitative approaches." In Norman D. Palmer (eds.), *A Design for International Relations Research,* monograph 10. Philadelphia: American Academy of Political and Social Science.

_____(1970b). *Truth and Power.* New York: Praeger.

_____(1973). *Politics Among Nations,* 5th ed. New York: Knopf.

_____(March 28, 1974). "Detente: the balance sheet." *New York Times.*

NADEL, S. F. (1957). *The Theory of Social Structure.* Glencoe, Ill.: Free Press.

NAGEL, ERNEST (1956). *Logic Without Metaphysics.* Glencoe, Ill.: Free Press.

_____ (1961). *The Structure of Science.* New York: Harcourt, Brace and World.

NAU, HENRY R. (Winter 1974–75). "U.S. foreign policy in the energy crisis." *Atlantic Community Quarterly,* vol. 12.

NEWHOUSE, JOHN, *et al.* (1971). *U.S. Troops in Europe.* Washington, D.C.: Brookings.

New York Times (December 5, 1977). "More boycott insurance, not less."

Newsweek (March 25, 1974). "Oil embargo: the Arab's compromise."

NICOLSON, NIGEL (ed.) (1966). *Harold Nicolson: Diaries and Letters, 1930–1939.* London: Collins.

NIXON, RICHARD M. (July 6, 1971). "President's remarks to news media executives." *Weekly Compilation of Presidential Documents,* July 12, 1971.

_____(August 5, 1971). "Transcript of the President's news conference on foreign and domestic matters." *New York Times.*

NOLTING, LOUVAN E. (September 1976). "The 1968 reform of scientific research, development, and innovation in the U.S.S.R." *Foreign Economic Report,* no. 11. US Department of Commerce, Bureau of Economic Analysis, Washington, D.C.: GPO.

NYE, JOSEPH S., JR. (June 30, 1977). "Time to plan: the international search for safeguardable nuclear power." *The Department of State.* Bureau of Public Affairs: Department of State.

O'CONNOR, JAMES (1970). "The meaning of economic imperialism." In Robert I. Rhodes (ed.), *Imperialism and Underdevelopment, a Reader.* New York: Monthly Review Press.

OECD: Organization for European Cooperation and Development (various years). *Economic Surveys.* Paris.

_____(1976). *Main Economic Indicators: Historical Statistics 1960–1975.* Paris.

OLSON, MANCUR, JR. (1965). *The Logic of Collective Action.* Cambridge: Harvard University Press.

ORGANSKI, A. F. K. (1968). *World Politics,* 2nd ed. New York: Knopf.

OSGOOD, ROBERT E., and ROBERT W. TUCKER (1967). *Force, Order, and Justice.* Baltimore: Johns Hopkins Press.

PANTIN, C. F. A. (1968). *The Relations between the Sciences.* Cambridge: Cambridge University Press.

PARK, ROBERT E. (1941). "The social function of war." In Leon Bramson and George W. Goethals (eds.), *War.* New York: Basic Books, 1964.

PEPPER, STEPHEN C. (1942). *World Hypotheses.* Berkeley: University of California Press.

PLATT, JOHN RADER (October 1956). "Style in science." *Harper's Magazine*, vol. 213.

POLANYI, MICHAEL (November 1941). "The growth of thought in society." *Economica*, vol. 8.

_____(1958). *Personal Knowledge*. New York: Harper Torchbooks, 1964.

_____(June 1968). "Life's irreducible structure." *Science*, vol. 160.

POPPER, KARL (1935). *The Logic of Scientific Discovery*. New York: Basic Books, 1959.

POWER, THOMAS F. (1944). *Jules Ferry and the Renaissance of French Imperialism*. New York: Octagon Books.

RAPOPORT, ANATOL (1968). "Foreward." In Walter Buckley (ed.), *Modern Systems Research for the Behavioral Scientist, A Sourcebook*. Chicago: Aldine.

_____ and WILLIAM J. HORVATH (1959). "Thoughts on organization theory." In Walter Buckley (ed.), *Modern Systems Research for the Behavioral Scientist, A Sourcebook*. Chicago: Aldine, 1968.

RIKER, WILLIAM H. (1962). *The Theory of Political Coalitions*. New Haven: Yale University Press.

ROBBINS, LIONEL (1939). *The Economic Basis of Class Conflict and Other Essays in Political Economy*. London: Macmillan.

ROBINSON, JOAN (1933). *The Economics of Imperfect Competition*. London: Macmillan.

ROBINSON, W. S. (June 1950). "Ecological correlations and the behavior of individuals." *American Sociological Review*, vol. 15.

ROSECRANCE, RICHARD N. (1963). *Action and Reaction in World Politics: International Systems in Perspective*. Boston: Little, Brown.

_____(September 1966). "Bipolarity, multipolarity, and the future." *Journal of Conflict Resolution*, vol. 10.

_____(1973). *International Relations, Peace or War?* New York: McGraw-Hill.

_____ and ARTHUR STEIN (October 1973). "Interdependence: myth or reality?" *World Politics*, vol. 26.

ROUSSEAU, JEAN J. (1762). "A discourse on political economy." In *The Social Contract and Discourses*. Translated by G. D. H. Cole. New York: Dutton, 1950.

ROYAL INSTITUTE OF INTERNATIONAL AFFAIRS (1937). *The Problem of International Investment*. London: Oxford University Press.

RUGGIE, JOHN GERARD (September 1972). "Collective goods and future international collaboration." *American Political Science Review*, vol. 66.

_____(1974). *The State of the Future: Technology, Collective Governance, and World Order*. Ph.D. dissertation. Berkeley: University of California.

RUSK, DEAN (August 13, 1963). "Text of Rusk's statement to Senators about Test Ban Treaty." *New York Times*.

SALPUKAS, AGIS (March 7, 1976). "Chrysler prunes its growth to thicken its profits." *New York Times.*

SCHEFFLER, ISRAEL (1967). *Science and Subjectivity.* Indianapolis: Bobbs-Merrill.

SCHELLING, THOMAS (1966). *Arms and Influence.* New Haven: Yale University Press.

SCHMIDT, HELMUT (October 7, 1975). "Schmidt, Ford 'cautiously optimistic' on world's economic recovery." *The Bulletin.* Bonn: Press and Information Office, Government of the Federal Republic of Germany, vol. 23.

SCHNEIDER, WILLIAM (1976). *Food, Foreign Policy, and Raw Materials Cartels.* New York: Crane, Russak.

SCHUMPETER, JOSEPH A. (1919). "The sociology of imperialism." In Joseph Schumpeter, *Imperialism and Social Classes.* Translated by Heinz Norden. New York: Meridian Books, 1955.

SHUBIK, MARTIN (1959). *Strategy and Market Structure.* New York: Wiley.

SIMMEL, GEORG (July 1902). "The number of members as determining the social form of the group." *Journal of Sociology,* vol. 8.

_____(March 1904). "The sociology of conflict, II." *American Journal of Sociology,* vol. 9.

SIMON, HERBERT A. (1957). *Models of Man.* New York: Wiley.

SINGER, H. W. (May 1950). "U.S. foreign investment in underdeveloped areas: the distribution of gains between investing and borrowing countries." *American Economic Review,* vol. 40.

SINGER, J. DAVID (October 1961). "The level of analysis problem." *World Politics,* vol. 14.

_____(1969). "The global system and its subsystems: a developmental view." In James N. Rosenau (ed.), *Linkage Politics: Essays on the Convergence of National and International Systems.* New York: Free Press.

_____; STUART BREMER; and JOHN STUCKEY (1972). "Capability distribution, uncertainty, and major power war, 1820–1965." In Bruce M. Russett (ed.), *Peace, War, and Numbers.* Beverly Hills: Sage Publications.

SMITH, ADAM (1776). *An Inquiry into the Nature and Causes of the Wealth of Nations.* Edited by Edwin Cannan. New Rochelle, N.Y.: Arlington House, n.d.

SMITH, BRUCE L. R., and JOSEPH J. KARLESKY (1977). *The State of Academic Science,* vol. 1. New Rochelle, N.Y.: Change Magazine Press.

SMITH, M. G. (July–December 1956). "On segmentary lineage systems." *Journal of the Royal Anthropological Institute of Great Britain and Ireland,* vol. 86.

_____(1966). "A structural approach to comparative politics." In David Easton (ed.), *Varieties of Political Theories.* Englewood Cliffs, N.J.: Prentice-Hall.

SNYDER, GLENN H. (1966). *Stockpiling Strategic Materials.* San Francisco: Chandler.

_____ and PAUL DIESING (1977). *Conflict among Nations*. Princeton: Princeton University Press.

SOREL, ALBERT (1885). *Europe under the Old Regime*. Ch. 1, vol. 1 of *L'Europe et la Revolution Francaise*. Translated by Francis H. Herrick, 1947. New York: Harper & Row, 1964.

STABLER, CHARLES N., and JAMES TANNER (October 31, 1977). "Energy breather." *Wall Street Journal*.

STALEY, EUGENE (1935). *War and the Private Investor*. Garden City, N.Y.: Doubleday, Doran.

STEPHENSON, Hugh (1973). *The Impact of Multinational Corporations on National States*. New York: Saturday Review Press.

STERLING, RICHARD W. (1974). *Macropolitics: International Relations in a Global Society*. New York: Knopf.

STIGLER, GEORGE J. (1964). "A theory of oligopoly." In Bruce M. Russet (ed.), *Economic Theories of International Politics*. Chicago: Markham, 1968.

STILLMAN, EDMUND O., and WILLIAM PFAFF (1961). *The New Politics: America and the End of the Postwar World*. New York: McCann.

STINCHCOMBE, ARTHUR (1968). *Constructing Social Theories*. New York: Harcourt, Brace and World.

STOESSINGER, JOHN G. (1976). *Henry Kissinger: The Anguish of Power*. New York: W. W. Norton.

STRACHEY, JOHN (1960). *The End of Empire*. New York: Random House.

STRANGE, SUSAN (January 1971). "The politics of international currencies." *World Politics*, vol. 22.

SULZBERGER, C. L. (November 15, 1972). "New balance of peace." *New York Times*.

Survey of Current Business (various issues). U.S. Department of Commerce, Bureau of Economic Analysis. Washington, D.C.: GPO.

TAYLOR, A. J. P. (June 4, 1976). "London Diary." *New Statesman*, vol. 91.

THOMAS, BRINLEY (1961). *International Migration and Economic Development*. Paris: UNESCO.

THUCYDIDES (c. 400 B.C.). *History of the Peloponnesian War*. Translated by Crawley. New York: Modern Library, Random House, 1951.

TOULMIN, STEPHEN (1961). *Foresight and Understanding*. New York: Harper and Row.

TROLLOPE, ANTHONY (1880). *The Duke's Children*, 3 vols. Philadelphia: Geddie, 1892.

TROTSKY, LEON (1924). *Europe and America: Two Speeches on Imperialism*. New York: Pathfinder Press, 1971.

TUGENDHAT, CHRISTOPHER (1971). *The Multinationals.* London: Eyre and Spottis-woode.

TURNER, LOUIS (1971). *Invisible Empires.* New York: Harcourt, Brace, Jovanovich.

ULAM, ADAM (1971). *The Rivals.* New York: Viking.

ULLMAN, RICHARD H. (October 1976). "Trilateralism: 'partnership' for what?" *Foreign Affairs,* vol. 55.

UN Department of Economic Affairs (1949). *International Capital Movements During the Inter-War Period.* New York.

_____ Department of Economic and Social Affairs (1961). *International Flow of Long Term Capital and Official Donations.* New York.

_____(1973). *Multinational Corporations and World Development.* New York.

_____ Statistical Office (1957, 1961, 1970, 1974). *Yearbook of National Accounts Statistics.* New York.

_____(1966). *Demographic Yearbook, 1965.* New York.

_____(1976). *Statistical Yearbook, 1975,* vol. 27. New York.

_____(1977). *Statistical Yearbook, 1976,* vol. 28. New York.

US Agency for International Development, Statistics and Reports Division (various years). *US Overseas Loans and Grants: July 1, 1945-.* Washington, D.C.: GPO.

_____ Bureau of the Census (1975). *Statistical Abstract, 1974.* Washington, D.C.: GPO.

_____ Bureau of the Census (1976). *Historical Statistics of the United States: Colonial Times to 1970.* Washington, D.C.: GPO.

_____ Department of Commerce, Bureau of Economic Analysis (1975). *Revised Data Series on US Direct Investment Abroad, 1966-1974.* Washington, D.C.: GPO.

_____ Department of the Interior (June 1976). *Energy Perspectives 2.* Washington, D.C.: GPO.

_____ Senate Committee on Finance (February 1973). *Implications of Multinational Firms for World Trade and Investment and for U.S. Trade and Labor.* Washington, D.C.: GPO.

_____ Senate Committee on Government Operations, Permanent Subcommittee on Investigations (August 1974). *Selected Readings on Energy Self-Sufficiency and the Controlled Materials Plan.* Washington, D.C.: GPO.

VAGTS, ALFRED (1956). *Defense and Diplomacy: The Soldier and the Conduct of Foreign Relations.* New York: King's Crown Press.

VEBLEN, THORSTEIN (1915). "The opportunity of Japan." In Leon Ardzrooni (ed.), *Essays in our Changing Order.* New York: Viking, 1954.

VITAL, DAVID (1967). *The Inequality of States.* Oxford: Oxford University Press.

VON LAUE, THEODORE H. (1963). "Soviet diplomacy: G.V. Chicherin, People's Commissar for Foreign Affairs 1918-1930." In Gordon A. Craig and Felix Gilbert (eds.), *The Diplomats 1919-1939,* vol. 1. New York: Atheneum.

WALLERSTEIN, IMMANUEL (September 1974). "The rise and future demise of the world capitalist system: concepts for comparative analysis." *Comparative Studies in Society and History*, vol. 16.

WALTZ, KENNETH N. (1954). *Man, the State, and the State System in Theories of the Causes of War.* Ph.D. dissertation. New York: Columbia University.

_____(1959). *Man, the State, and War: A Theoretical Analysis.* New York: Columbia University Press.

_____(Summer 1964). "The stability of a bipolar world." *Daedalus*, vol. 93.

_____(July 1965). "Contention and management in international relations." *World Politics*, vol. 18.

_____(1967a). *Foreign Policy and Democratic Politics: The American and British Experience.* Boston: Little, Brown.

_____(1967b). "International structure, national force, and the balance of world power." *Journal of International Affairs*, vol. 21.

_____(September 1967a). " The relation of states to their world." A paper delivered at the annual meeting of the American Political Science Association.

_____(September 1967b). "The politics of peace." *International Studies Quarterly*, vol. 11.

_____(1970). "The myth of national interdependence." In Charles P. Kindleberger (ed.), *The International Corporation.* Cambridge: M.I.T. Press.

_____(1971). "Conflict in world politics." In Steven L. Spiegel and Waltz (eds.), *Conflict in World Politics.* Cambridge, Mass.: Winthrop.

_____(1974). "America's European policy viewed in global perspective." In Wolfram F. Hanrieder (ed.), *The United States and Western Europe.* Cambridge, Mass.: Winthrop.

_____(1975). "Theory of international relations." In Fred Greenstein and Nelson Polsby (eds.), *The Handbook of Political Science.* Reading, Mass.: Addison-Wesley.

WATZLAWICK, PAUL; JANET HELMICK BEAVIN; and DON D. JACKSON (1967). *Pragmatics of Human Communication.* New York: Norton.

WEAVER, WARREN (1947). "Science and complexity." In Weaver (ed.), *The Scientists Speak.* New York: Boni and Gaer.

WEHLER, HANS-ULRICH (August 1970). "Bismarck's imperialism, 1862–1890." *Past and Present*, vol. 34.

WELTMAN, JOHN J. (May 1972). "The processes of a systemicist." *The Journal of Politics*, vol. 34.

WHITEHEAD, ALFRED NORTH (1925). *Science and the Modern World.* New York: Macmillan.

WIENER, NORBERT (1961). *Cybernetics, or Control and Communication in the Animal and Machine,* 2nd. ed. Cambridge, Mass.: M.I.T. Press.

WIGHT, MARTIN (1966). "The balance of power." In H. Butterfield and Martin Wight (eds.), *Diplomatic Investigations: Essays in the Theory of International Politics.* London: Allen and Unwin.

_____(1973). "The balance of power and international order." In Alan James (ed.), *The Bases of International Order.* London: Oxford University Press.

_____(1977). *Systems of States.* Atlantic Heights, N.J.: Humanities Press.

WILKINS, MIRA (1974). *The Maturing of Multinational Enterprise: American Business Abroad from 1914 to 1970.* Cambridge: Harvard University Press.

WILLIAMS, WILLIAM A. (1962). *The Tragedy of American Diplomacy,* rev. ed. New York: Dell.

WILLIAMSON, OLIVER E. (1965). "A dynamic theory of inter-firm behavior." In Bruce M. Russett (ed.), *Economic Theories of International Politics.* Chicago: Markham, 1968.

WOHLSTETTER, ALBERT (January 1958). "The delicate balance of terror." *Foreign Affairs,* vol. 37.

WOLFF, RICHARD D. (May 1970). "Modern imperialism: the view from the metropolis." *American Economic Review,* vol. 60.

WOODS, FREDERICK ADAMS, and ALEXANDER BALTZLY (1915). *Is War Diminishing?* Boston: Houghton Mifflin.

WOYTINSKY, W. S., and E. S. WOYTINSKY (1953). *World Population and Production.* New York: Twentieth Century Fund.

WRIGHT, QUINCY (1965). *A Study of War: Second Edition, with a Commentary on War since 1942.* Chicago: University of Chicago Press.

YOUNG, C. KENNETH (1976). *Stanley Baldwin.* London: Weidenfeld and Nicolson.

ZIMMERMAN, WILLIAM (1969). *Soviet Perspectives on International Relations, 1956-1967.* Princeton: Princeton University Press.

Index